Creating an
Australian Garden

Creating an Australian Garden

Angus Stewart

Researcher, Andrea Bishop

ALLEN&UNWIN

contents

introduction

One of the most gratifying experiences I've had in more than thirty years as a horticulturist has been seeing gardeners in ever-increasing numbers embrace the idea of giving our urban landscapes a more Australian identity. The cultural cringe that led us down the garden path of large lawns enclosed by shrubberies of camellias and azaleas has finally been overcome by an intrepid band of horticultural pioneers who are keen to celebrate the feel and smell of the Australian bush.

Australian plants are not only being used in greater numbers and variety, but are also being incorporated with considerable creativity into landscape designs, from informal 'bush' gardens to highly structured formal gardens with tightly clipped hedges and borders. In between are various approaches that blend Australian and exotic species together.

Along with this greater experimentation in design with Australian plants, a much broader selection of wild species has been brought into cultivation. As these wild species have become more widely grown, improved genetic forms have inevitably appeared and been selected for propagation as new cultivars. A great example are the many

and varied forms of the bower wattle (*Acacia cognata*), a species with gracefully cascading foliage. These forms range from 'Copper Tips' (a five- to six-metre shrub with dark-coloured growing tips) to 'Lime Magik' (a four- to five-metre shrub with golden foliage). A plethora of other forms less than a metre in height have become extremely popular as foliage features; these include 'Green Mist', 'Limelight', 'Mop Top', 'Fettucine' and 'Waterfall'.

While horticulturists have been selecting better forms within wild species, mad scientists have been breeding new cultivars by crossing various species. The kangaroo paw, for example, now comes in a profusion of hybrid cultivars. Indeed, it is now worthy to challenge Dame Edna Everage's gladiolus as the iconic Australian flower. While not all hybrid kangaroo paws grow successfully in a wide range of conditions, there has been an overall improvement in their characteristics, with longer flowering times, bigger flowers and stronger foliage. An additional benefit of these interspecific hybrids is that they are almost always sterile, so they're guaranteed not to spread into adjacent bushland from the gardens where they are planted. Like it or not, many Australian

TOP AND ABOVE The beautiful weeping foliage of *Acacia cognata* has recently captured the imagination of Australian gardeners.
FAR LEFT Various iconic Australian plants have assumed a far more prominent place in Australian gardens in recent times.

LEFT Anigozanthos 'Bush Pioneer' is an example of a tough new kangaroo-paw hybrid. *BELOW AND FAR RIGHT* Many spectacular forms of the red flowering gum *Corymbia ficifolia* are now available as true-to-type grafted specimens.

plants have just as great a potential to become weeds as their more notorious exotic cousins, such as agapanthus.

Another advance in the cultivation of Australian plants has been the increased use of grafting to widen the palette of plants available to the home gardener. An excellent example is the selection of superior forms of red flowering gum (*Corymbia ficifolia*). Formerly known as *Eucalyptus ficifolia*, this spectacular tree has for decades been frustrating gardeners who have bought it as seedlings with a bold, brassy red flower on the label. Years later, when the seedlings finally flower, the colour of the flower and the habit of the tree have often failed to live up to expectations. Thanks to grafting, colour forms ranging from the brightest

of reds to orange, pink, violet and even bicoloured pink-and-white are now becoming available in a range of heights from large trees to dwarf shrubs.

Grafting has long been a standard practice for exotic plants such as roses and weeping cherry trees, so it is about time we got with it and applied this time-honoured practice to Australian plants. It is a technique that promises to make many formerly difficult-to-cultivate Australian gems available to the home gardener.

I make no apologies for the fact that this book features the bold, beautiful new cultivars that are taking Australian flora into the 21st century. Now it's time for you to go out, sink the spade, and start to bring the bush into your garden. Go forth and propagate!

how to use this book

This book is intended to be both an inspiration and a practical guide to establishing a garden based on Australian plants. I imagine the pages getting dirty as you thumb through them while you're mucking around in your garden. The book is designed to take you right through every step of creating your dream, from planning the garden through to building and maintaining it.

The planning section—'Planning the garden'—encourages you to think about the look you want to create. I hope you will find it so inspiring and engrossing that you'll read it straight through. This section also encourages you to consider all the practical aspects of building your garden—which will save you the headache of having to move that thriving thryptomene just when it was starting to look like the one in the coffee-table book.

The next section is all about the hands-on reality of building and planting your garden: 'Building the garden'. This part of the book is not designed to be read from start to finish like a Mills and Boon love story. Rather, it is a reference section that will provide you with solid facts when you are ready finally to bring your plan to life.

'All about the plants' is my favourite part of the book—after all, plants make a garden. This is not a section for those minimalists whose ideal is a cluster of strappy-leaved cordylines and lomandras surrounded by a sea of pavers. It's for real plant people, who want to celebrate the biodiversity that is the Australian bush. In this part, I discuss all the major groups of Australian plants and how to use them in creating your dream garden.

'Garden examples' shows you a variety of real Australian-plant gardens. The idea is to show you how others have approached the task. This section will discuss common problems and how other gardeners have overcome them, as well as stunning successes and how they were achieved. Again, the aim is to provide practical examples that you can apply to your own space. Bush gardens are also included, which show examples of wild Australian flora that you can see on bushwalks, as are great public gardens that feature native plants.

Last but by no means least comes a reference section: the 'Native plant cultivar list'. This gives you an alphabetical list of some of the exciting new Australian plant cultivars that have been released in recent years as well as the best old cultivars that have stood the test of time. I have researched this section carefully, doing my best to ensure that the cultivars are commercially available, either through garden centres and hardware chains or via mail order. There is also a list of specialist native plant nurseries where you can find some of the more obscure plants, both those mentioned in the book and those you might discover independently.

planning
the garden

In a nation as young as Australia, we could be forgiven if we hadn't progressed very far with garden design. However, thanks to our culturally diverse forebears—who brought with them their own countries' accumulated knowledge of gardening, as well as a desire to recreate the gardens of 'home'—we have inherited a rich and loamy gardening legacy.

Not surprisingly, for many decades we emulated the horticultural fashions of other lands. However, more and more—as we've developed a sense of place and of national pride—we have evolved a sense of gardening style that is truly our own.

This shift to a distinctly Australian garden is gaining such momentum largely because our knowledge of native plants is increasing at almost the same rate as our appreciation of them. That isn't to say that our ancestors did not appreciate this continent's flora—they did, as is attested by Joseph Banks's extensive collection of Australian plants. But they didn't yet know how to grow them to best effect—which helped sow the seeds of a bad reputation for Australian native plants!

Nonetheless, the horticultural literature is dotted with the stories of brave souls who cherished native plants and persevered with them. Today, we have the benefit of their accumulated knowledge and are extending it all the time. We are also learning how to substitute native plants for the exotic plants we've previously reached for in particular situations. And, of course, the more we appreciate our Aussie beauties the more we want to learn about them—and on and on it goes! Breeders are well on board and are popping out brilliant new cultivars at a great rate. This combination of knowledge and accessibility makes for great possibilities when we're planning our own gardens.

When you make a garden with Australian plants, you literally bring the bush into your backyard. You may purchase your plants from the local nursery or propagate them yourself, but whether they are cultivars or species, they all initially came from one place—the amazing Australian bush. So you can pat yourself on the back, because as well as designing a modern Australian garden, you are helping to protect the life and diversity of our national flora.

The next section will take you through some information that is useful to consider when planning your garden. Now, you're probably busting to get into the garden and start ferociously digging and planting, and can't wait to head to the back of the book and choose your plants. But for the sake of your wallet, your sanity and the plants themselves, it might be wise to sit down with a cuppa and enjoy 'Planning the garden'.

ABOVE Water features create a soothing effect and also encourage wildlife into your garden. *FAR LEFT* Mass plantings of everlasting daisies can be used to create spectacular wildflower meadows.

TOP Existing trees in the garden are a great starting point for a new design.
ABOVE Raised beds can be used to create interesting effects in new gardens.

New or existing garden?

Whether you're remodelling an existing garden or starting from scratch, there are a few things to think about if you want to achieve the best possible result. Later in the book we will be discussing in detail all the practical considerations: soil types, climate issues, appropriate plant selection and so on. But before we get to that, you need to carefully consider what plants and structures are already present in your available space and decide how to incorporate them—or not—into your dream garden.

Before you go in boots and all, ripping out existing plants, take a few weeks to see if they are serving a useful purpose, such as creating habitat for fauna. For instance, an exotic tree may be a viewing platform for birds wanting to take a precautionary scan of your garden before they venture into it. Existing trees and shrubs may also be useful as 'nurse' plants, protecting new plantings from frost and other environmental stresses.

If you are starting from zero on a new block, it would be wise to consider what sort of stresses a bare site may create for your new plantings. Are there any strong prevailing winds whose impact could be lessened by fast-growing windbreaks such as wattles? In such a situation, you may want to create the garden in stages and wait until windbreaks are actually providing shelter before you put in more delicate plants. Or, if your garden is exposed to the west, do you need to protect new plantings from hot afternoon sun while they establish? Temporary structures supporting shadecloth can be erected in summer and removed as autumn brings milder temperatures. Are there any pipes or other conduits that need to be considered when selecting and placing your trees and shrubs? Are there any pockets of bushland nearby? If so, perhaps you can bring wildlife to your garden by, for instance, planting some of the local indigenous species.

Australian climate zones

Understanding climate is extremely useful when creating a bush garden. You don't need a degree in meteorology, but a bit of knowledge can save you time, dollars and heartache. If you're creating a bush garden from scratch, or if you don't know much about native plants, knowing which climate zone you're in narrows down your range of possible plants, which keeps the choices from becoming overwhelming. Also, understanding that the microclimate where you live might differ from the overall climate of your zone can help you create your own unique piece of paradise. For example, you may live in a built-up suburb where temperatures are warmer than average, or you may live in a small pocket where it tends to rain more than in the surrounding area.

Probably the best reason to pay attention to climate (both your own locality's and that of the places your plants come from) is that by doing so, you can learn to mimic plants' native environments within your own garden. That enables you to use a broader plant palette and create a more interesting garden—but more on that later!

SO, WHAT IS CLIMATE?

Climate can cover an area as big as a country and as tiny as your front verandah. Climate is the weather in a particular location that is averaged over a long period of time. It includes temperature, rainfall, humidity, atmospheric pressure and wind. Climate is determined by latitude, elevation and local topography, the temperature and proximity of oceans, the vegetation of an area, and prevailing winds.

AUSTRALIA'S CLIMATE(S)

Australia is the largest continent that is one single country. Overall, we can say that its climate is dominated by a sub-tropical high-pressure system whose movement north and south creates seasonal rainfall. But Australia is too vast to have a single climate. Given that it extends from 10ºS latitude (up near the Equator) to 45ºS, it's no surprise that a climate-zone map of the continent is more colourful than a Ken Done painting. Depending which climate map you're looking at, we have almost twenty zones, such as in the map on the right! And thanks to various mountain ranges, located mostly in the east, we also have mini-zones within zones.

We tend to describe climate zones in terms of *location* (tropical, sub-tropical), *temperature* (cool, temperate), *rainfall* or lack thereof (arid, semi-arid, desert), and even *plant type* (grassland, savannah). One climate term that gardeners from Perth, Adelaide and Melbourne hear often is 'Mediterranean'. But I don't see why we should use an area on the opposite side of the globe to explain our own climate—and if we've never been in the Mediterranean, what does that term tell us? Why not just say the plant grows well in areas with dry, hot summers and cool, wet winters? And for the record, Melbourne's climate is not Mediterranean—its winters are too cold.

When you've found your zone on a climate map, be aware that your garden may be subject to microclimatic effects, so you could be in a pocket that differs from the average in your zone in being, say, a little wetter. Following a local weather station's guide is useful as this will be more accurate than using the guide for the capital city. Your best approach is to keep a climate diary for your garden. Monitor conditions with a thermometer and a rain gauge. If you're really keen you could also consider using a maximum/minimum thermometer or installing a professional mini weather station.

EQUATORIAL
■ rainforest (monsoonal)
■ savannah

TROPICAL
■ rainforest (persistently wet)
■ rainforest (monsoonal)
■ savannah

SUB-TROPICAL
▨ no dry season
▨ distinctly dry summer
▨ distinctly dry winter
▨ moderately dry winter

DESERT
■ hot (persistently dry)
◪ hot (summer drought)
▨ hot (winter drought)
▨ warm (persistently dry)

GRASSLAND
▨ hot (persistently dry)
▨ hot (summer drought)
▨ hot (winter drought)
  warm (persistently dry)
  warm (summer drought)

TEMPERATURE
▨ no dry season (hot summer)
■ moderately dry winter (hot summer)
■ distinctly dry (and hot) summer
■ no dry season (warm summer)
■ distinctly dry (and warm) summer
■ moderately dry winter (warm summer)
▨ distinctly dry (and warm) summer
  no dry season (mild summer)
  distinctly dry (and mild) summer
□ no dry season (cool summer)

Australia's climate zones

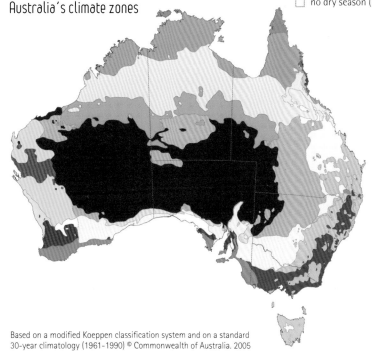

Based on a modified Koeppen classification system and on a standard 30-year climatology (1961-1990) © Commonwealth of Australia. 2005

CLIMATE STATISTICS TABLE

	Latitude	Elevation (metres above sea level)	Mean annual rainfall	Days with ≥ 1 mm rain	Mean annual min. temp.	Mean annual max. temp.
Hobart, Tas	42	51	614 mm	159	8°C	17°C
Launceston, Tas	41	170	676 mm	93	6°C	17°C
Melbourne, Vic	37	31	648 mm	100	10°C	20°C
Canberra, ACT	35	578	615 mm	72	7°C	20°C
Adelaide, SA	34	2	544 mm	120	12°C	22°C
Sydney, NSW	33	5	1213 mm	138	14°C	22°C
Perth, WA	31	20	752 mm	112	13°C	25°C
Geraldton, WA	28	2	449 mm	86	14°C	26°C
Brisbane, Qld	27	38	952 mm	114	15°C	25°C
Oodnadatta, WA	27	117	174 mm	34	15°C	29°C
Carnarvon, WA	24	4	229 mm	41	17°C	27°C
Bundaberg, Qld	24	27	1003 mm	104	16°C	27°C
Alice Springs, NT	23	580	280 mm	43	13°C	29°C
Townsville, Qld	19	4	1124 mm	90	20°C	29°C
Tennant Creek, NT	19	376	452 mm	37	20°C	32°C
Broome, Qld	18	17	601 mm	47	21°C	32°C
Daly Waters, NT	16	212	690 mm	55	19°C	34°C
Cairns, Qld	16	2	2005 mm	154	21°C	29°C
Darwin, NT	12	30	1712 mm	112	23°C	32°C
Cape York, Qld	10	40	1744 mm	98	23°C	29°C

LEFT AND ABOVE From the desert to the open bush and high mountains—
plants have adapted magnificently to Australia's diverse climate and geology.

Rainfall

Australia is the world's driest inhabited continent, and about 80 per cent of the country is classified as semi-arid or arid. The positive side of these potentially bleak realities is that they are the reason many of our plants are so beautiful. Think of the 700-odd species of our *Eucalyptus*, marvellously adapted to low rainfall with vertically hanging leaves that reduce exposure to sunlight and therefore transpiration. Or the Queensland bottle tree (*Brachychiton rupestris*), which stores water in its swelling trunk; the desert grasses that roll themselves up during the day to reduce their exposed surface area; and many of the *Melaleuca* or *Hakea* species, with their narrow, needle-like leaves. The very forms that endear these plants to us are practical adaptations to low rainfall. Another benefit of this evolutionary adaptation to drought is that it means many of our native plants, once established, need no further watering.

That in turn means there's no need for irrigation systems; no worrying about whether our entire garden is going to cark it if we go on holiday over summer. It also means we can be confident that if plants survive their first no-water test, they will likely mature into strong, healthy adults.

Ideas on 'establishment' watering do vary a little. Some think a single watering at planting should cover it; others keep watering for a few months or even a year. There is no one 'right' answer, because no two situations are exactly the same—different gardens have different soils, climates, microclimates, plants, and so on. The best thing is to experiment.

If we have success watering once, twice, a dozen times or more, then that is the formula we should stick to.

IT NEVER RAINS BUT IT POURS

This is certainly true of Australia's tropical and dry-tropical zones during the monsoonal summer months. For those in arid regions or southern climes, high summer rainfall sounds enviable, but in reality so much rain falling in such a short time can make life very frustrating for gardeners. Not only does it cause erosion and saturated soil, it also makes the task of choosing plants more difficult. High rainfall, coupled with the higher humidity of northern areas, means that fungal diseases proliferate. For those in the dry tropics the situation is even worse. Months of dry hot weather might tempt them to put in desert plants, but a month or two of torrential downpours can quickly devastate drought-loving species.

Of course, hundreds of species thrive in wet, humid conditions—including those lush, large-leafed shrubs and trees that epitomise the tropics. With warm weather, high rainfall and the right soil, these plants grow faster than queues for grand-final tickets. The trick to growing a native garden is the same wherever you are—understand your climate and become familiar with the preferred conditions of the plants you wish to grow.

Unless we have our own personal cloud-seeding program, it's difficult to get more of the wet stuff to fall whenever we want. Instead, we need to be cunning, and capture as much of the rain that falls on our property as we can. This means

TOP Natural and man-made swales help keep water where it's most needed.
ABOVE Creating a dry creek bed along a natural watercourse will assist with moving heavy rainfall safely through the property.
FAR RIGHT The trunk of the iconic Queensland bottle tree (*Brachychiton rupestris*) is a useful 'water tank' for drier times.

harvesting the rain with water tanks or ponds. It also means *channelling* the run-off (via swales, drains, and so on), *slowing* it (using mulch, strategically placed rocks and logs) and *preventing* it leaving the property (by using permeable materials for driveways and paths, for example, which allow rain to soak into the ground—this benefits plants on your property and prevents pollution washing into our creeks, rivers and oceans).

MEASURING RAINFALL

It isn't absolutely necessary, but measuring rainfall is fun. It's also a useful tool for planning when to plant. And it's nice to see how our own little patch compares to other areas of Australia. Rain gauges are cheap and easy to install, and the results are a guaranteed talking point with like-minded friends. Once you've been recording rainfall for a while, it can become a hobby, even a bit of an obsession.

Knowing exactly how much rain falls on our property, and when, is a good first step. Getting out into the garden when it's raining is the next. Take an umbrella, go into every corner of the garden, and watch what the water is doing—where it's coming from, where it's going, how fast it's moving and what it does on the way. Video it if you can, because quite often water behaves unpredictably, and it's easy to forget exactly how it moved through the property. Understanding what the water does will help you decide not only how to harvest and channel it, but also how to protect your plants, soil and property.

TOP A rain gauge can be incorporated as an unobtrusive part of the garden design.
ABOVE Even a small water tank will be useful during the height of summer.
RIGHT If space permits, a large water feature such as this will bring movement and tranquillity to the garden, while providing a habitat and breeding ground for many fauna.

Soil, Part 1

Any gardener knows that appropriate and healthy soil is one of the keystones of a successful garden. But what on earth is an appropriate soil, how do we know if we have one, how do we create one if we need to, and how do we ensure that it is healthy? These questions aren't necessarily as simple as they sound.

To answer the first question: an appropriate soil is one that suits the plants you want to grow. And, given that Australian native plants range from the ground-hugging, cold-loving *Abrotanella* daisy of Tasmania to the tall, lush-foliaged macadamia tree of tropical Queensland, taking in the shrubby, prickly *Triodia* grasses of our dry interior and a vast number of other species on the way, it goes without saying that there are more than a few appropriate soil types. In fact, if you

got nervous looking at the climate-zone map, you may not even want to peek at the soil-zone map on the next page. Like climate maps, soil-zone maps are useful as a broad guide, but it's far more useful to get outside and experience the conditions in our particular spot for ourselves.

There are two reasons for this: first, soil-zone maps give a generalised view of the soil of a suburb but there are always pockets of soil that are different within that suburb. Second, the topsoil on your property may not be the original soil. However, looking at a soil-zone map and reading about the geology of your area are still extremely useful things to do because they may be able to help you define, or at least narrow down, what your soil type is. To better understand whether that spot will suit the plants we want to grow, let's first have a look at what soil actually is.

BELOW, LEFT AND RIGHT Digging a hole to examine the layers in your soil profile will help you understand its strengths and weaknesses.

WHAT IS SOIL?

To a geologist, a soil is what is left after rocks wear away. To a builder, soil is what can crack walls if it shrinks or swells too much. But to a gardener, soil is what supports plants by holding them up as well as feeding and watering them. To ensure that it keeps performing all those functions properly, it also needs turning, amending and planting into. Fortunately, soil is a subject where a little bit of knowledge goes a long way. A good start to creating the right soil for your plants is to understand that soil is made up of various combinations of *sand*, *silt*, *clay* and *organic matter*.

WHAT TYPE OF SOIL DO I HAVE?

If you don't know your garden's soil type already, it's time to get outside and get dirty. You need to get up close and personal with a handful of the stuff and really look at it and feel it. When you've got a good handful, can you identify organic matter such as decomposing leaves? Is the soil moist or dry? Can you see sand granules easily? If so, is there a high or low proportion of them compared with other ingredients? Does it feel sticky, slimy or gritty? See how it behaves when you squeeze it. Does it fall apart easily when you stop squeezing or does it remain clinging together? The answers to these questions will help you identify your soil type. And not just the topsoil. You need to get down into the subsurface layers to see what your plants' roots will eventually have to deal with.

It would be nice if all we had to do was look at a soil zone map, see what kind

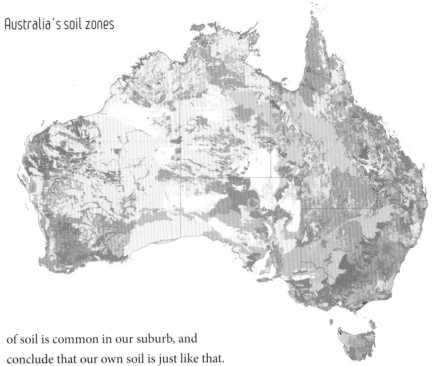

Australia's soil zones

of soil is common in our suburb, and conclude that our own soil is just like that. But geological processes don't understand zone maps. Soil can vary not only within suburbs but within gardens, particularly on sloping sites or ones that have a long human history, such as inner-city blocks. So check out different areas in your garden to see whether the soil type is consistent or not. It could help you to decide what to grow where.

Another thing to take into consideration (and one of the reasons we need to examine our soil closely) is whether or not soil was removed from your property before the house was built. These days it's common practice for much of the original topsoil to be carted away to create a stable building site. Later, new soil is trucked in. This causes several headaches for the gardener. First, we now have no way of knowing what the original topsoil was, so we can't imitate it even if we wanted to. Second, along with the topsoil has gone much of the microbial diversity that helps keep soil healthy

Soils generally without limiting chemical or physical properties
Soils with predominantly chemical limitations

Deep, highly structured soils with high initial fertility

Soils naturally low in nutrients

Calcareous soils

Saline soils
Soils with predominantly physical limitations

Deep, coarse-textured soils

Cracking clays

Hard-setting soils with dispersible clay subsoils

Soils with periodic subsurface waterlogging

Soils with periodic surface waterlogging

Shallow soils

Organic soils

Unallocated

(and which has evolved and adapted over aeons). Third, we're left with an exposed subsoil, which is usually very high in clay content, sets like a brick, and needs to be worked extensively before anything can be grown. And finally, developers often need to create a garden to sell the property, so they dump twenty centimetres of the cheapest soil mix they can find on top of the subsoil, then chuck in a few plants that have little hope of surviving. I can understand builders moving the topsoil to create a suitable working environment, but why remove the soil to replace it with an inferior product? If you are building or buying a new house and have any say in the matter, ask the builders to stockpile your soil for later redistribution.

I reckon there are three useful ways to work out your soil type:

1 SOIL TYPE IDENTIFIED BY EXPERIENCE

For the casual gardener (as opposed to the scientific one), soil descriptions are often experiential. If someone says, 'My back's aching from digging all afternoon with a crowbar, and I only managed to plant one lousy tree,' we understand that this lucky person probably has *clay* soil—quite likely with lots of rocks! If we hear, 'I've put enough compost into my soil to sink a ship, but it all just disappears,' we can be pretty sure this gardener has *sandy* soil. The wail 'My soil doesn't drain at all, and when it does dry it takes off in the slightest puff of wind' makes us think, 'Poor sucker,

FAR RIGHT A range of native plants, including the stunning black kangaroo paw (*Macropidia fuliginosa*) thrive in the naturally sandy soil at Kings Park in Perth, Western Australia.

that's definitely *silt*.' And when someone exclaims, 'My garden's looking amazing, everything's growing like crazy, and we planted a hundred windbreak trees yesterday,' we conclude that they have the holy grail of soil—*loam*.

2 SOIL TYPE IDENTIFIED BY SCIENCE

For the seriously scientific gardener, soil is made up of inorganic components that create its *texture*, living and dead organic components, water, air and various other gases. Many soils have a combination of all these materials, whose relative proportions determine the soil's type and characteristics. Also crucial is the way all the various components fit together to create a soil's *structure*. If our soil's texture and structure are in the right range, we will have an optimum balance of aeration and moisture to support good plant growth.

Basically, sand, silt and clay soils owe their textures to the different sizes of the mineral particles that make up their inorganic component. These particles

SOIL BREAKDOWN

	What does it look like?	What does it feel like?	How does it behave?
Sand	Large inorganic particles which are easy to see and relatively irregular in shape.	Gritty	It drains easily. It doesn't hold an electrical charge, so plants can struggle to absorb nutrients from it.
Silt	Particles which are smaller than sand but bigger than clay.	Mostly slimy, but your fingers will still make out a bit of grittiness.	It doesn't drain easily. The fine particles are prone to erosion by wind or water, and it can remain suspended in water. It has good nutrient content.
Clay	Tiny inorganic particles, which are not a uniform shape or size.	Sticky when wet	It has the largest surface area for its size because the particles are layered. It holds water well because of its shape. It also holds electrical charge, so plants can absorb nutrients from it.
Humus (decomposing organic material)	Particles of all shapes and sizes, depending on what they were originally and how old they are.	Loose and easily crumbled. It should also smell nice!	It aggregates or loosens soil. It holds water, as well as electrical charge, so plants can absorb nutrients from it.

come from the soil's parent rock, which might be weathered quartz, limestone, sandstone, or other materials, such as shells. They can also be transported to an area by wind.

A soil's organic components consist of the remains of once-living things: animals, leaves, flowers, fruits, insects, sticks; as well as living organisms such as fungi, bacteria, nematodes, worms, and so on.

Oxygen and other gases are important components of soil, and up to half of

the volume of a healthy soil may be air. Air pockets are essential not only for the movement of water, microbes and roots, but to let roots breathe. Oxygen in soil is just as vital to plant health as water and nutrients, which is one reason why we dig and loosen soil when we plant.

It's all these ingredients that determine the soil's type, its texture and how it behaves. What does *behaves* mean in the context of soil? Well, whether it drains easily or holds water; how it responds to amendments; if it can become compacted; whether it has a tendency to erode; how microbes work within it; how plants respond to it, and the like.

Although many soils contain all these components (see the table on page 24), our soil will be classed as sand, silt or clay depending on which component is *present in the greatest amount*. Loam, the fourth soil type, is the gardener's pot of gold because it contains fairly even percentages of sand, silt and clay (40–40–20). This means it drains well but holds moisture; that it can hold an electrical charge (essential for nutrient storage and uptake by plants); and that its particles cohere well, neither sticking tightly together nor falling apart too easily.

There are also peat soils and chalk soils, but they're less common in Australia, so we won't discuss them here. There are also more scientifically refined methods of classifying soil type (sandy loams, loamy sands, silty clays, and so on—all with varying percentages of the basic components), but they can be complicated and won't really help us in our quest to create the great Aussie native garden. If this section on soils gets you going, there are plenty of specialised books out there.

Spectacular Western Australian plants in Phil Vaughan's Bellarine Peninsula garden (see also pages 134–7) require good soil aeration to prevent root rot.

3 SOIL TYPE IDENTIFIED BY EXPERIMENT

On the right is a simple but extremely useful experiment in determining soil type. I call it the 'Sausage Experiment'. It can also be referred to as the 'Ribbon', 'Thread' or 'Roll' experiment. Give it a go!

SOIL LAYERS

When you collected the soil for the Sausage Experiment, you probably didn't dig too deeply. Now you need to. Why? Because soils aren't of uniform consistency all the way down. If you dig a hole, you'll see that the soil is made up of layers. By examining these layers, you can gain further insights into why your soil behaves as it does, and also determine the best ways to improve it.

Soil layers, also known as horizons, form because soil is constantly changing. As soil components weather, they become smaller and leach down deeper into the soil profile, particularly if they are small, like clay particles. The depth of each layer depends on things like what the soil's parent rock was, what plants grow there and how much litter they create, how exposed the soil is to the elements, and if it's already been amended or otherwise disturbed by humans.

There are four main horizons, but not every soil has all four. The O horizon is the thin uppermost layer, made up of decomposing leaf litter, grasses and other plants. The O layer is usually quite dark. Next comes the A horizon, often referred to as the topsoil. It consists mostly of the decomposing matter that's falling through from above. It still (usually) has a good

The sausage experiment
(a.k.a. scientific fun with mud)

Grab a large handful of soil and remove any stones, sticks and leaves. Break up any hard pieces until what's in your hand is uniform in size. Add a small amount of water until it's moist but not too wet.

Squash the soil into a ball. Does the ball hold its shape? — **NO** → You have sandy soil.

YES

Can you roll the soil into a sausage? — **NO** → You have loamy sand.

YES

Can you bend the sausage into a U-shape without cracks? — **NO** → You have loam, or silty loam.

YES

Can you bend the sausage into a ring without cracks? — **NO** → You have clay loam, or sandy clay.

YES

You have clay soil.

RIGHT In order to create a vibrant and colourful flower bed it may be necessary to improve the soil.
FAR RIGHT Plants from the semi-arid region of Western Australia require very well-drained sandy soils which can be provided through raised beds if required.

number of air pockets and is where living things such as microbes, worms and plant roots like to hang out. The B horizon is also known as the subsoil. It is more compacted and also usually paler than the layers above it, with less organic material. The photograph on page 22 (right) clearly shows a grey A horizon, with an ochre-coloured B horizon underneath. The C horizon, which sits just above the bedrock, contains relatively more of the parent rock that hasn't fully weathered yet.

Sometimes, erosion or human intervention causes horizons O and A to disappear. It's useful to recognise when this has happened, because it means you'll need to rebuild your topsoil layers before you can even consider planting anything. If there is no topsoil the ground will be compacted and very hard to dig into. It's also important to mix, mix, mix whatever top layers you do add with about fifteen to twenty centimetres of the subsoil. This will increase the proportion of your rebuilt topsoil that is well aerated and will help the different horizons to start working together. It will also help to guard against the culture shock that can occur when plant roots, after travelling happily through the topsoil for a few months, collide with the unwelcoming subsoil below.

SOIL MANIPULATION: THE WHYS AND HOWS

Now that you know what soil type you have, you're more likely to understand whether or not you need to manipulate it and how to go about your work if you do. What manipulation is required (if any) will depend, of course, on what you want to grow. Unlike the weather, soil is relatively easy to manipulate (assuming you have a strong back). Doing so allows you to optimise at least one of the fundamentals your plants require. But do you really need to fiddle with your soil to have an awesome native garden? It depends on what you have to start with and what you want to grow. But most soils will benefit from a bit of judicious handiwork.

SURVIVING OR THRIVING?

If a plant receives nutrients, water and sunlight, it will grow, because that's what plants are designed to do. But when plants grow, they don't know or care whether they're looking lush and healthy. They just want to survive and if possible reproduce and perpetuate their species.

Plants in the Australian bush are quite often merely *surviving* because they're constantly competing for extremely

limited food, water and light. They're doing a perfectly competent job of staying alive and producing seed in a good season (in the few years after a fire, say, when there are more nutrients available from the ash), but they're not exactly flourishing. We, of course, want the native plants in our gardens to *thrive* and look amazing. So we try to give them the best possible conditions, not just the bare bush minimum. This is one reason why we manipulate soil—to give our plants the very best chance to thrive. Our soil type may remain basically the same, but we'll tweak it here and there (add a touch of gypsum to clay, a lot of organic matter to sand, and so on) to help bring out its best qualities. We'll go into this in more detail later in the chapter.

TRICKING THE PLANT

Another reason for manipulating soil is so we can grow plants from another area. To do this successfully, we often need to trick them into believing they're at home. Naturally, we need a suitable climate to start with, but assuming we have it (or have created a microclimate that's close enough to it), manipulating the soil is the next step. The fact that we can do this is extremely exciting, because it means that within one garden we can create a variety of soil types, each supporting its own set of plants. We can have a mini-rainforest, with its deep, humus-rich soil; a dry, sandy rockery; and even a bog or pond garden edged with tall rushes that thrive in silty soil.

For this to work well in each case, we need to have a good idea of the plants' home soil. The good news is that this soil doesn't have to be replicated exactly: unless a plant hails from a tiny area, it's quite likely adapted to a range of soils. If—like many Western Australian plants— it loves sandy soils, for example, it will still feel at home in a variety of different sandy soils. And even if we can't create a sandy soil, we know that sandy soils drain well, so we can raise our garden beds to improve their drainage to mimic the effect.

DRAINAGE

Some plants prefer having wet feet and will thrive in boggy conditions, while others will curl up and die if their roots are waterlogged for any length of time. Most plants could cope with waterlogged soil for two or three days but any longer than that and they will start to show symptoms of stress such as leaf yellowing. The longer the soil remains waterlogged, the more the plant will die back, eventually reaching the point of no return and dying.

Part of our responsibility to the health of our plants is to understand the drainage conditions they like and to match these as closely as possible. Of course, some plants have a high tolerance for changes in soil moisture, while others have no tolerance at all. To satisfy our plants' needs, we also need to know the drainage conditions of our garden's original soil. This will tell us whether we should raise the garden bed, add more organic matter or sand, or just give up and plant lots of bottlebrushes, which love wet feet.

So—it's time to get our hands dirty again with another simple soil test. As with the Sausage Experiment, there are different ways to perform it. Here's our version, but you may prefer to Google for a version that suits you better.

RIGHT Before creating a garden featuring plants like this that require excellent drainage, it is strongly advisable to carry out the soil percolation experiment.

The soil percolation experiment
(a.k.a. scientific fun with water)

1. Dig a hole approximately 40 cm deep and 15 cm wide. Dig a few around your garden if your soil is variable.
2. Fill the hole with water and leave it to drain overnight.
3. Place a measuring stick or ruler into the hole. Ensure that it is long enough to go from the bottom of the hole to the top (or above).
4. Fill the hole with water.
5. For some very free-draining soils the water may sink out of sight within minutes, but for most soils it will take longer. Measure how far the water has dropped after an hour.

Less than 1.5 cm?
If the water level drops less than 1.5 cm in an hour, the soil is considered *poorly* drained.

Between 1.5 and 2.5 cm?
If the water level drops between 1.5 cm and 2.5 cm in an hour, the soil is considered *moderately* well drained.

Over 3 cm?
If the water level drops over 3 cm in an hour, the soil is considered *very well* drained.

BELOW Soil is the most important building block of your garden and should be closely examined to determine its structure, contents and type.

FAR RIGHT Some plants such as the waratah are fussier than others, so knowing your garden's direction(s) will be useful when deciding on plant placement.

AMENDING THE SOIL

Soil structure—the way our soil particles fit together—has a critical influence on the balance of water and aeration in our soil. Which brings us to another simple test. Take a pen and try to push it into your soil. If you have trouble doing that, imagine how much trouble the roots are having! A compacted soil needs to be broken up if our plants are to thrive.

CLAY

It probably goes without saying, but most clay soils need opening up. Space needs to be created for water, roots and microbes to move into. Lay into your clay with a mattock—or in extreme circumstances a crowbar—when it's slightly moist (if it is too dry it will turn to dust). Break it into fist-sized chunks (or smaller, if you don't have too many blisters) to a depth of about twenty centimetres. Before you add anything else, sprinkle gypsum at about 100 grams per square metre to begin with (a few good handfuls), and water it in well. When the soil has reached the slightly moist state again, turn it over with a garden fork, breaking the chunks up further. If you are really keen, you can also add coarse particles to the clay by mixing in coarse builder's sand (not fine sand), as well as stacks of mature compost or well-rotted manure. Generally speaking, the ratios for application are: one part clay (what you're starting with), one part sand, and one part organic matter. Adding even more organic matter can only help your plants in the long run—just make sure you work everything in well together.

SAND

Once again, mature compost comes to the rescue! You obviously won't have any problems digging it into sand, but it will be an ongoing chore. Sandy soil has a tendency to become hydrophobic (water resistant), and although organic matter helps it retain moisture generally, it can sometimes create a water-repellent surface on your soil. If you notice water beading and running off your soil at any stage, adding a soil-wetting agent will help overcome the problem.

SILT

Silt, being fine, has a tendency to erode and disperse. Adding organic matter helps combat this because (as with sand) it acts as a kind of glue that sticks the soil particles together. Silty soils will often tend to fall apart and form crusts on their surface that hinder the penetration of air and water. Silty soils also tend to become waterlogged owing to poor soil structure, particularly when they are disturbed, such as on building sites. Breaking up the soil and adding well-rotted organic matter will alleviate both of these problems.

Garden direction

Which way does my garden face? This always seems like an odd question, because surely gardens face every direction, particularly on a flat site. That is true, but if a site is sloping or bounded by a wall, it's useful to determine which way (north, south, east or west) it is most exposed to, because this affects how much sun it receives and how it is affected by prevailing winds. These factors in turn affect our design, plant choice and even how we manage our soil.

You can determine your garden's direction mostly by looking at where your home is situated on the block (and where most of the yard or open land is). First, use a compass or street directory to find out where north, south, east and west are in relation to your block. Another simple method is to point at the sun with your left hand in the morning and, while you're pointing at the sun, hold your right arm out directly to the side and point. This is roughly south. Alternatively, stop sleeping in and watch where the sun rises which, of course, is in the east.

Now sketch the outline of your block on a piece of paper. Add to it N, S, E, W on the relevant sides. Next, roughly sketch the house onto the paper. Where is most of the open land? We usually think of the house as 'facing', or looking into, the garden. This same direction is the *direction* of the garden. For example, if your block runs east–west and your house is roughly situated in the eastern section of the block (and you look out onto the western section), then you have a west-facing garden. If you have a small section of open land on the other side of the house, this is an east-facing garden.

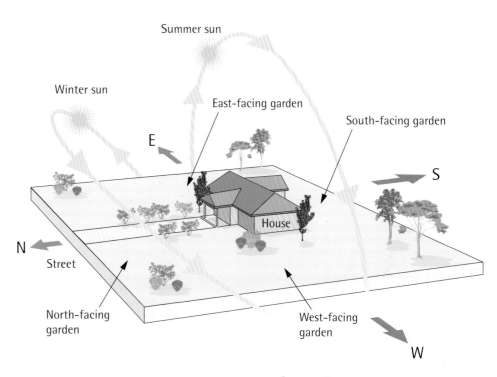

ELEMENTS THAT INDIRECTLY DETERMINE GARDEN DIRECTION

Sloping land: For example, you may have a rectangular block that runs north–south but is on a steep hillside that slopes towards the east. This garden is going to be in shade before a similar flat block because the sun is going to 'set' earlier there.

View: In this same scenario, your view to the east may be over a valley or it may look onto the surrounding neighbourhood where you can take advantage of the 'borrowed' landscape.

Street direction: Suburban blocks are generally rectangular, and houses are generally built closer to the street than the back fence, with the 'backyard' furthest from the street. If you know the street direction in such cases, you can quickly deduce which direction the garden faces.

It's all too easy to moan about the way our garden faces—'Woe is me, the garden faces west; it's too hot, everything shrivels up the first week of summer' or 'The garden faces south, so it's shady all the time, and in winter it's too cold to be out there'—but we really should be able to make our garden beautiful no matter which direction it faces. We can establish microclimates, adjust soil and carefully select suitable plants—after all, plants inhabit practically every land environment on earth no matter which way they face.

And while your garden as a whole faces a certain direction, different parts of it will face other directions. Each direction has challenges and positive attributes. Here are a few characteristics of gardens facing the four cardinal directions.

NORTH-FACING

This garden receives light for the whole day. In winter, when the sun rises and sets closer to north, this garden is lovely as it stays light and warm for longer. Plants in a north-facing garden need to be able to cope with a full day's sun. This can be too much for many plants during summer.

SOUTH-FACING

As could be expected, the picture here is pretty much the opposite. In summer, with the sun directly overhead, the southern orientation won't make much difference. But in winter the house will cast long shadows into the garden. South-facing gardens are usually relatively damp and cool, and this is, of course, more pronounced in winter. If you intend to install a pond, setting it in the south could be practical, as evaporation there will be somewhat reduced.

EAST-FACING

Many plants adore the rising sun and are quite content when the garden starts moving into shade after lunch. These are the plants you want in an east-facing garden, as they simply won't cope with the harsh afternoon rays. During summer the sun here still packs a hot punch, so keep the more delicate plants closer to the house.

WEST-FACING

Bearing the brunt of the sun in winter *and* summer, plants in west-facing gardens need to be tough. Soil will dry out excessively quickly and will need constant mulching and perhaps a soil-wetting agent to prevent hydrophobia. But you can still have shade-loving plants in a west-facing garden—you simply need to be smart with placement.

ABOVE If a garden faces the 'wrong' direction, boulders and other methods can be used to create a more favourable environment for plants.

FAR LEFT If you wish to grow the feather flowers (*Verticordia* species) of Western Australia in other climatic regions, you will need a microclimate created by a north-facing aspect.

RIGHT Freestanding walls, house eaves or large and small rocks are extremely useful for creating microclimates in a garden, as well as encouraging wildlife.

Microclimates

A microclimate is a small zone where the climate differs from that of the general area around it. Your whole garden may be a microclimate that allows you to grow plants that would not thrive on the other side of the street. On the other hand, most individual gardens will also have little pockets within them that create microclimates. Microclimates are created in various ways, usually unintentional but also by careful design. These can be broken down as follows:

Temperature: Stone and brickwork will absorb heat and radiate it back into the surrounding area, causing the temperature near them to be a few degrees warmer. This can help us mitigate the effects of frost. Courtyards therefore tend to be good places to grow plants that prefer warmer conditions.

Light: A north-facing slope will receive more sunlight throughout the day and thus be better for growing colourful beds of annuals such as everlasting daisies or brachyscomes.

Humidity: Areas of the garden where there is less airflow will tend to be more humid and would better suit rainforest plants rather than plants from drier climates.

Rainfall: A sheltered position may receive less direct rainfall, which will have an obvious influence on plant growth. As well, we can influence the amount of stormwater that gets channelled into areas of soil to try to create microclimatic effects.

Close acquaintance with your garden is probably the best way to identify microclimates. Why not grab a sun hat, a cool drink and your orange banana lounge and spend a day moving around your yard? As you go, note down microclimatic influences such as wind tunnels or variations in light at different hours and seasons.

Aside from the microclimates that form in your garden as an inevitable result of building and planting activities, you can create your own microclimates by various means. Rockeries and water features, for example, can form niches where you can grow those 'must have' plants that would otherwise struggle or die. Don't be scared to transplant a sulking specimen to a different part of the garden where you've identified a different microclimate. I have seen some astonishing variations in the performance of different specimens of the same cultivar or species in different spots within my own garden.

Garden location
COURTYARD AND BALCONY GARDENS

For my money, the key to making Australian plants work in a small courtyard-type garden lies in deciding what sort of 'look' we are after and ensuring that it can work within the constraints of prevailing light and climatic conditions. An urban environment will usually create a microclimate that is significantly warmer than otherwise, so our choice of garden style would ideally be tailored to these conditions. For instance, a lush look is easiest to create with rainforest plants. Or maybe we want a Zen-style garden, with formally topiarised plants combined with areas of raked gravel.

While small city gardens do often have some constraints such as shading, they also provide a wonderful opportunity. In small areas, you should be able to afford to create growing mediums in containers and raised beds that will be perfect for whatever plants you wish to grow. Dwarf kangaroo paws, for example, can be grown in containers to stunning effect. These hybrid cultivars have been bred to flower all year round, but they tend to be a bit touchy in the ground, as they require very good drainage but also good moisture retention in their growing medium. A high-quality potting mix will give them perfect growing conditions, provided you have a well-lit spot. Be aware, though, that to reach their best they will need extra water and feeding as well.

Another key to the small garden lies in careful selection of plants by size. I have occasionally seen the blunder of a large tree planted in the front yard of an inner-city terrace—and then, when its gargantuan size becomes apparent, having to be removed at great expense. There is now a wealth of compact Australian plant cultivars to choose from, and the palette grows larger every year. If you are in doubt about the size of a plant, then growing it in a pot will certainly limit it to manageable proportions. Then, if it does grow too big, you can always find a home for it elsewhere.

Another great opportunity in courtyard-sized gardens is to use some of the many new strappy-leaved cultivars of *Lomandra* and *Dianella* species. This style of plant will never have an invasive root system, is easily divided, and can be moved around the garden to create mass plantings with minimal effort and cost. Some of my favourites are the new grey-leaved *Lomandra* and *Dianella* cultivars.

SUBURBAN-STYLE BLOCKS

The average size of outer-suburban blocks has shrunk steadily over the past twenty years. New subdivisions now rarely exceed 500–600 square metres, while traditional quarter-acre blocks are increasingly being consumed by 'dual-occupancy' subdivisions where a second house is added to the existing one. The chief result of this radical change in suburban landscapes is that there is much less room for medium to large trees. In relatively confined spaces, biggish trees not only create potential hazards if they drop branches or are uprooted during storms; they also make it extremely difficult for smaller plants around them to thrive, since they compete with them for water and nutrients.

Creating a new suburban garden (or remodelling an old one that has

A slatted front fence allows privacy but doesn't exclude the landscape beyond.

been subdivided) requires very careful planning, particularly with respect to plant selection, to ensure that the result is safe and easy to care for. Using Australian plants not only makes a garden look good, it also attracts birds and other animals, adding fauna to our flora. As with the courtyard-style garden, it is useful to be realistic about the constraints that limited space creates and try to choose a 'look' based on the sorts of plants that will thrive without too much effort on your part.

Medium to large shrubs are particularly useful in the suburban garden, where we have a bit more room than a courtyard but not enough space for trees. Callistemons, grevilleas and melaleucas all provide numerous options wherever you are in Australia. These plants can create a framework that attracts birds but allows plenty of light into the understorey, giving you a much wider choice of plants to place around them. If you love flowering plants, then letting more light into your garden will broaden your planting palette as well as boosting the numbers of flowers the plants will produce. Very few native plants will continue to flower well in medium to heavy shade.

TOP AND RIGHT The constraints of a suburban block shouldn't dull creative inspiration for bringing the delights of the bush into your backyard.

Nothing could be more enticing to children or dogs than a large expanse of lawn!

BIG BLOCKS

If you are lucky enough to have plenty of space to play with, then your options really open up. You can let your hair down and plant avenues and feature trees to create a landscape that most gardeners only dream about. While it is exciting to be able to use large trees in landscaping, we need to be mindful of the large amounts of water and nutrients they need to thrive. A large tree will usually have a dramatic effect on anything planted within five metres of its base. So if you wish to have a vibrant garden of shrubs and low-growing plants, your large trees need to be planted well away from these areas. An avenue of silky oak (*Grevillea robusta*), with its glowing golden blooms, alternating with Illawarra flame tree (*Brachychiton acerifolius*), in its fire-engine-red glory, is a truly spectacular sight.

In larger gardens, topography should have a big influence on your design and choice of plant material. Sloping sites create opportunities for terracing and creating microclimates for species with particular requirements. On the other hand, flat sites lend themselves to a series of mounds that not only creates an interesting landscape but, again, allows the creation of microclimates and soil types that allow a much greater variety of species to be grown.

CLOCKWISE FROM TOP LEFT In a large garden, open spaces are as important as the plants for creating a sense of balance; A small rock outcrop is an lovely addition to a garden; A 'borrowed' landscape has been incorporated beautifully into this garden setting; A large block offers almost limitless possibilities; A steep slope has been used to create a garden feature as well as to help prevent erosion.

Garden style

A boisterous Australian businessman with a flair for all things horticultural once noted: 'A stylish garden may not have a particular style, and a garden of a particular style may not be particularly stylish.' For some people, creating a stylish garden is as natural as running downhill is for water. They don't *need* to follow a particular style—they just seem to throw plants willy-nilly about the garden and it all comes together beautifully.

Unfortunately, creating a garden that doesn't look excessively cluttered, haphazard or just plain weird is not as easy as the naturally gifted make it look. In fact, it can be downright confusing—and expensive! That's why, in my opinion, it's much easier to follow the 'rules' of a specific garden style to achieve the look you want. While this is by no means essential, rules can provide useful direction and boundaries. The trick is to know when to pull back so the garden doesn't end up looking contrived. We all know that some rules almost beg to be broken. But we need to know the rules before we know how we can break them to best effect.

Think of football, for example (any variety). Some rules for footy include: a set number of players; a specific duration for each game; a particular score each time the ball is kicked through the goalposts. We can't fiddle with these rules or it will be another game. Other rules or conventions, however, are open to interpretation. They're the rules that, when *our* team gets away with them, have us cheering, and when the *other* team gets away with them, make us curse the umpire! It's these rules that can (unofficially) be broken. And it's the varying interpretations of these rules that lend zing and excitement to the game.

It's the same with garden styles. Some rules need to be followed or our style becomes something else. Other rules are open to interpretation—indeed, breaking them adds that special zing of individuality to a garden. We just need to know which rules are set in stone for each style and which ones can be tweaked. So let's take a look at a few popular styles and their basic rules.

These bright yellow kangaroo paws would make a statement in any garden.

FORMAL

These gardens intend to show human dominance over nature. Historically, they tend to be on large estates, but their rules can be applied to large country properties, tiny city courtyards, and everything in between. The rules for formal gardens include neatly mown lawns with sharp edges, geometric (often symmetrical) designs, and clipped hedges. There are no rules for how large or small the lawn should be, what plants should be used, or which geometric patterns should be created. So have some fun with it.

CLOCKWISE FROM TOP The owner of this garden has thought laterally by using the bower of beauty (*Pandorea jasminiodes*) vine as a clipped hedge in his formal garden; New red growth on the topiary lilly pillies (*Syzygium* species) contrasts wonderfully with the vivid green hedges in this formal garden; Picket fences are almost obligatory in a cottage-style garden.

FAR RIGHT Australia's diverse daisy varieties, such as these brachyscomes and everlastings, are perfect for a cottage garden setting.

COTTAGE

Traditionally, cottage gardens were practical gardens, mixing densely planted edibles with ornamentals in wide beds. For a while, fashion swayed away from food and towards ornamentals alone. Now, however, we're increasingly using edibles again—especially those with good looks! Cottage gardens are cheerful, romantic and informal. To the casual observer, they may seem haphazard, even messy. In reality, they are examples of carefully organised chaos. These gardens are for gardeners with time on their hands.

What implicitly defines a cottage garden is … a cottage. But we can still create a cottage garden by having a structure or two of some sort overflowing with floral climbers. (Whether you use arbours, trellises or archways, ensure that they have a cottagey feel—putting a Japanese temple in a cottage garden is just asking for trouble!) Another common feature is a picket (or similar) fence to separate the cottage and its garden from the rest of the grounds. This can be useful on larger properties, but on suburban lots the main fence fulfils this purpose. Cottage-garden beds are usually quite wide (but keep yours to the scale of your house) and massed with densely planted alternating groups of flowers. Paths are another feature—straight or curved, and often made of brick or pebbles. These gardens have a mixture of small trees, climbers, annuals, perennials and shrubs, and the plants are notable more for their flowers than foliage. There may be a lawn or there may not—once again, there is plenty of room for individual interpretation!

TROPICAL

Tropical gardens are jungles. Australia is home to some of the world's great remaining jungles (also known as rainforests), and we are still finding plenty of new species in them, with fantastic horticultural potential. Tropical gardens are informal and densely planted. Green is the dominant colour, but there may be splashes of vibrant colours from accent flowers or foliage. Tropical gardens are vertical, because everything's heading upwards into the light, so vines and epiphytes suit this style well. Edges, paths, walls and sculptures tend to be simple and made from timber, rock or plant matter. Mulch and leaf litter is thick. That's it! Given that Australia has rainforests of all different types all the way from Cape York to Tasmania, with a bit of imagination you can create a 'tropical' garden in a wide range of climatic conditions.

BUSH

With such diversity in the Australian bush, a bush garden can include anything from cool, temperate or tropical rainforest to dry or wet sclerophyll woodland, and from heath shrubbery to desert or coastal landscapes. The rules of this informal garden style are comparatively loose, but including such elements as dead logs, bark or pebble paths and rough timber edging will help. Using recycled materials such as a corrugated iron divider or some carefully placed rusty farm implements also screams 'Aussie'!

ABOVE Tree ferns add drama to any tropical style garden—from Tasmania's cool rainforests to the Top End's steamy jungles.
LEFT AND BELOW A garden feels fresh and alive all year round with a basic palette of rainforest plants.
RIGHT With such colourful options, Australian bush gardens need never be bland!

JAPANESE

In traditional Japanese gardens, every element and its placement has symbolic meaning. But you don't need to understand the symbolism to create a garden with a Japanese feel. Most important is to remember that you are attempting to imitate nature. There will be no square ponds, no harshly clipped formal hedges, and everything will be carefully scaled to the dimensions of your block. It's also important to consider neighbouring properties—the borrowed landscape—and try to bring your garden into harmony with them. The garden is to be appreciated during every season, so when choosing plants, think deciduous! Japanese gardens are not cluttered, and the spaces set off the contents and vice versa. Often an enclosed courtyard-type retreat space is included, perhaps lined with pebbles and dotted with rocks. There may also be a water feature, a small bridge, a temple-style gazebo or archway, or a stone lantern. Just don't include them all (unless your garden is large): with a Japanese-style garden, less is definitely more!

RIGHT AND TOP Plants such as the coastal rosemary (*Westringia fruticosa*), *Lomandra* 'Tanika' and lilly pilly are perfect alternatives to those used traditionally in Japanese gardens. *FAR RIGHT* Use simple ornaments, sparingly, as finishing touches to your styled garden.

BALINESE

Balinese gardens are wild! In essence, of course, they are tropical gardens, so all the rules that apply to tropical gardens apply here, too. Balinese-style gardens should incorporate lots of large-leafed architectural-type plants to provide dramatic structure, but vividly coloured accent plants are also imperative. Although mostly informal, they can have some formal elements, such as straight paths. These are often created from square pavers set among pebbles and edged with low-growing, deep-green grasses. At the end of the path could be a focal point—a carved statue of a Balinese dancer or a water feature (not a fountain, but a spout dropping water into a concrete trough, or a round urn with still water and floating lilies). The requisite vibrant colours are provided by plants, flags, replica temple doors, and so on. A raised timber pavilion with thatched roof and grass matting—with or without a day-bed—also says 'Bali'. You may wish to include a statue of a Hindu deity set in a protective nook, where you can honour the spirit of the garden by burning incense or placing gifts of flowers.

While it may seem incongruous to include Japanese and Balinese-style gardens in a book about Australian gardens, I think it is high time we acknowledged our location and our burgeoning cultural connections with South-East Asia. Australians increasingly visit the region in preference to Europe, so it is not surprising that we should want to bring influences from Asian cultures into our own evolving culture and lifestyle.

CHOOSING YOUR OWN STYLE

You'll notice that when explaining these basic styles, I refrained from naming specific plants. This is because no matter where in Australia you live, you can create any one of these gardens with native plants suitable for your conditions. If you have a large property, you could even experiment by creating a series of garden rooms, each following a different theme. Just be sure they can't all be seen at once, or the effect will be utter confusion! For the same reason, in smaller gardens mixing styles is to be avoided at all costs.

Using a particular style as a template for your native garden is a great way of narrowing down plant choices and generally making the whole design process less overwhelming. Remember, though, that style is also about putting a personal stamp on your outdoor space. How can your passions, hobbies and indulgences be reflected in your garden to create a unique outdoor environment? How can your *styled* garden also be *stylish*?

Those are rhetorical questions because only you can answer them, but here's a quick note on stylishness: Sometimes we can follow all the right rules and tweak all the right rules and still, somehow, the garden doesn't work. After long and careful observation of many gardens, I've come to the conclusion that the secret is usually in the details. For example, a gardener might include too many ornaments for the size of the plot, making the garden look over-full and tacky. Another error is mismatched hard landscaping: square concrete pavers in a bush garden, or log edges around a formal lawn are never going to work.

A common mistake is to under-estimate the mature size of plants. When this happens, garden beds quickly become overcrowded, plant health and reputation suffer, and the design (if there was one) is shot to pieces. Another understandable but equally destructive error is impulse buys at the nursery. You're meandering along, trying to help your mother-in-law choose a shrub to replace the one that just died in the front garden next to the lemon tree, when a striking bloom grabs your attention or an unusual foliage form beckons you from the next aisle. Before you know it, there are three extra passengers spilling potting mix on the floor of your car. And that's the least of your worries. As much as you may have appreciated these plants in the nursery, in reality you have no idea where you're going to put them in the garden, and more often than not, they don't suit the style.

So the fundamentals of creating a stylish garden are quite simple: follow the right rules, break the right rules, and think about what you're doing!

ABOVE Recycled iron objects work perfectly in bush-style gardens.
TOP AND RIGHT Deciding how the garden will be used will ensure the garden *is* used!

Using the garden

There's no denying it—we Aussies are an outdoor mob and love to be in the garden. Whether it's playing cricket, cultivating vegies, or relaxing with mates and burning a bit of barramundi on the barbie, we can think of few better places to be than in our own backyard. Which is why, when planning your garden, it's important to consider how you will actually use it.

Most of what we do in the garden falls under one of three headings: general gardening, rest and relaxation, and chores.

GENERAL GARDENING

Pruning, weeding, feeding, propagating, digging, composting, planting, and other nice things—you may put these in the rest and relaxation category; others might call them chores. But for most people, general gardening falls in between.

To support your gardening, the garden may need to house the *shed* where you store your gardening tools and equipment, the *table* where you do your propagating and potting up (ideally close enough to the shed so we don't spend half of Sunday traipsing back and forth, and close enough to the driveway to make carting heavy bags of potting mix less arduous), and perhaps a *greenhouse*.

If you like rodents, cockroaches, snakes and gross smells visiting you at home, then ignore this piece of advice: don't place your *compost bin* close to the house. (Unless it's one of those tumbler types; they would be OK.) Find somewhere more practical—it may be

near the rubbish bins so you can take everything out together, or near the vegie patch to make moving the compost easier.

REST AND RELAXATION

Without a doubt, the reason we garden and do chores so diligently is because we just love to relax in the garden. So what do you do in yours? Read? Write? Sleep? Eat? Play? Swim? Sunbake? Entertain? Watch the fauna? Admire the flora? Answering the question of *who* and *how many* do *what* in the garden is imperative to working out what should be included within its bounds and where it should go. Consider things such as:

- *Kiddies:* sandpit, trampoline, swing, cubby, exploring, lawn, shade.
- *Teenagers:* hammock, separate entertaining area, pool.
- *Adults:* Pergola, entertaining/barbecue area, seats.
- *Pets:* Kennel, feeding spot, sheltered area, room to play and explore safely.
- *Fauna:* Remember—people are not the only ones using your garden! Plan for habitats (hollow logs, old pipes, fauna boxes) and water (ponds, baths, bowls), and keep your special guests safe from pets and vice versa.

Other R & R elements you could use in your garden are statues, pots, a pond, birdbath, bird feeder or water feature.

CHORES

Although we like to envision our time in the garden as being all fun and games, in reality that's seldom the case. But if your garden is planned with an eye to the practical, outdoor chores should become at least tolerable, which is more than you can say for vacuuming the lounge room. Garden chores include:

- *Mowing the lawn:* I know some would put this in the general gardening section, but really—who, other than sheep and guinea-pigs, likes mowing the lawn? When planning the garden, pay attention to edges: of garden beds, around trees, and so on. Raised edges are harder to mow close to, so if you have them you may need to whipper-snip as well. Also consider how much spare time you have, and perhaps adjust the size of your lawn accordingly. In the warmer months, lawns will require mowing at least every couple of weeks—that's a lot of weekends to waste every year! In fact, if you don't have any budding sportspeople in the family or if you've discovered fake tanning, why not dispense with a lawn altogether?
- *Hanging out the washing:* Apparently not everyone likes watching clothes dry—from the house. I'm not certain why, but in some circles clotheslines are regarded as an eyesore. If you're one of these people, when you're planning line placement look at the garden from inside the house, on the verandah, and so on, to find the least disagreeable spot.

Other considerations here are: *the direction of the sun* (avoid putting the line on the east or south sides of the house); *the type of line* (a Hill's Hoist is great for larger gardens or if you have kids, but folding or retractable lines are great for smaller gardens or if you need

to use the space for other things); and *the access path* (this should be safe to get to and from in a hurry during sudden downpours, made of material that won't be tracked into the house, and easy to wheel a trolley along if you choose. Remember to include a 'standing section' at the end of the path.)

- *Putting out the rubbish:* If you ever need proof that we've become a throw-away society (though hopefully a more responsible one), look no further than the variety of rubbish and recycling bins supplied by councils. Where and how your bins are placed in the garden deserves a bit of attention. Some people shove them down the side of the house, others leave them easily accessible (and visible) in the front yard, others lug them to and from the backyard every week, and others again create permanent homes for their bins. Until rubbish bins come in more attractive colours, I'm with the permanent-home folk, since all it takes to make one is four stakes in the ground and a bit of brushwood screening. There are plenty of how-to sites online, or you can buy a prebuilt unit.

Consider how you'll move the bins to and from the street, the path material (it's difficult pulling a heavy bin across pebbles) and what might be in your way (plants, cars, and so on). Making the chore easy will pay dividends down the track when even the teenagers aren't averse to it. (Dream on!)

Now, if you're thinking there's a lot to consider when planning how you'll use your garden, you're right. I know you've heard this before, but it's true: time spent planning is time not wasted.

Garden art

You've spent weeks planning the garden and months building it. Now it's finally finished, and the fun time begins. Yes, it's time to decorate. As with choosing finishing touches for your home, deciding what special pieces to add to the yard can be tricky. But it's also a great opportunity to bring your own creative style to the garden. Because art is so personal, you can get away with anything—up to a point.

Artistic items include:

- *Pots*—big, little, terracotta, timber, stone, concrete, mosaic, plain, fancy, empty, full of water/plants, single, grouped, standing up, lying down
- *Sculptures*—contemporary, cute, statement pieces, stylised, subtle, realistic, humorous
- *Practical items*—benches, water features, pergolas, gazebos, gates
- *Wall hangings*
- *Flags*
- *Logs*
- *Cast-iron anything!*

Original pieces of garden art add a touch of whimsy and are fun to encounter when exploring the garden.

TOP Simple focal sculptures are perfect adornments to a contemporary garden. ABOVE A quirky piece of Australiana is in keeping with the earthy feel of this bush setting. FAR RIGHT A creative touch can turn a simple path into a striking feature.

MATCH THE STYLE

Before you go rushing off to spend up big on your art (isn't that what connoisseurs do?), consider the look you're going for and the style of your garden. Nothing can make a garden look tacky quite as quickly as misplaced art! An ornate Venetian pot, for example, will look more at home in a formal garden setting than in a minimalistic contemporary one; likewise, a concrete statue of two girls skipping may blend into a cottage garden a tad more easily than into a Japanese-style courtyard.

The same is true for materials. If you have a bush garden, art pieces of stone, timber, concrete or terracotta would be good choices. In contemporary gardens, it's less about the material than the style—stick with simplified, plain pieces. For a formal garden you'd probably choose concrete or stone, while timber and stone will suit a Japanese, Balinese or tropical garden.

INSPIRE ME

For inspiration, visit public spaces, private gardens (with permission, of course), art galleries, vineyards (any excuse needed?), garden centres, potteries and markets.

WAYS TO USE ART IN THE GARDEN

- As a *focal point*—at the end of a garden or straight path
- As a *statement*—in the middle of a lawn
- As an *obstacle*—in the path to slow people down
- *Practically*—for sitting on, or distracting from an ugly view

HOW MUCH IS ENOUGH?

As for how many pieces of art you place strategically about your garden: that's up to you and your wallet. However, I offer the same advice as I did on matching the art to the style of your garden—too much can cross the border from tasteful to tacky. You don't need five miniature temples, eight stone lanterns and twenty-four moss-covered rocks to create a Japanese style garden. But if you simply must have the entire collection of fourteen concrete angels, then for goodness' sake position them subtly. Hide them in the shrubbery so they're unnoticed until you walk past—let them surprise. If you insist on placing them in full view, then follow a very simple design principle: group them all together. Very similar items—be they terracotta pots, shapely green bottles, pieces of driftwood or, heaven help us, concrete angels—can, when grouped together, make a real statement.

CONSIDER HOME-MADE

Rather than splurge on art, why not make it yourself—whatever you want—with new or recycled materials? You'll have fun, learn something and create a truly unique piece. Get the kids involved: they love nothing more than putting their own stamp on their play spaces. Give them their own area of the garden to design and decorate.

Paths

Being led up the garden path needn't be a negative experience. The right path in the right place and made from the right material can be attractive as well as practical, and enhance your garden experience. When planning a path, think how it will be used. This will help you make sensible decisions on things like width, route and material. Is the path to be used (mostly) for quick access, gentle strolls, one person, two people, kids, adults, dogs? Is the path in a damp, shady or uneven area? If so, you may choose to use gravel or mulch rather than pavers, which could become slippery and need to lie flat.

Consider the style and material of the house. If these don't especially match the garden style you're going for, a carefully considered path can help tie everything together. For example, if you have a plain red brick house and you absolutely *must* have a tropical-style garden, consider a gravel path with groups of similar bricks inset as stepping stones.

Be mindful when visiting other homes as to how the paths are used

PLACEMENT

When planning the garden, first consider the placement of the primary paths: front gate to front door; garage to back door; back door to washing line. Secondary paths should complement the primary paths: rubbish bins to street; back door to shed; general path through garden. By complement I mean echo the shape, flow and style. Where possible, multitask your paths—let them work as both primary and secondary paths.

People want to take the shortest route to wherever they're heading. This is apparent in most public parks, which feature well-worn 'cattle' tracks diagonally linking the main paths. If you don't want this happening in your garden, then pick the shortest route! You may appreciate the long winding path leading from the gate to the front door that lets you enjoy all the hidden delights of your garden, but you can bet any delivery people won't. So unless you don't mind your *Lomandra longifolia*, *Scaevola aemula* and *Syzygium australe* being trampled on and pushed through, pick the shortest route!

STYLE

These simple guidelines should make planning your paths much easier:

WIDTH

Choose a narrow path (70–90 cm) if:

- You want people to slow down—the ground might be slippery or uneven, or you may want them to admire something.
- You want people to walk in single file.
- The path is used only intermittently— by service people or such.

Choose a wide path (1.2 m) if:

- You want two people to be able to walk side by side.
- You have enough space and the path will still be in proportion to the rest of the area.

ROUTE

Choose a *straight* path if:

- You want people to get somewhere quickly.
- The distance is too short for a curved path.
- It's an amenity path (washing line, rubbish bin, service meter).

Choose a *curved* or *winding* path if:

- You want people to appreciate a particular plant or view.
- It suits the style of garden.
- You want to create a sense of mystery.

LEFT AND RIGHT Choice of path width, material and design can define and bring life to a garden's style.

MATERIAL

Always consider the style and material of the house. If mixing materials (pavers in gravel, flagstones in sand), ensure the colours and styles are complementary. Bricks set amid bark topping, for example, is a combination that's unlikely to work all that well.

Choose *gravel* or *pebbles* if:

- You want a cheaper option. Gravel or pebbles are probably the only materials that will suit any style of garden—it's their colour and size, and the edging, that will define a look.
- You require added security (it's very difficult to walk quietly on gravel!).
- You don't have to get somewhere quickly.

Choose *bark* topping if:

- Your garden style is tropical, bush or Balinese.
- You want an inexpensive path.
- A well-worn track is becoming slippery.

Choose *grass* if:

- Your garden style is cottage or formal.
- You need to cool an area.
- The path isn't used as the main drag.

Choose *brick* if:

- Your garden style is cottage or formal.
- You want to tie the house in with the garden.
- You want to get somewhere quickly.
- You need access for a stroller, wheelchair, bicycle or rubbish bins.

Choose *flagstones* if:

- Your garden style is cottage, Balinese or Japanese (use sparingly). In some cases, flagstones can also work in a tropical garden.
- You want a relaxed look.

Choose uniformly shaped *concrete* or *stone* pavers if:

- Your garden style is contemporary, Balinese, Japanese, or formal.
- You have an area in a gravel path that requires more stability.
- You need to get somewhere quickly.
- You need access for a stroller, wheelchair, bicycle or rubbish bins.
- You need particularly safe access.

COLOUR

Consider the house colour and garden style. What type of mood are you trying to create? Darker colours will convey a more sombre mood and could be suitable for Balinese, tropical and some contemporary-style gardens. Light colours will make a path more visible and 'vibrant', conveying a more active mood.

EDGING

This can be used in any garden—path function and garden style will determine what sort of edging will be most appropriate.

- Use natural edging such as *rocks*, *logs*, *treated timber* or *railway sleepers* if your garden style is tropical, Balinese or bush.
- Use *bricks* if your garden style is country or formal.
- Use *flexible metal*, *timber* or *plastic* edging with any style garden—just be careful how you use them and what the result looks like.
- Use *concrete* or *stone* if your garden style is formal, contemporary, Japanese or Balinese.
- Use *wire* edging if your garden style is country.

Water

Considering the movement of rainwater on your property is wise for a huge number of reasons. Do you remember this sentence from the section on Australia's climate zones?

'Australia is the world's driest inhabited continent, and about 80 per cent of the country is classified as semi-arid or arid.' If that isn't enough to make you think carefully about your water capture, storage, movement and usage, then you have my permission to stop reading this section! Even if you live in a high-rainfall area, knowing a few tricks for helping rain soak into the right parts of your garden and not flood other parts is just as important as learning how to keep water on your property in drier climes.

Many of the best ways to capture and keep water *on* a property are also used to move water safely *around* and *off* the property. Let's look at some passive ways to do this.

ABOVE AND FAR RIGHT: There are many ways to store and move water through the garden.

RAINWATER TANKS

This is the obvious place to store rainwater in large amounts. If you have gutters on every roof, shed and garage that are connected to a large tank or two (and you don't live in the desert), it's quite possible to survive on this water alone.

If you are considering installing tanks, you need to know how much rain you can harvest from your roof. To do this, first calculate the area of the roof in square metres (length in metres x width in metres). Then multiply the result by the average annual rainfall in millilitres. The answer will also tell you how many litres your tanks need to hold.

There are now so many types of tanks available (not to mention water barrels, large pots, and so on) that there's just no excuse for not harvesting at least a few thousand litres a year. Installing a small tank and using the water only for the garden during the dry months can really allay your worries about whether the garden will survive or not. No more watering on allocated days only—water when your plants need it!

Harvesting the rain is, of course, a passive measure. The water falls onto the roof, enters the gutters and makes its merry way into the tank. If the tank is up on a stand and its destination is lower than the tank, then gravity will move the water out. But this is really only useful if you are filling buckets and such. To water the garden effectively, you need pressure, and that means power. So if you have a tank, you'll also need a pump.

FROM ROOF TO GARDEN

An enormous amount of water goes into our stormwater systems every year, creating all sorts of pollution problems in creeks, rivers and oceans. So keeping as much water on our property as possible is good for our waterways as well as our plants. Collecting water in tanks is one solution. Dams—if you have the space—are another. But if neither of these measures is suitable for you, I have another suggestion. Divert your downpipes directly into the garden. A brilliant passive irrigation system following this principle was built by Tony and Yvette Gregorovich (you will find the plan and outline on page 140).

SWALES

Ah, I do love a swale! They are so useful in the garden—on flat land that may be prone to flooding or sloped land where you want to either slow the water down or keep it on your property. What is a swale? It's a dip or slight depression between a couple of ridges (though technically, if you are on a hillside you may just have one ridge and the area of the slope above the ridge would be considered the swale). Swales look like channels set into the ground—you've probably seen them running down the centres of freeways.

On flat land in flood-prone areas, it can be useful to channel water into a purpose-built swale so the water can subside at a slower rate in an area where it's not going to cause any problems. Water collected here can also potentially top up the groundwater. Flat-land swales are usually planted with turf and/or flood- and erosion-resistant plants.

Swales on sloping land are designed to run across the slope; as rain travels down the hill, it settles into the dip of the swale before hitting the ridge below. These kinds of swales are brilliant for slowing water and therefore helping prevent erosion, and

are perfect water collectors. Almost any plant can be grown in this situation and most are very thankful for the extra water!

Swales don't have to be large to be effective. When planting a tree on a slope, always create a mini-swale for it—just mound the soil in a semi-circle on the downside of the tree to capture the water as it runs down the slope. And if you're on an average suburban block, consider creating a few smaller swales throughout the garden that damp-loving plants can be planted into; those that prefer well-drained soil can be planted on top. When the plants grow and fill the spaces, you will hardly notice the swales.

SLOWING THE RAIN

Rain can travel downhill very quickly. Slowing the water helps prevent erosion as well as allowing more rain to soak into the ground. But sometimes water behaves unpredictably. So, next time there's a downpour, grab an umbrella and go into the garden. Watch where the water's coming from, where it's going and what it's doing on the way. It's a fascinating exercise, and it will tell you exactly where you need to slow or redirect the water.

Simple devices for slowing water on a hill include strategically placed rocks, logs, sandbags and such. You could even hammer in a few garden stakes and attach doubled-over shade cloth to it, digging the material a few centimetres into the ground to prevent water from flowing underneath. Any of these measures can be placed on the downside of specific plants if you need them to have more water. It's like making a mini-swale, only with solid materials more resistant to being washed away. A common sight now is 'walls' of heavy-duty wire filled with large stones. These are perfect, not only for slowing water near a plant but for collecting sediment, leaves and twigs, and keeping them out of stormwater drains.

Keeping water on your property is beneficial for wildlife and prevents pollution of our rivers and oceans.

PERMEABILITY

Probably one of the easiest ways to keep water on your property is to use permeable materials for driveways and paths so water can soak straight through.

IRRIGATION

Installing an irrigation system can be a great way to save water. These days they're extremely efficient, because they deliver set amounts of water and the sprinklers can be set to different spray patterns, eliminating overspray problems. Drip-line or seeper hoses are the most efficient, as they don't waste a drop of water—it's all delivered to the roots, exactly where it's needed.

Irrigation systems can be *manual*—just turn on the tap; *semi-automatic*—using a timer on the tap; or *fully automatic*—using solenoids and different delivery rates for different parts of the garden. You also don't need an engineering degree to be able to install them—they're just like Lego for big kids. But if it all seems a bit confusing at first, visit a professional irrigation system supplier—many will help you design your irrigation system free of charge as well as expertly explaining how the gadgets and gizmos work.

If you don't want your new garden to rely on supplementary watering, using an irrigation drip-line system solely for establishment watering might also be useful.

Plant functions and features

Plants grow all over Australia—which means there is a native plant suitable for virtually any spot. We simply need to decide what we want our plants to do—how we want them to *function* in the garden. If that seems like a strange expectation, consider that plants can:

- offer shade for us, our house and animals
- bring colour at all times of the year
- create differing height layers
- attract birds, insects and other fauna by providing food and habitat
- provide bush tucker
- bring pleasant scents wafting into the house
- help prevent erosion
- bring mystery to a garden
- offer a place to play
- bring interesting shapes and textures to a garden
- help create microclimates, and
- perform many of these functions at the same time!

You'll probably find that plants you like perform the functions you most appreciate. For example, you may be drawn to 'structural' or 'architectural' plants rather than 'shrubby' or flower-bearing plants. Since structural plants retain consistent form throughout the year, they can be used to great effect as focal points. They are used very effectively in modern landscapes, linking a contemporary house to the garden without spoiling the strong structural lines of the home. Another example: you may love dense prickly shrubs that become dotted with flowers during spring. These plants are havens for small birds and, when in flower, bees. Perhaps visits by birds and bees are what you appreciate in a garden. So look again at the plants you are attracted to, and think about what functions they could perform in your garden. Inversely, consider how you want your garden to function, and look at plants with features that fulfil that need. This thought process will help narrow down your plant wish-list.

Before choosing plants, carefully consider what's already in your garden and decide whether or not existing plants will stay or go. I think it's a mistake to become too attached to a particular plant simply because it's there—even one misplaced or unsuitable plant can detract from a garden's aesthetics. On the other hand, if you remove a plant simply because you don't know what it is or you want to start with a clean slate, you could regret it later.

TALL TREES

Trees are probably the most practical place to start when creating a plant wish-list, as it's much easier to arrange other plants around a tree than it is to add trees to the landscape later on. Because trees are tall, they're often placed on property boundaries—the eye is drawn towards them, so they help define an area. They're sometimes used (in conjunction with shrubbery) to break up larger spaces, and specimen trees—those with spectacular bark, unique form, or showy flowers or foliage—are used as focal points. Whatever its function, any tree should sit in a garden space comfortably, neither too big nor too small.

BELOW Versatile climbers such as (*LEFT*) wonga wonga vine (*Pandorea pandorana*) and (*RIGHT*) native sarsaparilla (*Hardenbergia violacea*) bring vertical *or* horizontal bursts of colour into the garden.

INFILL PLANTS

These are your mid-layer plants, which you can use to help break up a large space; create mystery by curving a path around them to 'hidden' areas of the garden; draw the eye from the ground up towards the trees; block a bad view; and serve as a backdrop to the garden. Mid-layer plants tend to cause the most confusion for garden designers, though that may be because this group of plants is usually the largest one used. To help reduce confusion, carefully assess the attributes of any mid-layer plants you want to use. Consider height, width, density, form, habit and maintenance requirements *before* colour and texture.

CLIMBERS AND CREEPERS

This is an extremely useful and versatile group of plants that can be used effectively vertically as well as horizontally. When trained well, climbers can cover a wire

ABOVE AND BELOW Consider flower form *and* colour when choosing plants for your garden. *FAR RIGHT, CLOCKWISE FROM TOP LEFT* A classic 'cottage' colour combination in an unusual 'cottage' setting; Contrasting vibrant colours such as red and purple (or pink and orange) add a sense of drama to a garden bed; Who says cottage gardens belong only in England?

fence and create a cheap and pretty screen. And a *Pandorea pandorana* or *Hardenbergia violacea* floating over an archway is an essential feature in a cottage garden.

PROSTRATE PLANTS

These plants may seem insignificant simply because they're at ground level, but they're important in creating an aesthetic buffer between hard and soft landscaping: tiny plants dotted among some crazy paving, or spilling onto a concrete path and softening its edges. Many ground creepers are very effective at preventing erosion. They also serve as living mulch—and make valuable lizard-protection zones!

COLOUR

Some plants blend into the garden environment for months on end and we hardly notice them until, almost overnight, they erupt in a vision of colourful delight. If a garden is planned carefully, these eruptions of colour can happen continuously throughout the year. Giving even the smallest consideration to colour in the garden will pay dividends. If plants you're using in the same area flower at the same time, will the colours work together? Flower size should also be considered, because large, vibrant-hued flowers will announce their presence much more loudly than tiny flowers of the same colour. The colours we choose will depend on personal taste and preference, but there are some colour schemes that are timeless:

- Blues and yellows make a classic combination; red and purple also make a striking pair.
- Single-colour gardens such as white are popular—or you could extend the idea, using only two or three colours throughout.
- Cottage gardens successfully mix pinks, blues and whites to great effect.

Using more than a few colours in the garden can potentially create a haphazard effect. To prevent this, use groups of plants of the same colour, rather than single plants, so that the eye is drawn from group to group.

RIGHT Up close and personal—with their spectacular colours, textures and forms, Australian plants have such a lot to offer. *BELOW* This beautiful specimen of *Indigofera australis* has been left to its own devices.

TEXTURE

Plants in the high-texture category almost beg to be touched. There are soft, wavy grasses to run your fingers through; fat, succulent leaves to squish (ever so gently!); velvety foliage to stroke; and even irresistible prickles to test.

FORM AND HABIT

Plant form and habit are inextricably linked, and both are important points to consider when choosing plants. *Form* is the shape of the plant—including all parts, such as the trunk, branches, flower stalks, and so on. *Habit* refers to the way the plant grows. For example, the habit of *Indigofera australis* is open, upright and slightly weeping. Its form—if left to its own devices—is a dome shape, usually slightly wider than it is tall. If we consider the form and habit of our plants, we can quite often match them perfectly to particular spots in the garden where they won't require excessive pruning or shaping. I reckon we've become a bit too obsessed with wanting to make all our shrubs dense and bushy at the expense of allowing them to show off their unique natural forms.

Australian plants and fire

The tragic bushfires in Victoria in 2009 graphically highlighted the need to reconsider the use of certain plants in fire-prone suburban gardens and public landscapes. Of particular concern are eucalypts and their relatives in the Myrtaceae family, whose leaves contain highly flammable oils. On days of extreme bushfire danger, when temperatures soar, humidity levels drop to near zero and high winds fan bushfires, these oil-laden leaves are capable of exploding into flames. Firestorms can race through the tops of myrtaceous trees and shrubs with disastrous consequences for nearby dwellings.

Of less concern but also containing flammable oils are many plants in the Rutaceae family (which contains genera such as *Boronia*, *Eriostemon* and *Philotheca*). Should we be using these potentially fire-prone plants in our gardens? While many suburban areas are relatively well protected from bushfires, others on the fringes of suburbia, near national parks and other bushland reserves, remain at risk. All homeowners in high-risk areas must have

Many Australian plants, such as these grass trees (*Xanthorrhoea* species), have evolved to survive blistering bushfires.

Mass flowering of grass trees (*TOP*) and kangaroo paws (*ABOVE*) after fire is a spectacular sight in the Australian bush.

even those that would normally survive a less intense bushfire.

The vulnerability to fire of the area you live in and its surroundings, together with the level of risk you are prepared to accept with regard to fire, are important considerations when designing a new garden or renovating an existing one.

Existing plants

If you are inheriting a site that has existing plants, it is worth pausing to review whether they can serve a purpose in your new garden before you reach for the chainsaw. Trees and shrubs certainly have a finite lifespan, and if they are on their last legs it is certainly easier and better to remove or renovate them before you start work. Dieback in outer branches or borer holes in the trunk and branches are telltale signs of ill-health and old age in trees and shrubs. With large trees, if there is any evidence of decay it may be worth consulting a professional arborist to establish whether the tree presents a safety hazard.

Another common issue for the native gardener is what to do when the existing garden is based wholly or partly on exotic species. Whether you choose to remove these plants is purely a matter of taste, as it is certainly possible to blend such plants into a garden based on Australian plants. In fact, they may be able to play a very useful role as 'nurse' plants, providing shelter from wind, frost and harsh westerly summer sun while your precious new plantings get established. Existing plants that form a screen around the house or garden may also play a role in protecting your privacy.

a comprehensive strategy for protecting life and property in the event of a bushfire.

If you live in a fire-prone area, you might consider the many Australian (and exotic) plants whose leaves contain little or no oil and may also store large quantities of moisture. An excellent example is the succulent pigface (*Carpobrotus* species). Such species can be planted as a fire-retardant buffer near your house; if you do want to grow fire-prone plants, these can be sited much further away from any structures on your property.

Another strategy worth adopting in fire-prone areas is to mulch with an inorganic, non-flammable material such as coarse gravel. Organic mulches such as barks and woodchips will burn in the face of firestorms, and in such conditions strong winds will convert these burning mulches into potentially dangerous flying embers. Not only do organic mulches burn, but the heat from their combustion can lead to the death of nearby plants,

An important issue to consider if you are going to leave existing plants in place is their fertiliser requirements. Plants such as roses need more fertiliser to perform well than some of the phosphorus-sensitive Australian plants, such as banksias, grevilleas and acacias. If possible, find out from previous owners what kind of fertiliser, and how much of it, has been ploughed into your soil.

Phosphorus can build up in soils where plants such as vegetables, citrus and roses have been fed on a regular basis with fertilisers designed for their needs. In such a scenario you would be well advised to stick with planting natives that are not as likely to be affected by elevated phosphorus levels, such as kangaroo paws and everlasting daisies (see 'Phosphorus needs of Australian plants' on page 74).

When moving into a new property, carefully consider the horticultural value existing mature trees can add to the landscape.

building
the garden

Soil, Part 2

One of the magic ingredients for making a garden soil healthy, productive and sustainable is humus (the black, soil-like stuff that is the end product of your compost heap). Humus gives 'body' to your soil, greatly increasing its water- and nutrient-holding capacity. It also helps to break up clay soils and improve their aeration and drainage, to the benefit of plant growth. Adding humus is not essential to create a successful garden, but it certainly helps.

With the exception of soils in rainforests and a few other areas, most natural Australian soils are very low in organic matter. Much of the continent is covered by dry eucalypt forest, where fallen leaves, bark, twigs and branches tend to accumulate on the forest floor until bushfires incinerate them. Fire releases the inorganic nutrients stored in the debris while burning all the organic material, which enters the atmosphere mainly as carbon dioxide rather than going back into the soil as humus (as happens in a rainforest). While plants from eucalypt-forest areas do not normally grow in soils rich in organic matter, that is not to say that they don't benefit from humus and compost when we add them to the soil in our gardens. That said, however, if you want to grow

phosphorus-sensitive native plants such as banksias and waratahs, then you should make sure you add the right type of compost.

How do you do that? Well, the nutrient content of the raw ingredients for a compost heap has a big influence on that of the finished compost. So, for instance, compost based on chicken manure (which is generally relatively high in phosphorus) is likely to be too rich for those phosphorus-sensitive plants. Your best bet is to either check the label on your compost and ensure that it has, say, less than two per cent phosphorus, or make your own.

To make low-phosphorus compost, you will need to avoid ingredients that contain high levels of that element. They

include manure from grain-fed animals and any fertilisers with more than two per cent phosphorus. Use ingredients such as lawn clippings and fallen leaves, and add a nitrogen-rich material such as urea to feed the microbes that break down the organic matter in your compost heap.

One of the pitfalls of compost is that if it is not fully matured before it is dug into your soil, the microbes responsible for decomposition will draw on nutrients in the soil to continue the breakdown process. This puts them in

FAR LEFT Many Western Australian plants, such as the black kangaroo paw, require a compost that has no added phosphorus. *BELOW* A simple composting bin such as this will provide an endless supply of soil conditioner for your garden.

A wide variety of organic materials can be used as mulches.

direct competition with your plants for nutrients, particularly nitrogen—hence the technical term *nitrogen drawdown*. If you are in any doubt about whether your compost is ready to use (whether it is a DIY or one you have purchased), a good and simple test is to plant some fast-germinating seeds, such as radishes. If the seedlings turn yellow or do not grow properly, then the compost is not ready. Compost that is still hot and produces steam when you dig it is definitely not ready to use.

MULCHES

Mulch is essentially a protective covering placed around plants to prevent moisture from evaporating, stop roots freezing in winter, suppress weeds and, in some cases, to nourish the soil as well. A multitude of materials can be used as mulches, and they have vastly different properties and outcomes, so it is important to select the one that best suits your needs and objectives. For instance, lucerne hay mulch will decompose to humus (in a way that woody materials will not) over a period of months, improving water retention and

absorption, building soil structure through aggregation of particles, and thus boosting aeration and drainage. Other mulch materials can also be used to create design effects through their colour and texture.

The choice of *mulch materials* will be influenced by what you wish to achieve by mulching.

WATER SAVING

The ideal mulch for minimising evaporation from the soil is a coarse, chunky material (pieces greater than 5–10 mm in diameter, but preferably much bigger) that traps lots of air to create an insulating blanket for the soil. Materials such as coarse eucalypt chips, pine-bark chunks and coarsely chopped straw are all good water savers. Coarse mulches can also help to trap stormwater that falls onto and flows over the garden, giving the water time to soak into the soil and thus preventing erosion as well.

WEED CONTROL

Once again, coarse, chunky mulch is best, as weeds will grow quite happily in mulch that contains a significant proportion of finer particles. Considering the type of weeds you are dealing with is also

important. In general, weeds growing from seed will be stopped by most mulch materials, if they are applied to a depth of five centimetres. However, creeping perennial or bulbous weeds such as kikuyu grass or oxalis respectively will need a continuous underlay of overlapping newspaper several sheets thick, or woven-fabric 'weed mats'. Some materials used as mulches, such as straw or manure, may also contain weed seeds, so care needs to be taken when sourcing mulching materials.

SOIL TEMPERATURE

Mulches also help to even out fluctuations in temperature, keeping soils warmer in winter and cooler in summer heat. Once again, coarse materials that trap air will provide the best result. Gardeners can enhance this temperature-control effect by choosing mulches of different colours depending on their objectives. For instance, dark mulch can be used in cold-winter climates to help maximise heat absorption, allowing spring root growth to start earlier and lengthening the growing season. Conversely, in hot climates light-coloured mulches such as straw will reflect heat, avoiding the high soil temperatures that can cause root damage.

FERTILISING AND SOIL IMPROVEMENT

Using mulches to feed your plants and build up your soil are also worthwhile objectives, but I would only recommend this in labour-intensive areas of the garden, such as where you grow annuals. Shrubberies are much better served by more permanent woody, chunky mulches that do not break down quickly. Some of the best materials for soil-improvement mulches are lucerne hay, pea straw, lupin mulch and fully mature composts. Worms will build up beneath the mulch and incorporate humus into the soil. Be very aware that these mulching materials will break down into fine particles fairly quickly, sacrificing moisture retention and weed control. A good way to retain these benefits while also feeding your soil is to use a high-nutrient material such as pea straw underneath a coarse woody mulch.

FIRE RETARDATION

Inorganic materials such as coarse gravel will help minimise the damage from an out-of-control bushfire and may also lessen the risk of a fire spreading from garden to house.

An inorganic mulch such as coarse gravel is a safe option in bushfire-prone areas.

AERATION AROUND PLANT CROWNS

Coarse, chunky mulches allow for better aeration around the base of plants. This can be particularly important for clumping, strappy-leaved plants such as *Dianella* (flax lily), which can be prone to root and crown rot problems if the base of the plant is moist. This problem can arise when fine mulches are used, particularly in more humid climates such as Queensland.

LAWN REPLACEMENT

Mulches can also be used to replace expanses of lawn to make gardens more water efficient. A coarse, chunky mulch will again be ideal due to its superior ability to suppress weed growth.

Some other points to consider when selecting mulches include:

- *Toxins*: Fresh wood chips and barks can contain toxins such as tannins that will damage plants. The trick is to age such materials by leaving them in a pile for several months to allow the toxins to dissipate before they are used in the garden.
- *Woody mulches*: If particles of mulches like eucalypt chips and pine bark become mixed into your soil, their decomposition will draw nutrients such as nitrogen out of the soil, depriving your plant roots of food. Woody mulch materials should never be dug into the soil for this reason.

TOP LEFT A very coarse mulch such as woodchip is important to ensure good aeration around the base of your plants. LEFT AND TOP RIGHT There are many ground-covering plants that can be used to create 'living' mulches.

An underlay mulch of manure, or some other nutritious organic material such as pea straw, will help avoid this problem.

- *Collar rot*: As a rule, mulches should also be kept away from the trunk or crown of garden plants to minimise the risk of rot caused by fungi that thrive in the humid conditions of the mulch. Some mulches can also become water repellent if they mat down (e.g. lawn clippings) or are allowed to dry out completely (e.g. composts). In these cases, a soil wetting agent will provide a solution.
- *Weed*: Make sure the mulch contains no weed seeds. Buy your mulch from a known and reputable source.
- *Cost*: Buying mulch can be an expensive business, particularly if you are looking to cover very large areas. Expect to pay at least $30–40 per cubic metre (enough to cover about twenty square metres). Fortunately, plenty of 'waste' materials can be used as mulch. These are readily obtainable either around the house or from other local sources such as tree loppers. They include: lawn clippings, home-made compost, wood chips, newspaper (shredded and unshredded), wood shavings, pine bark, sugar-cane residue, gravel, perlite, vermiculite, straw, lucerne hay, recycled tyres, and landscaping fabrics such as weed mat, plastic, rice hulls, manure, coconut fibre and pine needles.
- *Availability*: Materials from the home or garden that can be used as mulches include shredded paper, fallen autumn leaves and wood chips made from pruned plants.

FERTILISING AUSTRALIAN PLANTS

In the world of Australian plants, few topics are more controversial than fertilising. Some experts advocate not feeding your native plants at all, while others recommend feeding only with low-phosphorus fertilisers that are specifically designed for Australian plants. Recent research by the former CSIRO soil scientist Kevin Handreck has revealed an astonishing range of sensitivities to added phosphorus among a wide range of Australian plant groups; we will discuss this in a lot more detail later in this section.

In the meantime, what do we do about fertilisers in the native garden? The answer is that it really depends on what sort of result you want. While Australian plants in the wild have adapted to very low nutrient levels in their native soils, they are certainly capable of rapid surges in growth when extra nutrients are available. When a bushfire occurs in the wild, a burst of nutrients is released when all the fallen leaves, bark and twigs are incinerated. For the first year after a fire, most plants grow very fast, particularly if there is regular rainfall. I have seen waratahs, for instance, grow stems three to four metres long in a single season after a fire.

My own approach to feeding my native garden is to take it case by case as follows. First, a general comment with respect to *phosphorus levels*. A good general rule is that a low-phosphorus fertiliser will do no harm to native plants that are not phosphorus-sensitive. However, the reverse is certainly not the case. So if you have no information on your plants' phosphorus sensitivity, it is best to avoid using any fertilisers that are likely to have phosphorus content greater than two per cent. This includes fertilisers such as blood and bone or those that are based on chicken manure.

For *plants that are known to be particularly phosphorus sensitive* (see the list on page 76), I use urea, especially when establishing new plantings. This has zero phosphorus and is generally sufficient to give good growth.

When *establishing trees and shrubs*, I like to feed them well in the first couple of years so they form a decent flowering framework quickly. Once they are established, I will usually stop feeding them unless they are showing signs of nutrient deficiency. Most flowering shrubs and trees will flower quite happily each year. They only need to put on a small amount of growth each year to flower well, and heavy feeding usually just encourages excessive vegetative growth, which will get trimmed back after flowering anyway. And if you are really heavy-handed with established trees and shrubs, excessive feeding, especially with nitrogen, may inhibit flowering altogether.

Pruning native trees and shrubs is sometimes desirable if they have been let go for a few years. Most species (with the exception of most acacias and native peas) will respond well to *fertilising after pruning* if it is done coming into spring, when the plant is starting active growth, or when they have finished their annual flowering. If you are doing what I would refer to as a 'renovation prune', then a good feed at the same time will help the plant reestablish quickly.

Herbaceous plants include all those soft-wooded plants such as everlasting daisies, brachyscomes and most fan flowers (*Scaevola* species) as well as strappy-leaved plants such as kangaroo paws, flax lilies (*Dianella* species) and mat rushes (*Lomandra* species). These types of plants will generally not flower to their full potential if they are under-nourished. Kangaroo paws in particular will tend to sit and sulk, but they will produce abundant flower stems if they receive plenty of nutrients and water during their growing season (from autumn through winter in frost-free climates). In my experience, most Australian herbaceous plants (with the exception of lechenaultias) are not particularly phosphorus sensitive, which means they can be grown happily among exotic plants that require high nutrient levels to perform at their best.

Solid fertilisers need to dissolve before they can be absorbed by the plant, so apply them before rain or irrigation. Slow (controlled) release feeds let out a small amount of nutrient every time they come in contact with moisture, so are good long-term options, particularly for sandy soils where nutrients will leach away whenever the soil becomes saturated. Be aware, however, that slow-release fertilisers cost considerably more, so you need to weigh the benefits of their longer-term (and hence more efficient) nutrient release against their cost. I would suggest that the smaller the garden, the better value they are.

Phosphorus needs of Australian plants

Many Australian plants grow in the wild on extremely infertile, impoverished soils. These are, in fact, some of the oldest soils in the world, which explains why most of the nutrients have been leached out of them. Having evolved in such harsh conditions, our plants are able to survive and grow at nutrient levels that would have many exotic species turning up their toes.

Various Australian species have evolved root systems that are incredibly efficient at extracting the little nutrition that is available to them. One such example is the proteoid roots formed by many members of the Proteaceae family, such as banksias, grevilleas and waratahs (*Telopea*). Bundles of fine roots, not unlike cotton wool in texture, are formed among the normal roots. These roots are very efficient at extracting nutrients, particularly phosphorus, from the soil, enabling growth to continue in very infertile soils.

The very efficient extraction of phosphorus by proteoid roots can become a problem in garden soils, which have often accumulated fairly substantial levels of this nutrient over the years thanks to the application of fertiliser.

A lot of past gardening literature on Australian plants has assumed that most, if not all, of our flora is phosphorus sensitive. However, as I noted earlier, the research of soil scientist Kevin Handreck

Plants in the family Proteaceae, such as these grevilleas and hakeas, are particularly sensitive to phosphorus.

has revealed a surprising range of phosphorus sensitivity: while some species will turn up their toes at the slightest hint of added phosphorus, others will tolerate phosphorus just as well as common exotic plants, and even thrive on it. In a study done over several years, potted Australian plants of 810 different species were given—along with fixed and adequate levels of other nutrients—single superphosphate at rates of up to 0.9 grams per litre of potting mix. More than 80 per cent of the species tested showed no symptoms of toxicity from levels of phosphorus that would be considered 'normal' for most exotic species.

Australian plants that are generally accepted as being phosphorus sensitive and therefore in need of special attention when it comes to fertilisers include:

⊙ Genera in the family Proteaceae, including *Banksia*, *Grevillea*, *Telopea*, *Isopogon*, *Dryandra* and *Hakea*.

⊙ Various other miscellaneous genera from a range of families, including *Acacia*, *Bauera*, *Beaufortia*, *Boronia*, *Bossiaea*, *Brachysema*, *Chorisema*, *Daviesia*, *Eutaxia*, *Hypocalymma*, *Jacksonia*, *Lechenaultia* and *Pultenaea*.

In summary, the threat of phosphorus to Australian plants is nowhere near as great as we once believed. This is particularly relevant if you are starting a new garden with Australian plants in an existing garden that has been fertilised with 'normal' levels of phosphorus in the past. Your best option in such a scenario is to avoid using very sensitive species altogether or alternatively, to create raised beds for them.

Growing Australian plants in mounds

One of the keys to frustration-free gardening is to adopt an appropriate plant-growing philosophy. Perhaps the easiest solution is to use only plants that are foolproof for your soil and climatic conditions. On the other hand, if you are like me and most other gardeners, you will want to grow plants you desire that may not suit your local conditions, such as the spectacular flowering beauties of Western Australia. To do this you will often need to modify your conditions to suit those plants. One of the best ways to do this is to create raised beds and/or mounds in your garden.

Many of the most exquisite native plants require very good drainage in order to thrive.

The biggest problem caused by poor drainage, in my experience, is that plants become much more susceptible to soil-borne disease organisms such as *Phytophthora* and *Armillaria* fungi, which cause root rot. When plants succumb to

ABOVE Simple mounds will create raised beds that provide better drainage.
FAR RIGHT Stone walls provide a raised bed and make wonderful features in the garden.

such diseases, the top growth starts to die back, resulting in sick, tragic-looking specimens that are usually in terminal decline.

If your soil is not naturally well drained, there are various ways to address the problem. As mentioned in the section on soils, you can add gypsum and organic matter to develop a soil structure that creates better drainage. Another option is to take advantage of gravity and simply create raised beds and/or mounds.

RAISED BEDS

You can contain your growing medium (whether it's your natural soil or a medium you import) above the normal soil level using logs, railway sleepers, stone or brick walls, to name a few possibilities. This is particularly useful on sloping sites and in small gardens, where every bit of space is valuable if your desire is to create some feature flower beds. Raised beds are a perfect way to display low-growing colourful native plants that require excellent drainage to produce their best displays. If you make a raised bed for this purpose, try to site it where it will get maximum sunlight.

A couple of tips to ensure success with raised beds:

⊙ If your retaining wall is made of brick or stone, ensure that you provide weep holes every couple of metres at the base so that water can drain away in a heavy storm.

⊙ Do not skimp on the cost of the growing medium if you are buying it in. A good-quality 'garden mix' will likely cost up to $150 a cubic metre.

MOUNDS

Your raised area need not be an enclosed garden bed: you can also improve drainage by creating artificial mounds. The great advantage of this approach is that you do not need to spend money constructing walls. Simply plonk the growing medium onto the existing site where you want your mound to go. As well as improving drainage, the mini hills and valleys thus formed will help to create a more interesting and varied landscape. Having mounds of different heights and shapes lets you not only display plants to your advantage but also guide people around your garden on routes that will stimulate and surprise them.

Another benefit of creating mounds is the opportunity to create environments that suit particular groups of plants. This is especially so if you are on a sloping site, where mounds can be created along contour lines. Any stormwater that flows across the site will collect behind the mounds and gradually seep in, watering the plants from the base of the mound upwards. This creates a very water-efficient garden, as your plants are irrigated as much as possible by natural rainfall and receive its benefits long after the last shower, if there was enough rain to produce stormwater flow. It also helps limit the environmental damage caused when stormwater enters public drains and is deposited—along with loads of rubbish—into our waterways and oceans.

A very important point needs to be made before you start remodelling your garden. Wholesale changes to the surface drainage of your land can have profound effects on your neighbours. Alterations to a garden or house can create extra stormwater runoff, for example, that floods adjacent properties. With mounds, the opposite occurs, but your neighbours may also want to collect water, and may not in fact be pleased by a sudden lack of stormwater runoff. It would be a good idea to check with your neighbours and local council before you make any large-scale changes, just to be on the safe side.

Another practical consideration if you're planning to change water flows on your property is what will happen during any extreme storms. Torrents of water flowing through your garden are likely to cause an erosion problem, particularly while you are establishing new plantings. Once you've seen where the water will be flowing, it's a good idea to line its path with rock, creating a creek bed that will resist erosion.

DO-IT-YOURSELF BILLABONGS

We've seen how mounds on sloping sites can be sited along contour lines to maximise the use of precious water. But what if you have a totally flat site? By creating doughnut-shaped mounds, we can trap water in the centre, making what is in effect a raised billabong. In nature, billabongs are created when the course of a river changes, usually during a flood.

As the water surges straight ahead, bends in the river get blocked off and become small crescent-shaped dams that become ecological havens when the floodwaters recede.

To create our own raised billabong, we can simply excavate topsoil from the middle of the mound and pile it up around the mound's edges, forming a well in the centre. If we want a taller mound, we can bring in a little extra topsoil or commercial 'garden mix'. Raised-billabong mounds can be whatever shape you wish, as long as they have the well in the centre. Whenever it rains, the well will catch extra water, which will gradually soak into the base of the mound. You can also irrigate the mound by running water (preferably from a storage tank) straight into the billabong well with a hose.

As well as creating opportunities to harvest and store water, mounding also improves drainage, so the tops of mounds provide a niche for plants that prefer drier conditions as well as really good drainage. Conversely, moisture-loving species will do best at the bases of mounds, particularly where stormwater is able

to collect. Don't be scared to play around with your plantings by moving plants to different parts of a mound until you find the right niche.

Growing Australian plants in containers

As modern gardens become smaller, there is less opportunity to use many wonderful but relatively large trees and shrubs in the ways that the traditional Australian quarter-acre backyard once allowed for. By using containers of all sizes in the garden, you can present some of the most spectacular but difficult-to-grow Australian plants, such as Sturt's desert pea (*Swainsona formosa*) or black kangaroo paw (*Macropidia fuliginosa*).

Plants from very diverse environments require conditions that are very difficult to provide in-ground in the average Australian suburban garden. Growing plants in pots allows you to move your plants around to where they can be fully appreciated when they are at their peak as well as have optimum light, moisture, nutrient, aeration and humidity.

Growing in containers also means potentially large shrubs can be limited in size or 'bonsai-ed', thus suiting them to be in smaller garden spaces. Physically limiting the volume of growing medium available to the roots will automatically place a limit on the top growth. I use this strategy to keep a Norfolk Island pine (*Araucaria heterophylla*) as my Christmas tree. In its large container, new growth rarely exceeds a few centimetres a year, so the plant decorates my deck all year as well as being fully functional for a few weeks.

RIGHT A billabong can be created by constructing mounds at strategic points in your garden.
FAR RIGHT The swamp daisy (*Actinodium cunninghamii*) (LEFT) and a delicate pink crowea (RIGHT) are best grown in containers in many parts of Australia.

Container gardening can also give you an opportunity to express your creativity. Large pots can be painted to colour-coordinate with the plant in them, or a novelty item such as an old wheelbarrow can be used as a 'pot'. Mixing different plants in a container is another great way to express your design flair. You might use a vertical plant such as a kangaroo paw as a feature, surround it with a low grower such as a native bluebell, and have a spillover plant such as a scaevola dripping colour over the edge of the pot.

To maximise your success with container gardening, points to consider include:

- *Potting mix*. This is without doubt the most important thing to get right. My advice is not to skimp on the price of either a ready-to-use mix or the ingredients you purchase to make your own custom-made mix. If you go for a ready-to-use mix, make sure it carries the red Australian Standards mark. This indicates a premium-quality mix, which is likely to give you the best results all round. In addition to the Australian Standards logo, look for other 'bells and whistles' type ingredients that further enhance the quality of the mix, such as wetting agents to ensure that water is evenly distributed throughout the mix, and water-storing gels to increase the mix's moisture-holding capacity.

- *Container size*. Matching the size of your container to the eventual size of the plant you are putting into it is also very important. A plant that is too small for a large pot will tend to rot away, as it will have too much water available to it unless watered with very great care. It is good practice to establish a small plant in a temporary pot until it has completely filled the potting mix with roots before transplanting it into its permanent, larger-pot home. On the other hand, a plant that is too large for its container will tend to dry out easily and will be especially hard to keep properly watered in the hotter months. One episode of drying out can be enough to cause severe damage, such as loss of all the flower buds, and may even kill your plant.

- *Watering*. Keeping a potted plant optimally watered is easier said than done! Even experienced horticulturists have great difficulty with this one—trust me. A pot can be viewed as having a finite reservoir of water stored in the mix. If this reservoir is allowed to run out, disaster will often result. Plants growing in soil can draw on moisture that can move sideways in the soil as well as upwards by capillary action, so they have a bit more buffering than those in a container. If your pot plant does dry out, the potting mix can tend to shrink away from the edge of the pot and make it hard to rewet the root ball. A good remedy is to plunge the whole pot into a bucket of water to ensure that the mix expands again and removes any channels that have formed in air pockets within the root ball.

- *Feeding.* A good approach to feeding is to use controlled-release (also often referred to as slow-release) fertilisers in the mix initially. Good-quality mixes will already have it incorporated. When you observe growth slowing down or yellowing, it is time to supplement by top-dressing the pot. Liquid fertilisers are also a great way to feed your pot plants.

Fauna habitat

To sit and watch birds going about their daily lives in your own garden is a delightful experience. Over time, as you get to know each pair and they raise new young each year, they really do become part of your extended family. When your partner calls out urgently one morning, 'Honey, the magpie babies are out of the nest,' you come running as quickly as if the grandkids had arrived! And the two of you stand there murmuring how adorable the new twins are, and later tell friends proudly how quickly the little ones learned to eat on their own. And the cycle goes on

with every bird family in your garden.

And not only birds—your garden may also house possums, rats and mice, some slippery lizards, perhaps a few frogs, and many thousands of insects. Depending on where you live, you may also play host to—or have living nearby—koalas, kangaroos, wallabies, echidnas, wombats, blue-tongue or stumpy-tail lizards, birds, butterflies and bees, and everything in between. Just like you, they all need a secure place to rest and rear their young.

We all know that protecting our native fauna is essential and rewarding, but what is the best way to provide what they need as naturally as possible? The first thing to do is find out which creatures you have living nearby, then find out what you can about their requirements, and then set about meeting those requirements. If you're trying to attract a particular type of bird or animal to your property, you may need to supply a particular type of shelter or plant group. One of the best places to source information on fauna (and flora) endemic to your area and on their specific needs is local council websites. There are also plenty of specialist websites with a wealth of information, such as the brilliant *www.floraforfauna.com.au*.

Even if the fauna are not around now, when you create the habitat they *will* come! In fact, it's amazing how quickly word gets around that fancy new digs have been set up. I often hear stories of people in the suburbs who establish a native garden with habitat and can hardly believe how much fauna they now encounter on a daily basis.

FOOD

Fauna need food—protein as well as carbohydrate—year round. Providing a range of plants will offer them menu choices of nectar, pollen, seeds, fruit and leaves. And remember the food chain you learned about at school: if you attract certain insects, then protein-eaters like birds, bats, frogs and lizards will be appreciative. And so the chain continues.

Examples of food-providing native plants include:

- *Grevillea*
- *Callistemon*
- *Banksia*
- *Anigozanthos*
- *Eucalyptus*
- daisies
- grasses
- *Leptospermum*
- *Acacia*.

Etcetera! The more plants, the merrier your garden will be!

WATER

It's also important to provide water year round. Ponds are ideal, especially planted with rushes, shrubbery and such to provide cover from predators. A pond will attract frogs, birds and all sorts of other fauna—everything needs water. If a pond's not suitable for your garden, place bowls of different depths around the place (close to plants, with some on the ground and others higher) and fill them regularly.

LEFT Fauna habitat is created by providing shelter, water, stonework and plants appropriate for the species in your local area.

You'll find out very quickly that deep or straight-sided bowls (and bird baths) will be avoided by many fauna species and most birds. If your pond or water vessel is rather deep, pop in a few rocks to give birds and frogs something safe to hop about on and they'll soon be using it. With large, deep pots of water, I always put in a couple of sticks so that if a bird or animal does fall in, it has something to scramble up onto and won't drown.

HABITAT

A homely environment for fauna can be anything from leaf litter to prickly shrubs, holes or depressions in the ground, decomposing logs, high branches, hollows in trees and dense grass. So plants that provide fauna with food and shade may also be great for them to live in. But if you don't have such plants in your garden, don't fret. It's easy enough to plant a diversity of ground covers, shrubs and trees, and it's also easy to provide shelter. Various types of bird and possum boxes are available to buy, or you could make your own. For the ground dwellers, add some hollow logs, any type of piping— large and small diameters and various lengths, which can be partly buried under mulch if you choose. As well, place a few large rocks about the garden for lizard sunbathers. Butterflies and other insects also like to rest, and providing smaller wooden homes for them will keep them coming back to your yard.

HABITAT CORRIDORS

As new suburbs spring up, encroaching on more and more rural land, our native fauna become homeless and hungry and have to fight for survival. Apart from giving us delight and a sense of satisfaction, our Australian garden will help precious native fauna survive and hopefully thrive. If everybody in the suburbs planted just a few suitable shrubs, grasses and trees, they would augment the few habitat corridors still existing along railway lines and public walkways, and offer the birds, animals and insects their own housing estates. The way I look at it, they were here first, so we have a duty to provide for them—they are, after all, family!

Sustainable materials

If we appreciate the natural look in the garden, we're likely to select timber for garden edging, large rocks or boulders for visual interest, bark or pebble mulches, and gravel for paths. These things probably look fantastic, but what about the area they came from? Could we have contributed to the destruction of an ecosystem simply because we wanted materials that blend with our garden? Some products are more sustainable than others, so it is worth asking your supplier how 'green' the materials are.

TIMBER

We use timber for mulch, timber for edging and timber for garden walls and paths. That's a lot of wood to be sourcing from fragile native forests. Instead, use plantation timber from sustainable forests, or recycled timber. For edging, select from the many recycled-plastic alternatives.

PEBBLES

Getting stones and pebbles from active creek or river beds is more environmentally damaging than sourcing them from inactive watercourses or from local quarries. Many countries have limited or no laws preventing the removal of stones from streams and rivers, and as a result these environments can be severely degraded. Look for local quarried pebbles, recycled pebbles or even crushed bricks.

ROCKS

Large quartz or volcanic rocks are usually sourced from private properties and are not used to the same extent as pebbles, so the environmental impact is not as great. If you're still worried about the environmental effect, there are some great fake rocks available, which look surprisingly real and are a lot easier to move! On the other hand, you should also consider the energy and resources that go into making them and then weigh up which choice you are more comfortable with.

MULCH

If you're using bark chips, again select those from sustainable forests or plantations. If suitable, consider 'waste' products such as eucalyptus or sugar-cane mulch.

RECYCLED PRODUCTS

Many hard landscaping products are recycled, including soil, crushed concrete or brick, mulch, pebbles, stone and asphalt. Using the recycled alternative could save you a bundle and, in some cases, bring a unique aesthetic to parts of your garden, such as the use of recycled sleepers installed vertically in the Gregorovich garden (see page 139).

Planting philosophy

Another somewhat controversial subject in the world of Australian plants concerns the guiding philosophy behind plant selection. Are you a purist who wants to preserve the genetic integrity of the bushland in your local region? Do you want to collect plants from all parts of Australia? Or is your aim to create a show garden from the most spectacular native plants you can get your hands on? My own philosophy is a blend of these three. As well, I want a low-maintenance garden that is also a haven for wildlife.

INDIGENOUS GARDENS

Indigenous plants are usually defined as those that occur naturally in your local region. Anyone concerned about the decline in biodiversity on our planet will want to consider including at least some indigenous species in their garden. In the wild, plant species are constantly evolving in response to changes in their environment, so most species have considerable genetic diversity over their entire geographical range. For instance, the river red gum (*Eucalyptus camaldulensis*) is found all over mainland Australia, from the tropical north to the drier south, and numerous genetically different forms have emerged in adaptation to wide differences in climates and soils.

By growing plants from seed collected from local forms of a species, you are

FAR LEFT Sustainable and recycled materials can be used in all sorts of creative ways to provide features in your garden.
BELOW Non-indigenous species such as kangaroo paws have been blended with existing bushland to create a colourful feature.

helping to preserve a 'genetic snapshot' of plants that have evolved to fit your particular ecological location. The *provenance* of a plant is the location of the original plants it was propagated from. A plant of *local provenance* originated from your local area, and, in my opinion, there is great value in including such plants in your garden to complement plants that are grown for other objectives such as for food or as ornamentals.

NON-INDIGENOUS GARDENS

I am not a purist about the genetics of my garden. I certainly have a place in it for species indigenous to my local area, particularly the rare ones. However, I also want to grow plants from other areas of Australia, as well as the hybrid cultivars created by plant breeders and selectors, which often have great ornamental beauty. That said, I take great care to avoid any plants that have the potential to invade my neighbouring bushland.

Most of us are aware of the potential for plants to escape from gardens and become environmental weeds. This can happen just as easily with Australian plants as it has done with the notorious exotics such as lantana and privet. Cootamundra wattle (*Acacia baileyana*) is a prolific producer of seed, and this species has now become naturalised in bushland areas adjoining towns and suburbs where it's been planted. In such situations, it is competing with indigenous species for space and resources. An internet search will instantly connect you with a wealth of information provided by government and private bodies on

this subject. You can learn about the potential of a particular species to become a weed and how best you can avoid this happening. With a bit of thought and appropriate research, we can select plants wisely to give us a beautiful yet environmentally friendly garden that minimises weed risks.

THE GENETICS OF NATIVE PLANT CULTIVARS

Where do the new, improved Australian plant cultivars fit into the genetic picture? The answer depends on their origin, so they need to be looked at case by case. Some cultivars are simply selected variants of a species that may have a different flower colour or growth habit from the normal type of that species. For instance, *Acacia cognata* 'Limelight' is propagated from cuttings that all originated from a single dwarf seedling selected from a batch of *Acacia cognata* seedlings. This type of cultivar is almost always a fertile plant that is able to set seed and reproduce itself (unlike hybrids between different species which are usually sterile), which means that in theory, it could seed itself into areas surrounding the original plant and become a potential weed.

Many cultivars arise as hybrids, or crosses between two different species. These interspecific hybrids, as they are termed, are in the vast majority of cases genetically sterile (like a mule, which is a cross between a horse and a donkey) and will never set seed. *Grevillea* 'Robyn Gordon' is a good example of a sterile interspecific hybrid. Sterile hybrids

are very useful plants for areas near remnant urban bushland, reserves or national parks, as they allow us to have spectacular ornamental native plants in our gardens without having to worry that they will invade the bush and become environmental weeds, if you are concerned about the weed potential of a particular cultivar.

The right plant

One of the more unfortunate aspects of the cultivation of Australian plants over the years has been an 'us and them' mentality. Plants are classed as either native or exotic—and our ideas about them are instantly shaped by the stereotypes attached to those terms. No matter where in Australia a native comes from, for example, it is presumed to be extremely drought tolerant to the point where watering it is harmful; never to need feeding, spraying or pruning; and to

look rather drab for long parts of the year. An 'exotic', on the other hand, supposedly cannot survive without copious watering; has verdant foliage and spectacular flowers; but needs lots of fertiliser, regular pruning and various chemical treatments to keep it healthy.

That may be a slight exaggeration. Nonetheless, I still regularly hear the terms native and exotic used on gardening talkback programs to imply many of the above ideas. I know that the readers of this book are too discerning to fall for stereotypes. They know it is better to treat each plant individually, figuring out its needs on the basis of its geographical origins.

While it is always tempting to choose plants for your garden based on their looks or aesthetic appeal, you will spare yourself much heartache by researching each plant's climate and soil requirements. It might seem a bit boring or basic, but wandering around your own neighbourhood with a notebook, listing the plants you fancy that are thriving in environments similar to your own yard, will give you an enormous head start. A visit to one of the nursery industry's own endangered species, the specialist native plant nursery, will also provide you with a wealth of valuable information.

Unfortunately, the 'big-box' gardening stores, with their nationwide distribution networks, can also work against providing plants that will thrive in your particular garden. It is convenient for national retailers to promote the same plants across all of their stores, which increases the temptation for them to stock climatically inappropriate plants rather than take the trouble to limit distribution only to the plant's optimum areas. Let the buyer beware!

All of that said, it does not hurt to push the boundaries sometimes and take a chance on plants whose suitability for your garden is not a dead certainty. You can select microclimates and positions within your landscape that may be a little drier or less frost-prone, for instance. Also, plant breeding and selection have helped to adapt groups of plants, such as kangaroo paws, to a wider range of climates and soils. Another good example is the 'Summer' series of flowering gums that are the product of a cross between the red flowering gum (*Corymbia ficifolia*) from the dry southwest corner of Western Australia and the swamp bloodwood (*C. ptychocarpa*) from the tropical north. The result is a range of outstanding hybrids in a range of colours that are proving adaptable to a much wider range of soil types and climatic conditions than either of the parent plants.

As a general rule, plants from warmer, more humid climates, such as the coastal regions of central and northern New South Wales and Queensland, will tend to adapt better to drier and cooler climates than plants going in the reverse direction. That said, you will need to be much more careful with your selections in frost-prone southern and inland climates such as Canberra. Adapting to lower humidity is one thing, but to ask a plant from a warm climate to cope with heavy frosts is an entirely different matter. Tree species such as silky oak (*Grevillea robusta*) and native frangipani (*Hymenosporum flavum*) have proven able to adapt to frost once established in colder climates. Protective measures such as hessian guards around the tree will greatly boost the chances of survival during the establishment phase. Smaller plants, such as shrubs

FAR LEFT *Acacia cognata* 'Limelight' is a compact form of this species of wattle.
BELOW *Corymbia* 'Summer Beauty' is a hybrid flowering gum that is much better adapted to more humid climates of Australia.

and herbaceous plants from warmer areas (such as kangaroo paws), seem to find it much harder to cope with frost, probably because they are much lower to the ground and are hit much harder than established trees, which carry their foliage and flowers many metres higher. You may be able to mitigate the effects of frost for these lower-growing plants by planting next to a north-facing brick or stone wall or close to the protection afforded by the canopy of an established tree or a garden structure such as a gazebo.

ABOVE The sub-tropical species silky oak (*Grevillea robusta*) is surprisingly tolerant of frost once established in most garden situations.

FAR RIGHT Many of the more spectacular Australian plants require very good drainage and can be grouped together in a position that meets this requirement.

SOIL TYPES

It can also be difficult to know how a plant will adapt to your soil type. There are a number of aspects of your soil that need to be taken into account (see also Soil, Part 1, on page 22), such as texture, structure, pH (acidity) and nutrient content. If you are in any doubt about a plant's requirements, it's worth spending a little time researching it. Soil types can vary widely within a region and even within your own garden, particularly if you have a sloping site. So it also pays to spend a little time getting to know your own soil and seeing how it matches the requirements of any new plant you wish to grow.

If you have difficulty matching a 'must-have' plant to your soil type, a great solution can be to grow it in a container and choose a growing medium specifically suited to its needs. Potting mixes can be constructed to suit the requirements of plants from virtually any natural soil type. Ready-made mixes labelled specifically for native plants will suit a wide range of Australian species. However, there are plenty of exceptions— plants for which I would recommend making up your own custom-made mix. For example, Christmas bells (*Blandfordia* species) and other plants that grow naturally in swampy habitats will generally not thrive in the relatively open mixes that are designed more as a 'general purpose' mix for a wide range of native species. Specialist native nurseries will generally be able to tell you which species will need a specialised potting mix, as well as how to construct it. The website of the Australian Plants Society at *http://asgap.org.au/* is also a good source of information about this.

You might also plant non-local plants in raised beds and mounds, and create microclimates by planting 'nurse' trees or using rocks and walls as heat sinks (see page 36). These techniques let you fit your garden to the needs of some of the more challenging species.

GROUPING PLANTS WITH SIMILAR REQUIREMENTS

Good garden design is not just about aesthetics, it is also about practicalities. One of the keys to making a great garden is to group together plants that have similar requirements. There are many facets to this approach. To use it to best advantage, you need to observe and dig in your garden, getting to know all the microclimates and environmental niches within it.

Let us look at a few examples to illustrate the concept.

WATER

Certain groups of plants need more moisture than others to reach their full potential. Species that grow naturally along watercourses—such as bottlebrushes (*Callistemon*), many of the melaleucas and tea trees—will grow much better in an area where water tends to collect and the drainage may not be as good as elsewhere. Not only will these plants thrive in such places but they will also tend to pump away excess water, which can alleviate problems such as mosquitoes breeding. Siting these plants in dips and depressions also makes it easier to irrigate them if you ever need to supplement their water supply.

Wax flower and kangaroo paws both require full sun to flower to their full potential, and make stunning bedfellows.

Conversely, plants that prefer drier conditions will benefit from being together in areas of the garden where soil is less moist and the humidity levels around the base of the plant are lower.

HEIGHT AND LIGHT

Obviously we need to put taller plants behind lower-growing plants, but we also need to consider the spread of plants as well: generally speaking, plants chosen for their 'flower power' will flower much better the more sunlight they receive. This becomes particularly important as the garden matures over time. We often tend to overplant our gardens, as we are tempted to fill every possible gap early on without properly considering the expansion in height and width that will occur over time. Therefore, it is a very good idea to plant low-growing species together at the front of a bed or in their own separate beds. Also consider how the light changes over the course of a day and from season to season.

FERTILISER REQUIREMENTS

As we've seen, recent research is showing that Australian plants vary enormously in their nutritional needs, particularly with respect to phosphorus. It is therefore vital

that you group together plants that have similar requirements—banksias, grevilleas and waratahs, for example.

MAINTENANCE REQUIREMENTS

Some species need more attention than others, so consider leaving enough space to access them. A good example here is low-growing perennial plants such as everlasting daisies, which need regular dead-heading to perform to their full potential.

WHAT SIZE TO PLANT?

In establishing our plants, we have a number of options. Should we use seed, tubestock, semi-advanced, advanced or super-advanced plants? Obviously, the answers depend to some extent on the size of our budget. But let's consider the pros and cons of planting at each stage of development before we make a decision.

SEED

Plants with relatively large seeds are fairly easy to establish directly into garden beds. Plants such as everlasting daisies will establish very well in a disturbed bed of soil. Simply dig the soil and rake it level,

then distribute the seed, rake the soil over again, and keep it moist while the seedlings are establishing. This can give a lovely cottage-garden or wildflower-meadow effect. (Of course, seed can be sown in pots and then planted into the garden, which is a great idea for seeds from indigenous or other plants that you collect yourself from various gardens. This is a rather specialised activity that we do not have the space to cover in this book.)

TUBESTOCK

Tubestock refers to plants growing in small to very small pots of, say, less than 75 millimetres diameter. Such small plants are often in limited supply in mainstream

outlets, but they are available from many specialist native nurseries and mail-order outlets that can be found through the internet or gardening magazines. The great advantage of planting tubestock is that the plant has the opportunity to develop its root system *in situ* and unfettered rather than in the constricted environment of a pot. This is particularly important for woody plants. If you have a choice, ask for tubestock grown in long tubes, often called 'forestry' tubes because of their particular suitability to growing the good-quality root systems needed for establishing trees. The downside of tubestock is that the plants are smaller. However, if you do all the right things tubestock will often catch up and overtake plants established from pots at larger sizes, particularly if those plants were pot-bound, as they often are.

SEMI-ADVANCED

This refers to plants in pots from 75 to 175 millimetres in diameter. This is usually a pretty good compromise between tubestock and advanced or super-advanced stock, the idea being that the plants are relatively large for quick effect, but are less likely to be pot-bound than plants in larger pots. Again, this is particularly important for woody plants, which will potentially be in the ground for decades. If you decide to go for semi-advanced woody plants, it is a good idea to actually look at their root system before

you buy. Remove the plant from its pot and look at its roots, or, if you find it a bit too confronting to do this yourself, ask the staff at the retail outlet to do it for you. The roots should have just reached the perimeter of the pot and be ready to burst forth once you plant them. If there is any sign that the roots are curling around the bottom of the pot, then I would avoid that particular specimen.

ADVANCED AND SUPER-ADVANCED

This refers to plants in pot diameters of 200 millimetres and above. The larger pot size allows for a much bigger plant that will give you instant impact in the garden—the main advantage you get for outlaying a lot more money for such specimens. The downside is that it is much more difficult to establish how old such plants are, and also to knock them out of their containers to check whether they are root-bound. What may look like a bargain in the nursery can often turn into a bad decision down the track. Such stock certainly gives instant impact, but if the development of the root system is at all impaired by the plant having been pot-bound, then you run the risk that the plant will blow over in a big wind or that its curled-up root system will literally strangle itself as it matures.

In summary, if you are prepared to be a bit patient, then you will get a much better long-term result for a lot less outlay by establishing your garden with plants from smaller pots. I would add that there is also a lot more satisfaction to be gained by propagating as many of your own plants as possible—but it is OK to go the other way if you are not quite as obsessive a plant person as I am!

How to plant

Planting correctly will not only get your garden off to a flying start, but it will also ensure that your plants' root systems develop as healthily as possible, maximising their long-term stability. The ideal method depends on the type of plant you are putting in and, to some extent, the purpose of the planting.

First, here is a step-by-step guide that will work for any plant:

1. When preparing the planting hole, ensure that it is significantly wider than the root ball of the plant going into it. Loosen the soil in the base of the hole and in the pile of topsoil you will use to backfill around the sides of the root ball. You can mix in an appropriate compost, as well as a

Immersing a potted plant before planting ensures that it has the maximum moisture available during its establishment phase.

suitable quantity of fertiliser (follow the directions on the pack).

2. Carefully remove any weeds that may have invaded the pot.

3. Immerse the whole pot in a bucket of water until bubbles have stopped rising from the potting mix. This is one of the best tips for ensuring that your plant does not die of moisture stress in the first few weeks, particularly in very hot weather.

4. If there are any roots curling around the bottom of the pot when you remove the plant, don't be afraid to tease the roots out and cut away any that are badly curled. And resolve never again to patronise the retailer that sold it to you unless you can inspect or be shown plants' roots to make sure they are not pot-bound.

5. Place the plant into the hole and backfill with the topsoil 'cocktail' you have already prepared.

6. Create a 'well' around the plant that will hold water there while it soaks into the soil.

7. Mulch around the plant but leave a gap of five to ten centimetres around the stem to minimise the potential for collar rot.

8. Water the plant to remove any air pockets around the roots.

In the case of woody plants, it's a time-honoured custom to plant them at the same level in the garden soil as they were in their pot. But recent research has shown that much deeper plantings can have huge benefits, including faster establishment and better survival.

LONG-STEM PLANTING

When exotic willow trees were planted to stabilise eroding river banks in the Hunter Valley of New South Wales, Bill Hicks wondered why Australian trees and shrubs, particularly those endemic to the area, were not being used.

When Bill put this question to the authorities, they replied that native plants could not match the ability of willow trees to anchor the soil and prevent erosion. Bill asked whether anyone had tried planting the native species much deeper in the soil than was customary. This, he believed, would give them the chance to form roots along the stems, which in turn would make the plants much more stable in the soil and thus better at preventing erosion. At first, his suggestion was rejected as unworkable. Arguments against it included:

⊚ that if the stems of the plants were buried they would die because the crowns would rot out below the soil surface

⊚ that the root system of the plant would be deeply buried in the subsoil and would also rot out, and

⊚ that a plant with an elongated stem suitable for long-stem planting would have a pot-bound, dysfunctional root system to begin with.

Undeterred by conventional wisdom, Bill went ahead anyway and planted various native trees and shrubs—including eucalypts, callistemons, melaleucas and acacias—up to a metre deep. Not only did the plants survive, they rapidly overtook specimens of the same species planted

The long-stem planting method

Here's how to plant using the long-stem planting method:

1. Dig a hole using an auger or scissor shovel to a depth of about one metre. Pull out any loose soil by hand.
2. Pour at least a litre of water into the hole.
3. Carefully loosen the plant from its pot.
4. Support the root base with one hand and with your other hand, hold the plant a metre from the root base, which will be the depth you're planting it to.
5. Lower the plant into the hole.
6. Pack the dirt in around the root base and stem, and tamp down, creating a well around the stem.
7. Water the plant—the only time you'll have to!

alongside them using the conventional technique. Fifteen years and hundreds of thousands of successfully established native trees and shrubs later, Bill's long-stem planting method is increasingly being adopted for environmental restoration projects.

Having successfully used the technique in my own garden, I wholeheartedly recommend it for native trees and shrubs, especially if time and water are limited and you wish to dramatically reduce your maintenance load.

Reasons for adopting long-stem planting include:

- Only a single watering is required, and this can be done when the tree or shrub is planted.
- As the plant establishes, adventitious roots are established all the way along the stem. Once this happens, the plant is able to grow much faster.
- The tree or shrub will have a much stronger, better-formed root system. This makes for a much more stable plant that is less likely to blow over in the wind as the top increases in size—and ensures that several years on, you won't have unexpected gaps in your garden.
- The technique has been proven successful in a wide range of soil types and climatic conditions over the last fifteen years.

Several points need to be considered if you want to adopt the long-stem planting system:

- You will need specialist tools such as an auger or scissor shovel, particularly if you want the full benefit of planting up to a metre deep.
- You will lose some height in the plant, as you are burying all the top growth. However, experience has shown that while you may sacrifice an instant effect, you will gain much more in the long term.
- The technique is not suitable for many non-woody plants, including grasses and grass-like plants such as kangaroo paws.

Plant and garden care

Probably the single most useful piece of advice when it comes to plant and garden care is to put plants with similar requirements together wherever possible. That way you create 'zones' within which you can apply uniform watering, feeding or pruning regimes. This makes much more sense than rushing willy-nilly about the garden doing a little bit of this over here and a little bit of that over there, and trying to remember the likes and dislikes of each individual plant and whether or not you've paid it any attention this season. It's not as difficult as it sounds, either, since most plants aren't absolute sticklers for specific amounts of water, fertiliser, sun, and so on. Of course, some are more demanding, and it's these you'll need to pay particular attention to.

Caring for our plants should be enjoyable and easy. Unfortunately, that's not always how it turns out, and we end up expending much more time, energy, money and patience than we would like. The way to lessen the burden is to get the garden to look after itself as much as possible. Now, I know we can't expect a plant to uproot itself, head to the other side of the garden and prune another plant or turn on a hose, but our garden can certainly *help* look after itself when it comes to pests and diseases. The following explains how.

INTEGRATED PEST MANAGEMENT

IPM is a strategy for reducing pests and diseases in the garden using a range of sustainable and complementary methods. It focuses not on the eradication of every pest or disease but rather on maintaining a balance between 'good' and 'evil' in the garden. It has three stages: observation, prevention and human intervention.

OBSERVATION

This is the most important aspect of IPM. It entails continuously keeping an eye on (and recording if possible) pests and pest balances (thresholds); insect traps; plant condition (leaves, branches and bark); weather patterns; and generally everything in the garden.

Pests: It's helpful not only to observe what pests you have but learn all you can about their biology and life cycles. Understanding pests will help you find the best ways to deal with them. It can also be a fascinating education in biology, particularly if you have young children with a thirst for learning about nature. Catching their first Christmas beetle can be a great experience.

Pest thresholds: This refers to the levels of pests or disease you are prepared to tolerate before you intervene. These are a matter of personal opinion and will be specific to your garden and the pests and plants themselves. For example, you may tolerate a certain amount of scale or gall on a mature plant but understand that the same amount on a juvenile would be damaging and set out to control it before the damage causes the plant's death. For example, a common sap-sucking pest on lilly pillies and gum trees is the tiny psyllid. During its juvenile stage it lives underneath a hard covering called a lerp, and the adults are a few millimetres long, have wings and move about by flying or jumping. If there are lerps or psyllids on a few leaves only it's probably no cause for concern. However, if you notice clusters of lerps throughout the tree you may come to the conclusion that it's a good breeding environment for them and try to break their breeding cycle before the situation worsens.

Insect traps: If you are really keen, you can use these to determine what pests are in your garden and in what numbers. Keep a record of what you find in the traps so you can see when numbers increase. Insect traps use pheromones, food or visual attractants as bait, and can be purchased from hardware stores, or some basic types can be made at home. Aphids and other sap-sucking insects, for example, are attracted to the colour yellow. To help determine their numbers in the garden, paint a piece of cardboard bright yellow, and when it's dry smear Vaseline all over the board. Hang the trap in the garden and check it daily. You can trap wasps using an empty soft-drink bottle. Cut ten centimetres off the top

Banksias are very prone to iron deficiency, which appears as yellowing in the new vegetative growth.

RIGHT The 'Water Tube' is an innovative invention to provide a water reservoir that trickles out onto a newly established tree. *FAR RIGHT* Simple plastic sleeves provide a 'mini greenhouse' for new plantings with a weed-suppressing mat added around the base.

of the bottle. Insert either a piece of meat, or some cordial into the bottom. Invert the top section of the bottle and push it into the bottom section. Wasps will be able to find their way into the bottle but not back out. When plenty of wasps are trapped, fill the bottle with water to drown them.

Plant condition: Keep an eye on your plants and note how healthy (or not) they are looking. Check all parts of the plant for signs of problems: are the leaves displaying symptoms such as black spot or wilting? Chlorosis is a common symptom of a range of nutritional deficiencies and includes yellow splotches on (usually green) leaves, overall yellowing of leaves, and green veins with yellow leaf tissue. Die-back will be noticed first on the tips of leaves, before spreading to the whole leaf, stem and possibly, eventually, the branch and whole tree.

Weather patterns: Yes, it's important to watch these, too, as the weather plays an important role in the life cycles of pests. For example, aphids like it wet and warm, so if a colony is beginning to get out of hand and rain is forecast, it would be wise to deal with it beforehand. Hot, humid weather will also encourage many fungal diseases to take off in a big hurry. Fungal spores spread easily in the wind or rain, so if a storm is brewing and you have already noticed sooty mould or such on your

plants, tackle these diseases without delay by spraying (if rain is not imminent in a few hours) with a fungicide or removing affected leaves.

PREVENTION

As with our own health, this is usually better than attempting a cure. A healthy soil will help sustain healthy plants. Healthy plants are less susceptible to predators and can overcome their attacks more easily. Also, practise good garden hygiene: clean secateurs between pruning plants, clean cultivating tools regularly, throw diseased plant material in the rubbish, not the compost, and be mindful of sources of compost, manure and mulch—it's all too easy to bring pests and diseases into the garden from other areas.

HUMAN INTERVENTION

Human intervention is also needed to keep a garden healthy. As the gardener, it's your job to help limit pests by adjusting microclimates and by applying mechanical, biological or chemical controls.

Microclimates: If an area's microclimate is too humid, it can promote fungal diseases. To make a microclimate drier, add or remove plants (or parts of plants), allowing more sunshine to penetrate and air to circulate; eliminate overhead watering; and clean up leaf litter. A microclimate may be too dry and plants become stressed, encouraging pests or diseases to move in. This could be altered by mulching, providing shade (taller plants, built structures etc.) or increasing the water.

Mechanical control: This entails physically removing pests from the plant or stopping them from getting onto it. Removal can be done either by hosing or picking them off (preferably with gloves). Insect barriers include double-sided tape wrapped around a tree trunk (or plastic strips, in the case of possums). Insect traps can be made at home. For example, a beer trap is useful for catching slugs and snails. Simply quarter fill a jam jar with beer and push the jar into the soil with enough of the jar above ground so it doesn't fill with soil. Slugs and snails will be attracted to the beer and drown. Earwigs will happily find refuge in a rolled up newspaper—leave it where you suspect there are earwigs and check regularly. You may like to have a bucket of soapy water to hand to shake them into.

There are plenty of variations of these and other traps to be found online.

Biological control: A range of insects, bacteria, fungi and nematodes can be your allies in the fight against pests, devouring them or making conditions unpleasant for them. For example, ladybirds love to feast on aphids and can eat hundreds a week. Ladybirds can be purchased or encouraged to the garden by including their favourite plants, such as herbs and artichokes. A common control for caterpillars is a bacteria called *Bacillus thuringiensis* which is sprayed onto leaves and kills by ingestion. Parasitic wasps can be useful in controlling a range of pests such as lawn grubs. These beneficial organisms can be purchased from either garden stores or companies specialising in biocontrol.

Chemical control: Then there are pesticides. Some of these, of course, are more toxic than others, and have more potentially damaging side effects. But because it combines a variety of approaches to pest control, integrated pest management allows you to use plant-based and less concentrated chemicals. They may not be as strong as more powerful alternatives, but you'll be using them as a back-up, not your sole weapon.

Soil care: 'Feed the soil and the plants will feed themselves' is a saying well worth remembering. Add a variety of well-composted organic matter to the soil beneath your mulch at least once a year, and let the soil organisms do the rest. Rock minerals are another useful addition to any garden-care regime, as they add essential trace elements.

I started this section with perhaps my most important piece of garden-care advice: *group plants of similar requirements together*. Here is my second top piece of advice: *apply liquid seaweed emulsion regularly.* By helping to create strong root zones and plant cells, seaweed emulsion fortifies plants against the stresses of heat, drought, and pest attack. It also stimulates the activity of beneficial soil microbes, the invisible key to a healthy soil and therefore healthy plants.

all about the plants

Acacias

Acacias are almost ubiquitous in Australia: virtually every region has its own set of wattles that are adapted to the local conditions. They are one of the great pioneer plants, always among the first to colonise areas disturbed by fire or other environmental upheavals. As well as their utility in the landscape, they have a lot to offer from an ornamental perspective. At any given time of year, you can find a species of wattle in bloom somewhere around the country, so there's one to suit every garden. And their variety of colours, textures and growth habits (weeping or upright, for example) lend themselves to a range of garden designs.

Wattles have been genetically improved to make them more versatile, especially for smaller gardens. In particular, numerous compact and ground-covering types have been released in recent years. The foliage of many of these new cultivars is as much an ornamental feature as the classic yellow blossoms. The river or bower wattle (*Acacia cognata*) has given rise to many of the best new compact wattles, with forms ranging from tight bun-shaped plants less than half a metre tall ('Green Mist', 'Limelight' and 'Mop Top') to beautiful weeping shrubs several metres high, with features such as golden foliage ('Lime Magik') or purple-tipped new growth ('Copper Tips'). These cultivars are reliable and long-lived garden plants in southern Australia, but can be a bit prone to root-rotting diseases in more humid coastal areas such as Sydney and Brisbane. In such climates, they are best considered as short-term (one- to three-year) plants.

It is not often that an entirely new colour appears in a plant family, so the advent of the red 'Scarlet Blaze' *Acacia leprosa* is very exciting. It has a tendency to be a bit open and straggly, but regular tip pruning while it is in the establishment phase will turn it into a more compact shrub with lots more flowers.

As well as looking at the exciting options among the old and new *Acacia* cultivars available, I highly recommend growing the indigenous wattle species of your area. This will give you a plant adapted to local conditions. For instance, frost tolerance varies enormously among the different wattles, so if you live in a frost-prone area you will be well served by choosing your local species.

ABOVE *Acacia* 'Scarlet Blaze' is a unique new red-flowered wattle cultivar.
FAR LEFT Many species of acacias are grown for their striking foliage.

GROWING AND MAINTENANCE TIPS

Acacias belong to the legume family, which means their roots are able to fix nitrogen from the air and use it as a nutrient. As a result, they grow fast and need little if any fertiliser—another reason to include them in your garden. The only thing you need to watch out for is deficiencies in or sensitivities to particular nutrients. A number of species are sensitive to added phosphorus, which also points to a minimalist approach when feeding wattles.

Unlike most woody Australian plants, wattles do not usually respond well to heavy pruning. To be on the safe side, it's a good rule of thumb not to cut into wood any thicker than a pencil. Most *Acacia* species do not need pruning to keep a good shape, though if you want to stop them from seeding it is a good idea to give them a light prune after flowering. This is particularly important if you live near bushland, as wattles can tend to invade surrounding areas and compete with your local species. The seed is also very long-lived and can remain dormant in the soil for decades, just waiting for the right conditions to germinate.

Borers are often a problem with wattles and can wreak havoc on the trunk and branches. Healthy, actively growing wattles have a built-in borer defence mechanism: they exude a gum that drowns the insects in the holes they are drilling. If a wattle is badly damaged by borers, then this mechanism has probably broken down—a sign that the plant is approaching the end of its useful life. Another common problem is gall wasps, which pupate inside little balls on the stems and foliage. These damage only the part of the tree they are infesting, so the best remedy is to cut off the balls, or galls, with secateurs and destroy them.

USING ACACIAS IN THE GARDEN

In the bush, as we've noted, acacias are one of the great pioneer plants of disturbed areas. After bushfires and in cleared areas, they are among the first plants to return unaided. The upshot is that fast-growing wattles will fill a gap in your garden while you are waiting for slower-growing species to do their stuff. On the flip side, wattles are often short-lived, which may influence your decisions about where to plant them and what to plant beside them.

If you want to provide shade or shelter around the perimeter of a large garden, there are several large tree species of wattle that will do the job, including cedar wattle (*A. elata*), Gosford wattle (*A. prominens*), and blackwood (*A. melanoxylon*). A number of other wattles grow into small trees, and these are very handy garden plants as they tend not to have invasive root systems. Some great examples include the Cootamundra wattle (*A. baileyana*), black wattle (*A. decurrens*), and Australian golden wattle (*A. pycnantha*). As we noted above, small to medium shrub-sized wattles have emerged as great garden plants in recent times. Many are mentioned in the cultivar list at the back of the book.

The vibrant yellow flower is a signature of Australian wattles.

Kangaroo paws: *Anigozanthos*

This remarkable group of Australian plants embodies many of the qualities that make our native plants so distinctive. Their vibrant, almost iridescent flower colours are combined with a bizarrely furry texture created by the hairs that cover the stems and flowers—and provide the latter's colour. Another oddity is the way the colour varies according to temperature, with cooler days producing more intense shades. Thus the same kangaroo-paw species in bloom can look completely different in different environments.

Kangaroo paws also typify the frustrations of growing many of our native plants, since many varieties can be rather unreliable in cultivation. Nonetheless, they are now well established as garden plants, particularly the many named hybrids that have been released over the past twenty-five years. Having been responsible for a number of the new cultivars, I would like to give you my perspective on choosing the right kangaroo paw for your garden.

I would divide the kangaroo paws into three groups for home cultivation:

Group 1—Tall cultivars (flower stems approximately two metres). These are long-term perennial garden plants and comprise two basic types. First, there are hybrids between *Anigozanthos flavidus* and *A. pulcherrimus,* whose flowers are yellow, orange, and red-and-yellow. Then there are the *Anigozanthos flavidus* x *rufus* hybrids. Their blooms range from

The bright colours of kangaroo paws are created by a dense felt of hairs on the flower surface.

burgundy to bright red or orange-red. All of these hybrids are long-lived; I have seen them survive for over twenty years as garden plants if the clumps are divided every few years. The plants in this group are very vigorous growers, and are also resistant to the fungal disease leaf rust, and generally resistant to *Alternaria* leaf spot, the other major fungal disease in kangaroo paws, and the crown-rot diseases that kill many of the shorter paw species and cultivars in garden situations.

Group 2—Smaller cultivars. Many new cultivars have resulted from crossing the species *A. flavidus* (which confers a degree of adaptability on hybrids) with other smaller-growing species that are naturally short-lived, including *A. humilis*, *A. bicolor* and *A. gabrielae*. Because the second parent usually lives for a couple of years at most, these hybrids also tend to be short-lived in the garden, even though they are technically perennial plants. So it is best to think of them as plants that will flower their heads off for their shortish lives but need to be replaced within a few years.

Another strength of the shorter cultivars is their long flowering; some, including *Anigozanthos* 'Bush Pearl' and 'Bush Diamond', flower all year in frost-free conditions. An outstanding way to grow these cultivars is in containers. In a good-quality potting mix, you can grow a plant with fifty or more flower stems that can be moved around the garden for maximum effect. These stems can also be cut for indoor arrangements.

Group 3—Species. There are twelve species of kangaroo paws, and every one of them is worth growing. Each has its own unique beauty, from the diminutive red-and-green flowered *Anigozanthos gabrielae*,

with flower stems only a few centimetres tall, to the towering tall kangaroo paw (*A. flavidus*), whose flower stems can top three metres. Then there is the bizarre black kangaroo paw (*Macropidia fuliginosa*), which creates a 'wow' effect in any garden, or the Albany catspaw (*A. preissii*), with its spectacular claw-like flowers. Then, of course, there is the floral emblem of Western Australia, the red-and-green kangaroo paw (*A. manglesii*), which also comes in a host of other colour schemes.

GROWING AND MAINTENANCE TIPS

As mentioned above, the different types of kangaroo paws vary enormously in their ease of cultivation. Unless you are prepared to give them some tender loving care, it is best to stick to the taller types, with flower stems around the two-metre mark. These will generally perform well over a wide range of conditions, except in areas that receive heavy frosts (a proviso that applies to all the paws). Maintenance of these taller varieties is simple. They can be chopped right back to ground level each year to clean up any dead or blackened foliage.

A handy tip to prolong the flowering season of the taller kangaroo paws is to cut out the top half of the flower stem as soon as the first flower opens and use it indoors as a cut flower. Its removal stimulates the growth of the dormant flower buds that remain on the bottom half of the flower stem, the part still on the plant. These dormant buds develop into side branches that extend the flowering period (usually from late spring to mid-summer) by at least a month or two.

With the smaller hybrid cultivars, it takes a bit more work to maximise their relatively short lives. Each flower stem arises from a fan of leaves (usually six), which gradually die and turn black as the flowers finish. A number of dwarf paws, such as 'Bush Pearl' and 'Bush Diamond', flower all year. A savage cutback will often kill the smaller hybrids, so rather than chopping the whole plant down to ground level, it is best to remove the spent flower stems one at a time. As you do so, make sure you take the old leaves that are associated with them.

With the exception of the tall kangaroo paw (*A. flavidus*), the wild paw species tend not to be long-lived in the garden, particularly if drainage is poor. Give them a well-drained position with as much sun as possible, such as in a rockery. Otherwise they can be grown quite happily in containers, where I have had them flower well for ten years or more. A good tip with pots is to use a free-draining mix but apply plenty of food and water while the plants are actively growing and flowering. The flower stems are very succulent while they are developing and do not react well to lack of moisture.

USING KANGAROO PAWS IN THE GARDEN

It is hard to go past kangaroo paws when you're looking for a vibrant splash of colour in either pots or garden beds. The crucial point is to select the right variety for your purpose. Although the smaller varieties tend to be short-lived, they can provide a spectacular display in a feature garden bed, particularly if you have a smaller garden, and of course they are also fabulous in pots. The dwarf varieties will, to put it bluntly, pump out colour and then cark it.

If you want a more permanent display of kangaroo paws, the tall varieties are ideal and can survive for many years in most non-frosty areas of Australia. Placed at the back of garden beds, they are a perfect backdrop for low-growing plants of contrasting or complementary colours. The tall varieties will also provide long-lived cut flowers.

The tubular flowers of kangaroo paws are adapted for pollination by nectar-eating birds with long beaks, so try to position them where you will be able to watch the delicate spinebills and honeyeaters that will seek out the flowers in many parts of Australia. Placing paws near the windows of your house or the deck, where you can sit still and observe, will bring you a wonderful wildlife reward.

FAR LEFT The dwarf species of kangaroo paw such as *Anigozanthos humilis* are perfect for rockeries or containers.
LEFT *Anigozanthos* 'Bush Diamond' (TOP) is great for short-term displays, while *Anigozanthos* 'Lilac Queen' (BOTTOM) is a long-lived kangaroo paw better suited to permanent plantings in the garden.

Australian climbers: *Hardenbergia, Kennedia, Pandorea, Sollya, Tecomanthe and others*

Australia has a wonderful array of evergreen climbing plants, many producing abundant and spectacular flowering displays. The bower of beauty (*Pandorea jasminoides*) flowers for many months of the year and has become popular in other parts of the world as well. Native sarsaparilla, or happy wanderer (*Hardenbergia*), is another star in the garden, with numerous cultivars detailed in the list at the end of this book.

GROWING AND MAINTENANCE TIPS

Climbing plants can only fill a vertical space if they have something to climb on, so an appropriate support such as a trellis or fence is essential unless you want them to grow as ground covers. Most Australian climbers are known as twiners, because the stems twist around their supports rather than clinging to them with aerial roots. Their supports must therefore have an open structure. A bare wall will not support twining climbers; you will need to put lattice or wire over it.

Prune and feed your climbers immediately after they finish flowering to keep a compact, bushy habit as well as produce better flowering next time.

USING CLIMBERS IN THE GARDEN

Climbers can double as ground covers if they have nothing to climb on, so they can potentially fill horizontal spaces as well as vertical ones. Bear in mind, though, that they will climb on living supports as well as fences and trellises. Over time they will strangle trees and shrubs if allowed to. Decide what you want your climber to do, then plant and train it accordingly.

Australian daisies come in many shapes, colours and textures.

Australian daisies

The daisy family, Asteraceae, is one of the wonders of the botanic world, having spread all around the globe. Australia is very well represented, and its Asteraceae have produced some excellent garden plants. The daisy flower is actually a composite of numerous tiny florets. Each gives rise to a seed with its own 'parachute', enabling it to ride the wind and put down roots if it happens to land on a patch of bare and preferably disturbed soil. You will therefore find your native daisies seeding themselves spontaneously in other parts of your garden. This promiscuous voyaging can be curbed by deadheading the spent flower stems once they finish flowering. There are a number of groups of Australian daisies worth considering for the splashes of colour they are able to provide at relatively short notice.

Herbaceous daisies: *Brachyscome*

Plants of the versatile *Brachyscome* genus can provide colour and movement in your garden for many months of the year. For the home garden, two distinct groups are of special interest: suckering and non-suckering types.

The suckering types, such as the Pilliga daisy (*B. formosa*) and its various hybrid cultivars, are extra useful because they can sprout again from their root system if they have been cut or have died back after a flush of flowers. This means they will go on and on flowering, bursting into islands of colour after rain and when temperatures are favourable. These clumps are also very portable and can be sliced and diced—with a trowel instead of a knife. The resulting subdivisions can then be replanted straight into other parts of the garden.

The non-suckering types, such as the cut-leaf daisy (*B. multifida*), can provide shorter-term bursts of low-growing colour. These brachyscomes grow from a single point or crown, so if anything detrimental happens to that growing point you will lose the whole plant. Fortunately, they are very easily propagated by soft-tip cuttings, which will strike roots, so you can easily renew the plants from year to year or multiply them for special displays.

Special mention must also go to the Swan River daisy (*B. iberidifolia*). This species is an annual and provides flowers unique in this genus. My particular favourites are the black-centred types, which come in a variety of colours from dark purple to blue, white and pink. The colourful annuals are best raised from seed, which can be bought from specialist seed retailers. Sow the seed in pots or directly in garden beds.

Everlasting daisies: *Rhodanthe* (a.k.a. *Helipterum*)

and *Xerochrysum* (a.k.a. *Helichrysum* or *Bracteantha*)

These groups of daisies are wonderful sources of vibrant colour. The starry, paper-like bracts that provide the colour in the flowers retain their colour when dried, and can be preserved in arrangements for a year or more—hence their alternative name, everlasting daisies.

The xerochrysums comprise a somewhat mysterious chapter in the history of the cultivation of Australian plants. Some time in the mid-nineteenth century, a strain of *Xerochrysum bracteatum* (at the time it was known as *Helichrysum bracteatum*) appears to have been bred in Europe in a range of colours that do not appear in the wild in Australia, where this species is yellow and, rarely, white. The colours of the European strain include purple, red, orange and pink. The original strain is an annual plant that is sown in autumn and flowers in spring. Seed companies around the world have carried it on, and it is now possible to buy tall strains (up to two metres) as well as dwarf ones.

Over the past twenty years, a number of forms of *Xerochrysum bracteatum* have come into cultivation from different areas of Australia. The most exciting of these is a perennial large-flowered, grey-leaved form from south-east Queensland. It has given rise to a number of outstanding garden plants, including the cultivars 'Cockatoo' and 'Dargan Hill Monarch'.

In recent years, the large-flowered perennial forms have been crossed by breeders around the world with the variously coloured annual forms to create an ever-increasing array of xerochrysums (often sold under their old botanic name, *Bracteantha*), from low-growing domed plants to metre-high shrubs. Cultivars such as the 'Sundaze' series (listed at the back of this book) will provide colour in your garden for several months, starting each spring. The plants strike very readily from tip cuttings, so they can easily be renewed when they start to look a bit tired.

The chamomile everlasting (*Rhodanthe anthemoides*) is a fabulous garden plant that can go on for several years in good growing conditions. The grey-green foliage becomes covered in delicate little flowers for several weeks in spring. This species has several excellent cultivars, including 'Paper Baby', 'Paper Star' and 'Chamomile Cascade'. All are worthy of a spot in your garden.

As well as the xerochrysums, several annual species of *Rhodanthe* (also known as *Helipterum*) were the subject of much breeding work in Europe in the nineteenth and twentieth centuries. *Rhodanthe chlorocephala* and *R. manglesii* both have annual strains (often sold as *Helipterum*) that will provide wonderful annual displays in a wide range of climates and conditions.

The shrubby Australian daisies are somewhat underrated, in my view. There are two major groups, both charming. The rice flowers (belonging to the genera *Ozothamnus* and *Cassinia*) feature masses of tiny everlasting daisies reminiscent of rice grains in showy terminal clusters at the ends of the shoots. The second group, belonging to the genus *Olearia*, have soft daisy flowers which make an effect in the garden similar to that of the exotic perennial asters. Look out for the outstanding cultivars from these groups in the list at the back of this book.

GROWING AND MAINTENANCE TIPS

A light trim after a heavy flush of flowers is all the pruning you need to do to keep your various Australian daisies looking good. The shrubby daisies should be cut back by about twenty to thirty per cent behind the flowers to keep them as compact, free-flowering plants. *Ozothamnus* and the various everlasting daisies are also good as cut flowers, and cutting them serves to prune the bush.

Shrubby daisies can be somewhat prone to attack by borers, and unfortunately it is very hard to control this problem short of replacing the plant. With the herbaceous daisies, such as brachyscomes, and with the *Xerochrysum* genus, watch out for caterpillars. The bacterial insecticide Dipel can be used as a non-toxic way to prevent caterpillar infestations.

USING AUSTRALIAN DAISIES IN THE GARDEN

Brachyscomes and everlasting daisies are some of the best native plants for providing low-growing colour at the front of garden beds, in rockeries and in hanging baskets and pots of all sizes. The shrubby daisies are excellent background plants for shrubberies and can be used as container plants as well.

Everlasting daisies are not only good in the garden but also last indefinitely in the vase.

Australian rainforest plants

Australia is home to one of the largest collections of rainforest plants left on the planet. Our rainforests range from true tropical rainforest in the Daintree, in north Queensland, to the cool temperate rainforests of Tasmania, with many intermediate types between. This means that no matter where you live, there is a way to bring that emerald-green rainforest lushness to your garden. Many rainforest species also have fleshy fruits that attract birds and other animals—and often humans, too, lending a bush-tucker aspect to your garden.

Stream lily (*Helmholtzia glabberima*) is a fantastic plant for shady conditions. I consider it to be the perfect Australian alternative to clivias for its ability to flower continuously in heavy shade, such as those awkward spots under trees. The metre-high flower heads are white with a pink blush and last for many weeks on the plant.

Davidson's plum (*Davidsonia pruriens*) is often mentioned as a bush-tucker plant. The plum-shaped purple fruits do make a delicious jam, but that is not all there is to this interesting small tree. Its textured, deeply cut leaves also make it an outstanding indoor plant that will survive if given a well-lit spot near a window. Give it an occasional rest outdoors to soak up a bit of rain and refresh the foliage and it will look great for years.

The mat rush (*Lomandra hystrix*) forms a beautiful glossy green-leaved clump that works well even in shady conditions. It is as hardy as its cousin, the spiny-headed mat rush (*Lomandra longifolia*), which has become a standard fixture along roadways and in roundabouts. A tidy-up of old flower stems and dead leaves at the end of spring is all that is required to keep the mat rush looking its best.

Lilly pillies have become a popular choice as hedge plants thanks to their outstanding response to regular pruning. A couple of species that perform extremely well include the brush cherry (*Syzygium australe*) and the small-leaved lilly pilly (*S. leuhmannii*). As well as producing edible fruits, they put on pretty displays of powder-puff flowers. But perhaps their best feature is the colourful new growth that both species produce during the warmer months. It is important to give both these plants plenty of space, however, as they do grow into sizeable trees.

For a bold statement in the garden, the spear lily (*Doryanthes palmeri*) is unsurpassed. Its close relative the Gymea lily (*D. excelsa*) has been the focus of horticultural attention for some years now. Like the Gymea lily, the spear lily performs well in either shade or sun and responds brilliantly to extra water and nutrition, as do all rainforest plants. The large strappy leaves can reach a metre or more in length, while the bright red flowers, borne in a toothbrush-like arrangement on the metre-long flower stalks, attract birds.

This is but a small selection of the numerous native rainforest plants that have now found their way into the nursery industry. Specialist native nurseries are the place to go to find some of the more unusual species. Look for these at *www.angusstewart.com.au*.

GROWING AND MAINTENANCE TIPS

Rainforest plants come from an environment where the soil generally has lots of humus created by natural means, so adding plenty of well-rotted compost is the way to ensure healthy, thriving specimens. In the natural environment, the rainforest provides shelter from harsh winds and westerly afternoon sun, so choosing sheltered spots or providing supplementary shade if need be will also help establish your rainforest plants.

Generally speaking, rainforest plants tend to look after themselves and do not need a lot of attention. However, if you do want to create bushy flowering specimens, tip pruning when they are young and an annual 'haircut' after flowering will do the job. It is also worth mentioning that most rainforest plants are not particularly phosphorus sensitive and can be planted in areas where lots of fertiliser has been used in the past.

USING AUSTRALIAN RAINFOREST PLANTS IN THE GARDEN

Rainforest plants tend to share the broad emerald-green foliage that lends itself to the tropical garden look. They are also a great way to bring shade and shelter to your garden. A different suite of bird life tends to be attracted by these plants as well. Many rainforest species have fleshy, edible fruits that persuade animals to help with seed dispersal. Cassowaries play this role in the rainforests of north-east Queensland, for instance.

FAR LEFT AND LEFT Australian rainforest plants provide an endless array of flower and foliage types that thrive in warmer climates but will also adapt to protected spots in cooler areas.

Australian Rutaceae: Boronia, Correa, Crowea, Diplolaena, Eriostemon and Philotheca

Some of the most delicate and beautiful of all Australian plants belong to the citrus family, Rutaceae. One of the defining features of this family is the presence of essential-oil glands in the leaves, which often exude a strong scent if they are crushed. A number of these species, notably the brown boronia (*B. megastigma*), have some of the most delightful perfumes in the plant kingdom. Another common feature is the starry shape of the flowers of many species such as boronias, eriostemons and philothecas—though correas and diplolaenas offer totally different flower shapes as well.

Most of the Australian Rutaceae flower in spring, but there are exceptions. The delightful croweas provide a show right through the autumn, while correas are a mainstay of bird-attracting colour throughout the winter.

My favourite in the Australian Rutaceae is the genus *Philotheca* (most of these plants used to be called *Eriostemon*). The species *Philotheca myoporoides* (long-leaf waxflower) and the various cultivars derived from it are incredibly tough but very showy garden plants. Some have pleasantly aromatic foliage and almost demand to be planted near a path where you can deliberately brush against them or crush a leaf to delight a visitor.

TOP AND ABOVE Various forms of *Philotheca* are not only outstanding garden plants, but are also good as cut flowers.
LEFT The delicate star-shaped flowers of boronias normally appear in spring.

GROWING AND MAINTENANCE TIPS

It needs to be said at the outset that this is not always the easiest group of plants to cultivate. While there are some very tough plants in this family, such as the long-leaf waxflower (*Philotheca myoporoides*) and the white correa (*C. alba*), the majority, and particularly the boronias, have proven to be short-lived in many parts of Australia.

The plants of this family generally grow in the wild as understorey shrubs in eucalypt forests, so a sheltered position with very good drainage and strong but filtered sunlight for most of the day is ideal for them. It is often claimed that they like a cool root run and that planting next to rocks helps create such a situation. My own observations confirm this theory; certainly, they are often found growing near rocks in the wild.

When it comes to fertiliser, some species of boronia are known to be very sensitive to phosphorus, so it would pay to err on the side of caution and use low-phosphorus feeds generally with this group of Australian plants. Once established in the garden, they are usually fairly tolerant of dry conditions, but they are certainly not happy in waterlogged soils, so avoid planting them in situations where this could occur.

Most species flower only once a year, so give them a light haircut straight after flowering and you will be well rewarded. Most also make excellent and long-lasting cut flowers, and using them this way will help to prune the plant. If you do cut off flowers, just be sure to return at the end of the flowering season and even out the shape by cutting back any stray stems.

USING RUTACEAE IN THE GARDEN

Many of these delightful shrubs make wonderful small- to medium-sized feature plants that are particularly good for areas of dappled shade around larger shrubs and trees. Some of the tougher members of the Rutaceae can also be useful as compact hedges, in particular the long-leaf waxflower (*Philotheca myoporoides*) and its cultivars, such as the very tough 'Profusion'. If you are one of the many gardeners who have been tempted by the perfume of the brown boronia in the nursery but had it die a few weeks after you planted it in the garden, then consider growing the touchier members of the Australian Rutaceae in a pot.

Banksias

There has to be a place for at least one banksia in every garden. The incredible range of sizes and shapes in flowers, foliage and growth habit make these a 'must have' that adds not only beauty and texture but attracts wildlife as well. If you want a perch from which birds can gauge whether your garden is safe for an extended visit, then the coast banksia (*B. integrifolia*) or old man banksia (*B. serrata*) are good options. There are also many shrubby banksias, too numerous to mention in detail, and even ground-covering banksias, such as the intriguingly named southern blechnum banksia (*B. blechnifolia*) from Western Australia.

Without doubt, one of the greatest breakthroughs in breeding Australian plants for the home garden has been the dwarf banksias selected over the past twenty years. Perfect for today's smaller gardens, these low growers deserve a place in gardens of any size and are particularly good for container gardening. In my opinion, the best dwarf selections have undoubtedly come from the hairpin banksia (*Banksia spinulosa*). The cultivars 'Stumpy Gold', 'Coastal Cushion', 'Birthday Candles', 'Cherry Candles' and 'Honey Pots' all form low-growing mounds that are festooned with the candle-shaped flower heads that are such a distinctive hallmark of the Australian bush.

Other banksia species have also provided some very useful dwarf and ground-covering cultivars. From the coastal banksia (*B. integrifolia*), we have the ground cover 'Austraflora Roller Coaster'; the old man banksia (*B. serrata*) has yielded the prostrate 'Pygmy Possum';

and the excellent compact shrub 'Mini Marg' is a selection of *B. marginata*.

Large flower heads are also a feature of many *Banksia* species. The cultivar 'Giant Candles', a probable hybrid between the heath-leaved banksia (*B. ericifolia*) and the hairpin banksia (*B. spinulosa*), is one of the most spectacular banksias for the garden, with flower spikes over half a metre long.

GROWING AND MAINTENANCE TIPS

Probably the most important factor in growing banksias is nutrition. They are generally among the most phosphorus-sensitive of Australian plants, so be sure to use a low-phosphorus fertiliser when you feed them coming into spring.

Another important feature of banksias is the fact that their peak of flowering usually comes in winter. This means that if you are going to prune them, the ideal time is at the end of winter, immediately after they've finished flowering. Cut them any other time and you risk removing the flower buds or potential flowering wood. Banksias can be divided into two broad types based on their growth habit, which also influences pruning. Species such as the hairpin banksia (*B. spinulosa*) have a *lignotuber*, a swollen stem that can be seen at the base of the plant. This produces new shoots after bushfires have killed all the existing above-ground shoots. The *non-lignotuberous* type includes species such as *B. ericifolia*. This type tends to die completely after a bushfire, so when pruning it is best not to cut the plants back to stems any thinner than your thumb.

When pruning banksias, it's also

Banksias create long-term interest in the garden through foliage, flower and fruits.

important to choose the kind of look you want them to bring to your garden. As the flower heads finish blooming, you must decide whether you want to let them go to seed or not. Species such as *B. serrata* have rather ornamental seed pods, which display themselves prominently long after flowering and seeding. I prefer to leave the seed pods on the plant to give the garden a 'big bad Banksia man' feel, but this is purely a matter of personal taste. If your preference is to remove the pods, then the best time to do it is straight after flowering.

USING BANKSIAS IN THE GARDEN

There is a tremendous range of growth habits in the genus *Banksia*. If you are looking for trees that will not only attract birds but give them a safe haven from cats, then species such as old man banksia (*B. serrata*) and coastal banksia (*B. integrifolia*) will grow to between ten and fifteen metres depending on climate and soil conditions. A number of banksias form large shrubs that are ideal as screening plants along fence lines; these include heath-leaved banksia (*B. ericifolia*) and its excellent large-flowered hybrid 'Giant Candles', scarlet banksia (*B. coccinea*) and bull banksia (*B. grandis*). For small to medium shrubs that will bring birds into your garden at eye level, there are again numerous options, including the hairpin banksia (*B. spinulosa*), possum banksia (*B. baueri*), mountain banksia (*B. canei*) and Wallum banksia (*B. aemula*). For ground cover, there are the numerous dwarf cultivars mentioned above, as well as the extraordinary species *B. blechnifolia*.

It is well worth researching the geographical origins of any banksias you are contemplating for your garden. In general, the Western Australian species become more and more difficult to grow reliably on the east coast the further north you go. By contrast, the eastern states' banksias are fairly reliable in most parts of Australia.

Banksias also make terrific cut flowers, especially the larger, shrubby Western Australian species such as *B. prionotes* and *B. menziesii*. A couple of the eastern species, such as the Hinchinbrook Island banksia (*B. plagiocarpa*) and swamp banksia (*B. robur*), are also great cut flowers, while the coast banksia (*B. integrifolia*) has leaves with silvery-white undersurfaces that make wonderful long-lived cut foliage.

Bottlebrushes and paperbarks: *Callistemon* and *Melaleuca*

Callistemons go by the very descriptive common name of bottlebrush, while the melaleucas' common name is paperbark. Both genera are among the most adaptable Australian plants when it comes to soil conditions. They will mostly thrive in waterlogged conditions that would be the death of many other native plants. Conversely, they can also survive well in dry conditions.

Callistemon and *Melaleuca* are very closely allied, and this becomes very obvious when their flower heads are compared. The main distinguishing characteristic is that the fluffy, colourful stamens are held singly in *Callistemon* and bundled together in little groups in *Melaleuca*. There is reportedly some talk among botanists of eventually bringing *Callistemon* and *Melaleuca* together in one genus, but we needn't worry about that for now. However, it does explain why these two plant groups tend to behave similarly in the garden.

While we normally think red when it comes to these plants, they show many gorgeous colour variations, including white, yellow, mauve, purple and even green. Another useful feature is the variety of growth habits, from procumbent ground-covering shrubs to substantial trees and everything in between.

GROWING AND MAINTENANCE TIPS

These genera are among the easiest of all Australian plant groups to grow. They adapt well to a wide range of soil types and will tolerate waterlogged as well as dry soils.

As far as maintenance goes, a once-a-year pruning is all they require to stay at their best. The timing of this is rather critical, though, as the plants will develop a leggy, twiggy appearance if they are not pruned straight after their main flowering flush, in spring. Simply cut directly below the spent flower heads to stimulate the growth of new shoots; this will result in more abundant flowering the following year.

USING CALLISTEMONS AND MELALEUCAS IN THE GARDEN

The adaptability of these groups makes them a candidate for a number of roles in the garden. Their ability to be pruned back to ground level (if necessary) means that they can be kept to whatever dimensions you require, making them great screen plants. The fact that they are not particularly susceptible to root rot makes them a great choice for hedges, which are unlikely to develop unwanted gaps, as can happen with less reliable plant groups. Choose smaller-leaved varieties for this purpose, such as *Callistemon* 'Great Balls of Fire'. For a low-growing hedge, the excellent grey-leaved 'Little John' works very well.

Some of the more spectacular callistemons, such as 'Kings Park Special' or 'Purple Splendour', are useful as feature plants for prominent parts of the garden.

These cultivars will usually flower twice a year, in spring and again in autumn, if they get sufficient water and nutrients during the growing season.

Gum trees: *Eucalyptus* and *Corymbia*

Gum trees dominate the Australian landscape as no other trees do on any continent. It is no wonder, then, that these versatile trees have been increasingly adopted by gardeners as varieties better suited to cultivation have emerged. Gum trees must be chosen very carefully for the garden, as they can create fire hazards and their root systems can be invasive. However, with a little forethought and research it will generally be possible to find a gum tree that will suit your situation. In particular, a number of new cultivars that feature spectacular flowering are well worth considering.

The red flowering gum (*Corymbia ficifolia*) has given rise to numerous selections and hybrids that are being propagated by grafting. This means that you can now choose the exact colour you want for your garden, from bright red to orange, violet, pink and white, and even bicoloured types. The height of the various cultivars varies enormously, from bushes a couple of metres high to large trees, so it is very important to research the qualities of each cultivar so you end up with the one that best suits your needs. Another point to make about the genus *Corymbia* is that

CLOCKWISE FROM TOP LEFT Eucalyptus macrandra; E. macrocarpa; Corymbia ficifolia; E. torquate; E. leucoxylon; E. 'Torwood'.

The mottlecah (*Eucalyptus macrocarpa*) has the largest flowers of any gum tree.

unlike most of the *Eucalyptus* gums, its species hold their flowers in clusters at the ends of the branches.

The terminal flower heads of the red flowering gum can appear between December and February depending on the cultivar and the latitude. The ideal way to choose one is to see it in flower at your local gardening retailer.

The genus *Eucalyptus* contains many spectacular flowering types. Many are classified as mallees, which means they grow as multi-trunked shrubs rather than trees. In addition to beautiful flowers, many of these small gums also have highly ornamental barks—notably the gungurru (*Eucalyptus caesia*). As with the new red flowering gums, a number of new cultivars of *Eucalyptus* are being made available through grafting. It is very important to keep an eye on such grafted plants, as they are likely to sucker from the base of the tree. Such shoots should be removed as soon as possible after they appear.

GROWING AND MAINTENANCE TIPS

Eucalypts and corymbias are generally very adaptable and easy plants to grow. They are generally not phosphorus-sensitive and will tolerate a wide range of soil types and climatic conditions. When choosing a particular plant for your garden, the most important consideration, in my opinion, is to ensure that it has a good healthy root system.

Normally I would recommend pruning behind the flowers immediately after they have finished blooming. However, you may want to consider leaving the flowers in place to form gum

nuts. In many species these are beautifully ornate, and some stay on the tree for months at a time, creating year-round interest in the garden. Whether you prune your gum trees or leave them alone is a matter of taste, entirely up to you.

USING EUCALYPTS AND CORYMBIAS IN THE GARDEN

With growth habits ranging from the multi-trunked mallees (technically, these are shrubs) to the tallest flowering plants in the world (the mountain ash, *Eucalyptus regnans*), the gum tree family has something for everyone. The key, as mentioned earlier, is to do your homework and choose the right species or cultivar for your particular situation. For smaller gardens, though, do consider some of the new, very compact cultivars. For patios and decks, bear in mind that many smaller gum trees grow happily in containers.

Goodeniaceae: *Dampiera, Goodenia, Lechenaultia* and *Scaevola*

The family Goodeniaceae offers some of the most spectacular and useful herbaceous natives for the garden. Dampieras have some of the richest blue flowers imaginable, to which goodenias—with their buttercup-yellow flowers—make a stunning complement. The lechenaultias come in an extraordinary range of almost iridescent colours. Scaevolas are perhaps best known by gardeners for their rich purple flowers, though a range of other shades is progressively being made available by plant breeders.

Dampiera

Blue is not a common colour in the botanical world, so a whole genus with predominantly royal-blue flowers is a wonderful asset to gardeners. Dampieras are perhaps not the easiest plants to grow, but with a little attention to detail they can provide a wonderful splash of blue for an extended period of the year. The species *Dampiera diversifolia* is perhaps the best known in cultivation, but a number of others are becoming more widely grown.

Goodenia

The genus *Goodenia* contains a range of types, from ground covers to more upright herbaceous and even slightly woody plants. Some goodenias have proven to be extremely tough and adaptable in cultivation, such as the east-coast species hop goodenia (*G. ovata*). My own prostrate selection of this species, 'Gold Cover', grows vigorously under a very wide range of conditions and is proving to be a long-lived, reliable ground cover that flowers for many months of the year. The more typical upright form of *G. ovata* has been extensively used around Melbourne freeways as a tough, drought-tolerant landscaping plant. By contrast, many of the spectacular *Goodenia* species from Western Australia need more specialised growing conditions.

Lechenaultia

This exclusively Western Australian genus is a darling of the many visitors who flock to the west to view its wildflowers. The almost impossibly bright flowers of the various species stand out on roadside verges, which seem to suit these mainly ground-covering plants down to the ground. From the bicoloured red-and-cream wreath lechenaultia (*L. macrantha*) to the royal blue of *L. biloba* and every colour in between, there is something for everyone in this amazing group of herbaceous plants. Although they are technically perennial plants, capable of living for a number of years, in most gardens these are definitely short-term plants and should be treated as annuals.

Scaevola

This versatile genus has been the subject of intensive development by plant collectors and breeders over the past fifteen years. In particular, the low-growing herbaceous species *Scaevola aemula* is now widely grown around the world as a long-flowering pot and garden plant, and there are now numerous cultivars available. This species grows in every state of Australia in a variety of habitats, which perhaps explains its outstanding adaptability in cultivation. It provides a stunning floral display for six to nine months of the year, from spring onwards. Although a perennial plant, it often struggles to come back with the same vigour and display as in the first year. In my own garden I treat it as an annual, replacing it every year to ensure the best possible display.

FROM TOP Lechenaultia biloba; *Scaevola* species; *Goodenia* species; *Dampiera wellsiana.*

Of the other herbaceous species, *Scaevola albida* is an outstanding garden plant. It is tough, thrives in coastal situations as well as elsewhere, and generally lives much longer than its more spectacular cousin *S. aemula*. *Scaevola albida* comes in a variety of colours, from mauve to purple, pink and white, forming dense mat-like plants that flower throughout the warmer months of the year. Having bred the cultivars 'Mauve Carpet' and 'White Carpet' myself, I can vouch for their good garden performance.

As well as herbaceous ground-covering plants, the genus *Scaevola* includes a number of attractive shrubby species that are also finding a place in the garden. One of the best is the dark-blue *S. nitida*, from the coastal areas of south Western Australia. Flowering in spring, this two- to three-metre-high shrub should be trimmed lightly after it blooms to keep a nice rounded form.

GROWING AND MAINTENANCE TIPS

All members of the Goodeniaceae will thrive in a sunny, well-drained position. If your soil's drainage is a bit dodgy, then growing in containers is a very good alternative. This will also allow you to mix plants of different heights and colours, creating a feature that can be moved around the garden.

Most species are not phosphorus-sensitive and will respond well to general-purpose fertilisers. A light trim after each flush of flowers will help prolong flowering and keep the plants tidy. Most species also last well in the vase, and by taking out the odd stem for cut flowers you will be pruning the plant at the same time.

TOP Scaevola albida 'White Carpet' is a relatively long-lived fan flower when planted in the garden.
ABOVE Scaevola aemula 'Aussie Crawl' is a ground-covering form of this attractive species.
RIGHT Australian grasses and grass-like plants are generally long-lived plants that create vertical accents in the landscape.

USING GOODENIACEAE IN THE GARDEN

Scaevolas and dampieras are generally in the purple-to-blue range of the colour spectrum, with an intensity that makes a perfect contrast to yellow- or orange-flowered plants such as goodenias and hibbertias. You can create an especially striking effect by combining classic yellow-flowered plants such as *Hibbertia* or dwarf *Acacia* (such as the prostrate form of Cootamundra wattle, *A. baileyana*) with *Scaevola* in pots, rockeries and smaller garden beds.

Many species of Goodeniaceae also work well as container plants, particularly in hanging baskets. That way, you can not only provide them with a perfect growing medium, but you can also grow them on sun-drenched balconies and decks, where they will have ideal light conditions and good aeration to prevent fungal diseases.

Grasses and grass-like plants: *Dianella, Lomandra, Pennisetum, Poa* and *Themeda*

I have grouped these plants together because they tend to have similar growth habits as well as performing similar roles in garden design. The past twenty years have seen an explosion in the availability of new cultivars of all these plants.

Lomandra has become extremely popular as a tough, reliable landscaping plant. Though it's far from spectacular, it can survive and thrive in harsh conditions. The species *Lomandra longifolia* stands out as the most adaptable species for

gardeners. Going by the fantastic common name of spiny-headed mat rush, this species has given rise to a number of cultivars, the best of which is the very narrow-leaved 'Tanika'. Its grass-like foliage makes this plant look quite unlike its more widely used, broad-leaved cousin, *L. longifolia*.

Dianellas get their common name, flax lily, from their tough, fibrous leaves, from which Aboriginal people spun string and wove baskets. *Dianella caerulea* has been the stand-out species in cultivation, giving rise to a number of great new cultivars that are listed at the back of this book. In contrast to their tough foliage, dianellas produce delicate sprays of blue, pink or white flowers, followed by beautiful blue or purple berries.

Various native grasses have also been selected for cultivation, such as the rather spectacular swamp foxtail (*Pennisetum alopecuroides*). Some caution should be exercised with this plant, as it does have potential to seed itself and invade surrounding bushland. The various native species of poa, as well as kangaroo grass (*Themeda triandra*), have also given rise to some useful ground-cover options. Check the cultivar list at the back of this book for some of the new native grasses.

RIGHT Grass trees are wonderful grass-like plants that add vertical accents around the garden.
FAR RIGHT The diversity of flower types offered by the genus *Grevillea* has made them arguably the most popular group of Australian plants in the garden.

GROWING AND MAINTENANCE TIPS

Most of the plants in this group are very tough, low-maintenance garden plants that require only one annual tidy up to keep them looking good. After flowering, go through and individually cut out each flower stem and remove any dead or tired-looking foliage to make way for fresh new growth. A handful of low-phosphorus fertiliser at the same time will also help to rejuvenate the plant.

USING NATIVE GRASSES AND GRASS-LIKE PLANTS IN THE GARDEN

All of the plants in this group have a tufting habit, with leaves varying from needle-like to strap-like. This means they add vertical accents to a garden design, as well as being tough ground covers that do not require constant work to maintain.

Grevilleas

The genus *Grevillea* is undoubtedly among the jewels in the Australian floral crown. There are something like 500 *Grevillea* species, spread over a wide range of wild environments: desert, semi-arid, sub-alpine and rainforest, as well as dry eucalypt forest. *Grevillea* is also arguably the Australian plant genus that has seen the greatest advances in genetic improvement: selection and deliberate breeding have created hundreds of new, improved cultivars that often combine the best characteristics of two or more wild species. Alternatively, a number of cultivars have arisen as improved or unusual forms of a wild species—with a differently coloured flower, for example, or a more compact habit.

Grevilleas can be divided into several different groups:

Large-flowered grevilleas, also known as 'tropical' or 'Queensland' grevilleas. Cultivars such as 'Misty Pink', 'Honey Gem' and 'Moonlight' have become a prominent part of many Australian gardens and have proved to be long-flowering, bird-attracting plants that thrive in a wide range of climates and soils. When given ideal conditions, some of these grevilleas can grow into small trees, so it is important to bear this in mind when selecting a grevillea variety for your garden. All the large-flowered grevilleas originate from a group of species from Queensland, such as *G. banksii*. The best for my money is 'Moonlight', whose creamy-white flowers are produced all year round in a range of climates (excepting frosty areas) and soil types. It will form a small tree if left

There is a grevillea suited to
every climate in Australia.

unpruned, but regular trimming will help
to keep a more compact shape. As many
large-flowered grevilleas have a reasonable
vase life, an ideal way to prune is by
cutting stems for indoor decoration. A
host of new large-flowered grevilleas have
appeared over the last ten years; many of
the best are listed in the cultivar section at
the end of this book, and many more are
in the pipeline.

A second, and even more popular, type
of large-flowered grevillea is what I call
the 'Robyn Gordon' group. It was started
by David Gordon in the 1970s, when he
selected a hybrid seedling that had come
up in his garden and named it after his
daughter Robyn. Perhaps the most widely
planted grevillea of all, 'Robyn Gordon'
turned out to be a hybrid between the
Queensland species *G. banksii* and a
spectacular Western Australian species,
G. bipinnatifida. Since then, a number
of people have repeated the hybrid
combination of these two species to
create a range of grevilleas that form
dense shrubs up to a couple of metres
tall and bear spectacular flowerheads
all year round. These new crosses have
also extended the colour range, from
bright-red 'Robyn Gordon' to the yellow-
and-orange 'Peaches and Cream' and the
orange 'Superb'.

Spider-flowered grevilleas. These have
relatively small clusters of flowers, but
what they lack in flower size they make
up for in subtle beauty. An outstanding
example is the Deua grevillea (*G.
rhyolitica*), which produces bright-red
flowers all year round and has given rise
to some great new hybrid cultivars such
as 'Lady O'. The plants of this group are
generally much smaller than the large-
flowered grevilleas and can be kept
trimmed into very neat small to medium-
sized shrubs.

Toothbrush grevilleas. The last major
group of grevilleas is characterised by
one-sided flower heads that look just like
toothbrushes. While this group's flowers
are not as spectacular as those of the
larger grevilleas, their foliage is fascinating
and varied. They provide a wonderful
range of ground covers and shrubs of all
sizes that make excellent screen plants.

Some of my favourite toothbrush
grevilleas include 'Bronze Rambler',
an outstanding ground cover that is
extremely adaptable to differing climates
and soil types and has interestingly
textured foliage with beautiful coppery
new growth. Another tried and trusted
ground cover is 'Poorinda Royal Mantle',
probably the most widely planted low-
growing grevillea of all, with its red

flowers and divided foliage. It can cover many square metres and is ideal for spreading over sloping sites as well. It can also be used as a weeping standard when grafted onto a rootstock such as silky oak (*Grevillea robusta*). 'Poorinda Peter' is a large spreading shrub with bronze-coloured new growth, which harmonises well with the pinkish flowers.

GROWING AND MAINTENANCE TIPS

Grevilleas are sensitive to even moderate amounts of phosphorus in the soil, and can die if their soil is not managed carefully (please read the section on fertilising phosphorus-sensitive plants on page 74). Particular care should be taken with organic fertilisers such as blood and bone and chicken-manure based products, as their phosphorus levels are generally too high for grevilleas. If in doubt, use products that are specifically designed for native plants, as these are guaranteed to have appropriate phosphorus levels.

Grevilleas respond very well to pruning, and most will tend to become open and leggy if left to their own devices. Tip-pruning at planting time and during the first few years of life will develop sturdy, bushy plants that are more resistant to being blown over in severe storms. With established grevilleas, light pruning to just behind the flower heads after flowering will help keep them compact. A common conundrum is when to prune the ever-blooming types such as 'Robyn Gordon'. Their branches all terminate in a series of flower heads that will bloom for months on end, but eventually accumulate a lot of 'sticks' where the flowers have dropped off. Simply cut these back when they become unsightly and you will stimulate new flowering branches. Alternatively, you can give the plant a big 'renovation' prune once every few years. Grevilleas that have been let go can be reshaped: the ideal time for a drastic pruning is spring, when the plant is ready to bounce back with active growth.

Grevilleas are generally fairly trouble-free as far as pests and diseases go. Probably the main problem with this family is root rot caused by a variety of soil-borne fungi such as *Phytophthora*. A well-drained soil is the key to prevention here. Sooty mould on the leaves and stems can also affect plants, particularly as they get old and leggy. In my experience, the best solution to this is to cut them back hard in spring and encourage vigorous new growth.

USING GREVILLEAS IN THE GARDEN

This is an extremely versatile group of plants that can be used in many ways. The spectacular large-flowered 'brush' types are stunning when in full bloom and make great *feature plants*. Ever-blooming cultivars such as 'Robyn Gordon' and 'Superb' should be planted in positions where their numerous bird visitors can be readily observed. Most grevilleas are outstanding either as informal or formal hedges that serve as excellent *screens*. Larger-leafed types such as 'Orange Marmalade', 'Ivanhoe' and 'Poorinda Peter' are best used as informal hedges, while smaller-leafed types, such as *G. rosmarinifolia* and *G. lanigera* and their hybrids, can be used as lower-growing formal hedges, as they retain a neat appearance when clipped. There are also a number of *ground-covering* grevilleas that are ideal for dry exposed embankments or other relatively well-lit areas. With their vast variety of flower types and foliage, grevilleas are also great for providing *background colour* and *texture* in the garden.

The silky oak (*G. robusta*) has long been used as a street *tree* or feature plant—not just in Australia but around the world. In full bloom, it is arguably one of the most spectacular choices for this purpose. Another lesser-known tree grevillea is the white silky oak, or white yiel yiel (*G. hilliana*), which has long sprays of white flowers and a lovely large divided leaf. Another great reason to plant it is that it is now an endangered species in the wild.

Hibiscus and hibiscus-like plants

The cotton family, Malvaceae, contains some of the world's most useful and also most ornamental plants, with many spectacular examples in the Australian flora. As well as the true hibiscuses, such as *H. splendens, H. tiliaceus, H. heterophyllus* and *H. divaricatus,* there are two outstanding species in the genus *Alyogyne* that have very hibiscus-like flowers and are excellent garden plants. They are *A. huegelii* and *A. hakeifolia,* and both are from Western Australia. The cultivar 'West Coast Gem' has proven to be the pick of the crop in this group over a wide range of climatic conditions.

GROWING AND MAINTENANCE TIPS

Hibiscuses and alyogynes are very fast-growing plants that need judicious pruning to bring out their absolute best. Tip-pruning right from the start will develop a compact shape as well as a vegetative framework that will allow them to flower their heads off through the warmer months of the year. Once they are established, take them back by about twenty per cent after flowering. These plants are not phosphorus-sensitive, so general-purpose complete fertiliser will work well.

USING HIBISCUSES IN THE GARDEN

These are definitely feature plants when they are pruned and shaped for maximum flowering. If you can't be bothered with pruning, they can serve as screening plants, as they will develop into large shrubs.

Pimeleas

The pimeleas are, in my opinion, the most underrated group of Australian plants in terms of ornamental horticulture. With species scattered all over Australia, this genus contains enormous diversity. Species such as *Pimelea ferruginea* have long been popular as garden plants, but there are many others with equal or greater potential. Pimeleas generally are small, compact floriferous shrubs whose large clusters of small tubular florets attract butterflies. Most species flower in spring, but there are others, such as *P. linifolia,* that flower throughout the year. One of my own selections, *P. linifolia* 'White Jewel', is a low-growing mound that simply never stops flowering.

The Qualup bell (*P. physodes*) is now becoming available to gardeners as a grafted plant that has a life span of a few years when given a well-drained position in full or almost full sun. It is also a wonderful cut flower that will benefit from the pruning effect that the removal of a few stems for the vase creates. *P. rosea* is yet another species that has become more available in recent years; my own selection, 'Deep Dream', has lovely cerise flower heads.

GROWING AND MAINTENANCE TIPS

The pimeleas need plenty of light and a well-drained soil to reach their full potential. Tip-pruning while they are young and a light pruning after flowering are all that is generally needed to keep your pimeleas compact and flowering profusely. Fertilise them with a handful of low-phosphorus feed at the same time.

USING PIMELEAS IN THE GARDEN

Pimeleas vary from low-mounding plants to small shrubs and make great feature plants for shrubberies. Place them where you will be able to observe the many butterflies they will attract. They also make fabulous container plants for the small garden.

ABOVE LEFT Alyogyne 'West Coast Gem' is an outstanding cultivar for temperate regions. *RIGHT* All species of pimeleas are a great way to attract butterflies to your garden.

Waratahs: *Telopea*

The floral emblem of New South Wales, *Telopea speciosissima*, is one of Australia's iconic plants. While we usually associate waratahs with the rich red of picture postcards, recent breeding has created a whole new palette of colours, including white, pink and yellow.

There are five species of *Telopea*, and breeding between these has also created an array of new forms with better adaptability to frost and more compact growth habits. *Telopea speciosissima* is by far the most spectacular species of the genus in terms of flower size, but it also tends to be the most unreliable in cultivation. Crosses of *T. speciosissima* with the Gippsland waratah (*T. oreades*) tend to be much more adaptable to conditions along the Australian east coast, and the cultivar 'Shady Lady Red' has been a solid performer.

Hybrids of *T. speciosissima* and *T. mongaensis* have created a useful group of relatively frost-tolerant waratahs. This breeding began at the National Botanic Gardens in the 1960s, and the resulting plants can still be seen thriving in various spots around the Gardens.

In twenty years of breeding waratahs, three breeders—horticulturists Paul Nixon and Brian Fitzpatrick and the Victorian doctor-horticulturist Graeme Downe—have produced an impressive range of new types. A couple of the most interesting arose from the Tasmanian waratah (*T. truncata*), which in the wild has perhaps the least striking flowers of the species. As an example, Graeme has crossed a very rare yellow-flowered form of *T. truncata* with a *T. speciosissima* x *T. oreades* hybrid to create the small-growing but relatively vigorous yellow-flowered cultivar 'Golden Globe', currently being marketed as 'Shady Lady Yellow'.

GROWING AND MAINTENANCE TIPS

Success in growing waratahs depends very much on your soil type. The best such plants I have ever seen grow in the heavy clay soils of the Dandenong Ranges, east of Melbourne. These soils are derived from the volcanic rock basalt, and while they are predominantly clay they are also well structured, with good moisture retention and nutrient content but good drainage as well. Bear this in mind if you have tried your luck with waratahs in the past and found the results disappointing. Sandy soils built up with compost to retain moisture and provide nutrients are your best bet for growing waratahs.

Waratahs are great vase flowers and should be cut just as the first florets open at the base of the flower head. If you take each flower with a stem at least forty to sixty centimetres long, you will have effectively pruned that shoot for the year. After the plants finish flowering, come back and prune the same distance below any spent flowers. Leave intact any shoots that have not flowered, as they are the ones most likely to produce next year's blooms.

Waratahs are susceptible to scale insects, which can be controlled with persistent applications of pest oil. Waratah-stem borer is much more difficult to control, as the damage is usually done before you notice the pest. I adopt a philosophical approach to this problem: I prune off affected stems and flower buds and terminate the grubs inside with extreme prejudice.

USING WARATAHS IN THE GARDEN

If there were Oscar awards for garden plants, then waratahs would be obvious candidates, as they are stand-out performers in any landscape. They can also be grown in large containers. Place these in sunny spots where you can enjoy watching the nectar-feeding birds that visit. If you are blessed with a fertile, well-drained clay soil like that in the Dandenongs near Melbourne or the New South Wales southern highlands, then you will have small trees with dozens of blooms, so give them a few metres to spread out. Rockeries are another good place to display waratahs, where you can provide the combination of nourishing soil and good drainage they like best.

ABOVE *Telopea speciosissima* has the largest flower of the five waratah species.
RIGHT Several new colours in waratahs have recently been released to gardeners.

garden
examples

jacobs garden

The perfect native garden

It's no surprise that over fifty species of birds call the Jacobs garden home. The exquisite property, set on just over two hectares, combines areas of endemic bush with a cultivated garden overflowing with bird-attracting native flora. For nearly two decades Elspeth and Garry Jacobs have been propagating and planting, arranging and rearranging their plants, paths and garden beds. They are not trained horticulturists, but their garden is a testament to their deep appreciation and understanding of plants and their aptitude for creative design. The success of this garden is no accident. It results from thoughtful planning, clever management and lots of hard work.

The Jacobses live in a suburb in the foothills of Melbourne's Dandenong Ranges. Their property faces a mountainside covered with towering eucalypts. What a view! With much indigenous vegetation remaining in their suburb, a bush flavour lingers here, too. You go through the gate, along the curved driveway hugged by native bush, stop at the brick house, and immediately fall head over heels in love with the garden. But this is not just one garden. As you discover only when you begin exploring it, the property has three distinct parts: the bush, the nursery, and the rear garden, all linked by open spaces, winding paths and plenty of surprises.

PART ONE: THE BUSH

The first section of the Jacobs garden that visitors encounter is part of a pocket of remnant native woodland. Weeding is the main activity carried out in this section, so the vegetation—which includes more than 100 species—remains as it has been for thousands of years. The decision to leave this area uncultivated is one reason for the garden's success: this section, its public face if you like, blends perfectly with the bushland character of neighbouring properties and of the suburb as a whole, and unites the property with the mountain near which it is situated.

ABOVE Actinotus helianthi is known as the flannel flower because of the furry texture of the leaves.

FAR LEFT With its winding paths, diverse plants and distant views, Elspeth and Garry Jacobs' Montrose property, near Melbourne, epitomises Australian bush gardens.

PART TWO: THE NURSERY

Located just off the driveway and away from the house (which is set towards the rear of the block), the nursery area was initially a commercial enterprise established by the previous owner. The Jacobses use the facility for plant propagation.

ABOVE On the rear verandah plants are placed directly outside windows, seemingly bringing the outside in.
TOP, FROM LEFT The man-made pond, home to numerous duck families, looks as though it's been part of the landscape forever; Hard landscaping is limited to sleepers, boulders and pebble paths—plants define the look of this garden; Elspeth and Garry have done such a great job with plant placement it's impossible to tell where their garden ends and where the 'borrowed' landscape begins.

PART THREE: THE HOME GARDEN

The endemic bushland of the front yard runs up to the house and also forms a wide fringe around the entire property. The property slopes uphill, so the garden at the rear of the house occupies its highest point. The native and cultivated trees in this garden can be seen from the bush front yard, serving as an appealing endpoint to the overall design. Towering even higher is the mountainside, which is visible from the front and rear gardens as well as from within the house. Judging by the many seats dotted about, the property's delights are often appreciated from these vantage points. But the views from all of the house's picture windows are magnificent, so it makes sense that the owners have based much of their garden's design on how it appears from within.

If you choose an uncultivated look, keep edges soft and ornaments in keeping with the overall theme

GARDEN STYLE

This is a bush garden through and through. Bed edges are defined only by paths or lawns. Most beds are mounded, which improves drainage and also creates separate large 'islands' within the garden. Plants tumble onto and overhang the paths, softening their edges and adding to the bush feel. Bark mulch protects the plants and visually ties the beds together. Boulders, tree stumps and a few terracotta pots dotted about also provide visual continuity and follow the bush theme. There isn't much hard landscaping here, just pebble paths, a few large rocks, and steps made from railway sleepers.

THE POND

Every bush setting deserves a billabong, and this garden has one of the loveliest I've seen. To ensure that the levels, positioning and lining were correct, the Jacobses had the pond installed by a professional. But to prevent it from looking *too* professional, they planted it up themselves—so successfully that families of black ducks and wood ducks live here.

HOW SPACE IS USED

The property is, in a sense, a series of loosely enclosed spaces. The cultivated and bush parts of the garden seem to radiate out from the house, starting with groundcovers, then low shrubs, then taller shrubs, and finally the large eucalypts that surround the property. The open spaces of the rear garden are irregularly shaped lawns surrounded by wide garden beds. The open spaces of the front yard are irregularly shaped wide garden beds with mostly low-growing shrubbery, linked by a series of winding pebble paths. These open spaces bring balance to the garden as a whole.

HOW PLANTS ARE USED

Living for many years in Western Australia, Elspeth and Garry Jacobs developed a strong appreciation for the west's native flora, particularly the mallees (including *Eucalyptus preissiana* ssp. *lobata*, *E. multicaulis*, *E. diversifolia*, *E. pleurocarpa* and the well-known *E. caesia* ssp. *magna* 'Silver Princess'). They have used these smaller-growing eucalypts as feature trees and to define the garden edges, helping to move the eye up from the open spaces and low shrubbery into the taller canopy and the borrowed landscape beyond.

With more than 800 species of Australian plants, Elspeth and Garry's garden contains an enormous diversity of form, colour, size and growth habit. There are hundreds of shrubs, including waxflowers, grevilleas, hakeas, daisies and emu bush. Ground covers include grasses, *Hibbertia empetrifolia* and *Scaevola*.

The Jacobses say their 'rules' for positioning a plant are that it should look good from inside the house and that it can't block a view. They also follow the simple design principle that if a bed can be viewed from a few angles, then the tallest plants are placed in the centre and the lowest at the edges, but if the bed can be seen from only one angle, the taller plants are usually grown at the back.

GARDENING PRACTICALITIES

Soil: With the exception of a small area in the rear garden, the soil on the property is original.

Pruning: The owners believe that pruning is one of the keys to growing native plants successfully, and constantly tip-prune to encourage bushiness. After the main flowering, a heavier prune is carried out and old woody growth removed.

Water: Until 2008, when a 20,000-litre tank was installed to hold rain captured from the roofs of the house, garage and shed, watering was done by hand via buckets carried from the house. The tank means the garden can be watered whenever necessary—not just on authorised days.

Propagation and planting: The Jacobses propagate their own plants. They usually grow several examples of the same species to use throughout the garden.

Emulating this garden may seem like a daunting task, since its success rests on so many different elements. However, bear in mind that Elspeth and Garry were horticulture novices when they began. They sought advice from a variety of sources, such as the Australian Plants Society, and they have taken many years to create this relaxing bush garden. There's hope for us all yet!

vaughan garden

A plant collector's native bush paradise

My favourite private Australian plant garden is on the Bellarine Peninsula in Victoria, and belongs to plant collector extraordinaire Phil Vaughan and his family. This is also the site of their retail nursery, which specialises in rare and unusual Australian plants and carries one of the most extensive ranges of any nursery in the country.

Phil and his family wanted to show that you can create an amazing and colourful garden with Australian plants. Phil also wanted a place where he could indulge his passion for collecting the finest and most spectacular members of the Australian flora. Finally, he wanted somewhere to showcase the latest cultivars from his nursery and the results of his experiments with grafting hard-to-grow Western Australian species.

THE CHALLENGES

Not surprisingly given its owner's passions, the garden holds an extraordinary array of Australian plants. But that's not the only thing that makes it such a special place. In fact, being such an avid collector created challenges for Phil—one of them being how to make the garden work aesthetically. With such a diversity of genera, it could easily have ended up looking cluttered or confused. Another challenge arose from the types of plants he chose. Phil loves Western Australian natives, which thrive in the sandy, well-drained soils and low humidity of their home state but are notorious for displaying signs of homesickness when grown in other parts of the country—they tend to slowly deteriorate, often succumb to the fungal disease botrytis, and may eventually die.

ABOVE Eremophila nivea and *Darwinia* species (front) thrive in sandy soil.
FAR LEFT Phil Vaughan's intention for his Bellarine Peninsula garden, in Victoria, was to combine plants from around the country in a naturalistic setting.

Create 'rooms' in your garden by mounding and by graduating plant sizes

THE SOLUTION

Phil's rare talent for naturalistic garden design has led to a very distinctive style that helps to overcome the problems of trying to display such a huge array of species being grown out of their natural conditions. To overcome these problems, he has settled on a couple of simple techniques. First, Phil created large mounded beds throughout the garden that are separated by meandering gravel paths. This helped provide visual interest in the flat landscape and created a wonderful foundation for displaying plants of varying heights and habits. With plants graduated by size, from taller specimens at the top to ground covers spilling onto the paths, the mounds also create natural 'rooms', so you see mostly the section you're walking through, rather than the entire garden—thus preventing visual overload. The same technique is just as effective in smaller gardens than Phil's: the trick is to keep mounds in proportion to the property, and provide access all around each mound so the plants can be appreciated.

Mounding the beds also overcomes the drainage issue, as the plants never get wet 'feet' and, with water draining away rather than pooling beneath them, humidity is kept to a minimum. The plants are manually watered only when planted: rain does the rest.

ENHANCING THE BUSH STYLE

Phil has placed rocks and logs along the paths and within the garden beds. These reinforce the naturalistic theme of the garden, provide habitat for fauna and help create microclimates where smaller plants thrive. Phil also uses bark mulch, which he keeps away from plant trunks to prevent diseases like collar rot.

AMAZING PLANTS

Another feature of the Vaughan garden is Phil's innovative use of grafting to propagate plants from all areas of Australia. This enables him not only to produce plants that are often impossible to grow from cuttings, but also to add much more adaptable root systems to some difficult-to-grow plants, such as the magnificent large-flowered mint bush (*Prostanthera magnifica*), which is grafted onto the ever-reliable rootstock of the coastal rosemary (*Westringia fruticosa*). Feather flowers from the semi-arid country north of Perth grow alongside spectacular flowering gums from the Western Australian south coast.

PHIL'S TIPS

- Create mounds for visual impact in any size garden, and to improve drainage.
- Combine a range of species for interesting forms, textures, and year-round colour.
- Create temporary colour with herbaceous plants that are regularly renewed.
- Use rocks and logs to create microclimates and that lovely bush feel.
- Tip-prune plants regularly to encourage flowering and a bushy habit.
- Incorporate any foreign topsoil into your home soil to a depth of about twenty centimetres.

Phil has combined a profound love of Australian plants with a sound knowledge of horticultural principles to create an amazingly diverse and beautifully designed garden. His garden is successful for many reasons, but for me the main one is that when I visit I'm not wandering around an old horse paddock in Victoria—I'm exploring one of the world's most diverse floral regions, in the Kwongan country of Western Australia. What could be nicer?

ABOVE LEFT Everlasting daisies (*Xerochrysum bracteatum*) bring, as the name suggests, long-lasting vibrant colour to any garden. *RIGHT* A stunning array of predominantly Western Australian species thrive in raised beds created on a flat site.

gregorovich garden

A family-friendly, suburban native haven

Installing a new garden takes skill, patience and careful planning, and many people prefer to leave the job to the experts. But Yvette and Tony Gregorovich are proficient DIY-ers, and they chose to tackle the project themselves. It was certainly a good decision, because not only did they save themselves a lot of money, they have created—on an averaged-sized suburban block—a unique garden perfectly suited to their needs.

They had three main aims. They wanted to use predominantly native plants; the garden should need minimal water and maintenance; and both front and back yards should be suitable for the whole family, including their two young children.

SOIL

Getting the right soil for a new garden can often be a nightmare, but the soil on the Gregoroviches' block is a sandy loam to a depth of one metre. This is generally easy to dig, which is handy, but it's also quick to drain, letting nutrients and water leach through before plants have a chance to use them. To counter this, the owners dug rubble into the soil during setup, and regularly add organic matter and mulch.

RESPECT FOR NATURE

It took a couple of years for local fauna to work out that what had previously been some lawn, a weedy tree and a few random shrubs was now a haven in the 'burbs. In this sustainable garden, Tony and Yvette try to create a balance between actively creating a refuge for fauna and letting nature do its own thing. They leave pests to sort themselves out, randomly distribute compost and blood and bone at various times of the year, and provide rocks and decomposing logs for habitat. Grasses are cut back hard towards the end of summer—when bushfires might do the same in the wild—so they grow back strong and lush. The owners' respect for nature is also demonstrated by their preference for recycling wherever possible. Reusing hard landscaping materials and plants cuts costs, helps the environment and brings a touch of individuality to any garden.

ABOVE Being slow growers, grass trees (*Xanthorrhoea* species) are perfect as pot specimens.

FAR LEFT, CLOCKWISE FROM TOP LEFT Carefully placed trees, pergola and sails bring much-needed shade into the west-facing front yard; Natives and exotics in perfect harmony; To Tony and Yvette's surprise, plants thrive in the sails' dappled shade; Tony's home-made seat—perfect for hours of lolling about; Smooth gravel has been used as mulch to good effect in various parts of the garden; With its spreading crown, attractive bark and maximum height of 12 metres, the Wallangarra white gum (*Eucalyptus scoparia*) is a perfect addition for smaller gardens; The large granite boulders are a hit with butterflies and lizards, as well as the Gregorovich family.

Preventing stormwater from leaving your property helps your plants and is a clever way to help reduce pollution of our creeks, rivers and oceans

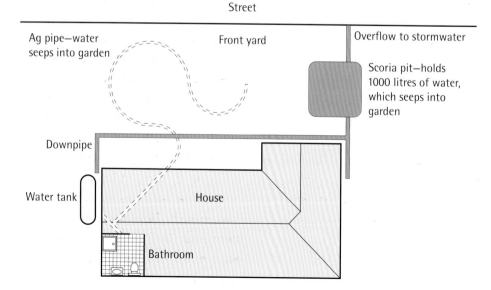

WATER

To help their garden survive on rainfall alone, Yvette and Tony chose to install simple passive-watering systems that divert rain from the roof into the garden rather than into the stormwater system.

As they were giving the original garden a complete overhaul, it made sense for them to install this system at the start. But because it's such a simple concept, it could fairly easily be retrofitted to any garden. In the Gregoroviches' front garden, the underground terracotta piping, which ran from the roof downpipe to the stormwater drain, was badly cracked. They replaced it with PVC piping connected to the stormwater system by a T-junction. Under the T they dug a deep pit a metre square and filled it with scoria. Rain now runs down the downpipe as usual, fills up the pit (which holds about 1000 litres) and *then* overflows into the stormwater drain. The water in the pit slowly filters through the garden.

Another clever passive system diverts the family's bath and shower water into the front garden. (They use only biodegradable soaps and shampoos.) To the PVC piping from the bathroom, they attached a length of 100-millimetre ag pipe (flexible black-plastic tubing with slots that allow water to drain out). Embedded in scoria, this pipe runs through the garden at a depth of 200 millimetres and ends at a large *Eucalyptus scoparia*—the feature tree of the front yard.

The back garden has similar passive systems. A garden bed behind a covered barbecue area receives extra water when it rains, as the roof overhanging it was designed without guttering; and the fernery is watered from a gravity-fed PVC pipe system that runs off the shed.

The owners have also installed two 3000-litre tanks, which they plan to use for additional watering requirements. Their passive systems can be switched off, allowing the tanks to fill and preventing the gardens from being overwatered during the wetter months.

STRUCTURE

To make their garden more appealing to the eye, the Gregoroviches once again used a few simple but clever devices. First, they edged all garden beds with railway sleepers laid either horizontally or vertically. To add interest in the front garden, they built a raised section using railway sleepers laid horizontally, and filled the resulting mound with soil taken from the backyard, where a new shed was planned. (A similar effect can be created by mounding large areas of soil.) They also used railway sleepers as anchor points for shade sails that they installed in the front garden. These sleepers create vertical lines as well as a sense of visual continuity.

Street

Ag pipe—water seeps into garden

Front yard

Overflow to stormwater

Scoria pit—holds 1000 litres of water, which seeps into garden

Downpipe

Water tank

House

Bathroom

An echoing of colours, textures and materials unifies the front and back yards.

POSITIONING

The Gregoroviches' property is on a gentle slope running east–west, with the front yard at the highest point and facing the hot afternoon sun. To help prevent it from baking in the afternoon, they planted a fast-growing Wallangarra white gum (*Eucalyptus scoparia*). As this feature tree was one of the first plants into the ground, it offered some shade to other plants during their establishment phase. Another reason the owners planted the tree in this position was to help cool the two front bedrooms. It wasn't as effective as they would have liked, so they installed the shade sails. These give plenty of shade, but at first Tony and Yvette were concerned that the plants beneath them would suffer from lack of light and water. They needn't have worried—the plants are thriving.

The backyard is slightly lower than the front, and the north corner slightly lower still. Because water naturally flows to this point, and it's the coolest section of the garden, the fernery the owners created here is also flourishing.

PLANTS

The Gregoroviches' love for native plants is evident, but their garden also contains exotic species. Diversity is the key in this garden, which consists of focal plants, including a spectacular firewheel tree (*Stenocarpus sinuatus*); structural plants, including bird's nest ferns (*Asplenium australasicum*), New Zealand flax (*Phormium tenax*) and cycads; movement plants, such as swamp foxtail (*Pennisetum alopecuroides*) and *Acacia cognata*; and plants that add colour, including various *Correa* cultivars, Austral indigo (*Indigofera australis*), liriopes and fringe lilies. *Hakea bakeriana* line the side fence, creating a sense of unity within the garden, and a couple of newly planted mallees (*Eucalyptus lehmannii*) will eventually provide a mid-height layer.

HARD LANDSCAPING

Pavers are laid close to the house for practicality, positioned to allow room for either pebbles or small plants between them. The gaps allow water to seep into the garden rather than rush down the driveway into the street. The Gregoroviches replaced the original fence with a higher one, but its open horizontal timber slats provide privacy without seeming to exclude the neighbourhood. The fence gives passers-by a glimpse of the unusual front yard and also brings in the borrowed landscape across the street, creating the illusion the garden is bigger than it actually is.

WHAT GROWN-UPS LOVE

- Identifying the birds and seeing new varieties turning up
- Having only a small patch of lawn to mow
- Knowing the kids are learning about nature
- Propagating their own plants

WHAT KIDS LOVE

- Running through the garden and around the trees
- Playing in the sand pit
- Watching the ants
- Finding caterpillars building cocoons
- Identifying spiders
- Pulling bark off trees
- Climbing on rocks

WHY THE GREGOROVICH GARDEN WORKS

It wasn't created in a day—or even a weekend. Sticking to their native-garden theme, the owners took their time to create a garden that suited them and their budget. Similar hard-landscaping materials (railway sleepers, recycled timber, rocks, paving and mulch) are used in both front and rear yards. This reinforces the native theme and creates a sense of continuity. Plants of all height layers are included, from ground covers to tall trees. This creates visual interest for humans, and food and safety for a range of birds and other fauna. Using predominantly native plants with similar requirements makes maintenance a breeze.

angus's garden

A plant breeder's experimental garden

Buying a forty-hectare rural property in 2005 gave me the opportunity to create my dream garden on a virtually unlimited area. Like any keen gardener, I tore into the task with reckless abandon. Here are some lessons I learned along the way that may benefit you in your quest to create your own Australian native garden.

SETTING AND SOIL

The property is on one of the numerous sandstone plateaus on Sydney's northern outskirts. The soil is a rather impoverished sandy loam overlying a clay-based subsoil. I created the main garden on a north-facing slope to take advantage of the natural light.

STYLE

I decided early on to try to create an informal bush garden that blended as well as possible with the Sydney-sandstone vegetation around the site. The surrounding bushland is dominated by the fabulously gnarled Sydney red gum (*Angophora costata*), with an understorey filled with all kinds of botanical delights, including flannel flowers (*Actinotus helianthi*), waratahs (*Telopea speciosissima*) and several species of grevillea and banksia. As a professional plant breeder, I also wanted a natural setting where I could continuously trial my 'experimental' native plants, as well as new Australian cultivars, to get a feel for how they would work in home gardens. I used rocks, timber sculptures and natural logs throughout the garden to enhance the bush style.

ABOVE Raised beds allow me to grow species from all over Australia that require very good drainage.
FAR LEFT Tall kangaroo paws provide the major colour in the garden for several months during spring and summer.

CONSTRUCTING THE GARDEN

To give me a reasonable chance of success with plants from all over the continent, I decided to experiment with mounds of varying heights created with various types of soil. I obtained topsoil from the local area from sources such as swimming-pool companies that had excavated suburban backyards and a commercial development in a nearby area of virgin bushland, which yielded truckloads of weed-free topsoil.

I built up long mounds running along the contour lines of the sloping property. This is a very effective water-harvesting technique: any rainfall collects along the upper base of each mound, slowly soaking in and watering whatever is planted on the mound. Creating the mounds involved much shoveling, barrow pushing, and even the occasional assist from an earthmover, but the hard work was well worth every drop of sweat. The growing conditions vary enormously, even within each mound, and I tried to match my plants to these differing microclimates and soil environments.

As a professional horticulturist, I have access to many free or cheap plants. Most of the plants in my garden were established from tubestock, mostly in pots fifty millimetres or less in diameter. Overall, the establishment rate from this stock has been outstanding. An occasional bout of hand watering during dry spells has been necessary for newly planted material, but on the whole the garden copes without irrigation.

LESSONS LEARNED: THE GOOD, THE BAD AND THE BODGY

Generally speaking, the various mound gardens I created have been successful. A very good example of what can be achieved with mounding was where I used one of my favourite landscaping plants—*Callistemon* 'Great Balls of Fire', a dwarf cultivar with gorgeous pink new growth through the warmer months. One of the earliest mounds I constructed traps copious amounts of water during heavy rain. As it gradually seeps through the mound, it irrigates a stand of 'Great Balls of Fire' planted on the other side of the mound. Through spring, summer and autumn, a flush of brightly coloured new growth regularly appears a week or two after rain.

Another idea that worked really well was to use fast-growing 'pioneer plants' during the first couple of years to prevent soil erosion and give a burst of colour while the slower growers established. For this task I used everlasting daisies (*Xerochrysum* cultivars), rice flowers (*Ozothamnus diosmifolius* 'Radiance') and *Acacia cognata* cultivars such as 'Lime Magik' and 'Copper Tips'. This was extremely successful, giving plenty of foliage and lovely splashes of colour during the couple of years it took for the slower growers to fill out and take over the garden.

Something I can also recommend is mass plantings of the taller kangaroo-paw cultivars. Not only are they very easy to

Use fast growers to fill the garden with colour while other plants become established

grow and maintain, but the practically solid walls of flowers they produce attract a continuous array of nectar-feeding birds from surrounding bushland. Eastern spinebills, wattlebirds, New Holland honeyeaters, rainbow lorikeets and eastern and crimson rosellas all have their turn raiding the flowers for their sweet treasure.

Along with the success, I've also had plenty of failures that proved instructive. What has surprised me the most is the degree to which native plants established in the understorey have struggled in dry weather. I was quite dismayed, for example, to see well-established kangaroo paws collapse in a heap during a three-month dry spell at the end of one winter, coming into their spring flowering period. The paws bounced back as soon as it started to rain, but I lost the flowering for that year. Experiences like this have reinforced my view that although Australian plants are drought tolerant on the whole and will survive dry periods, they will not thrive in them, still less produce the stunning floral displays you see in this and other books. Nevertheless, Australian plants do survive environmental adversity better than many exotics. When times get tough, they can shut down their systems, and when the rains come again they will burst back into life, often looking better than ever.

TOP AND CENTRE Mounds have been created to trap any natural runoff to allow it to gradually soak in over time.
BOTTOM Callistemon 'Great Balls of Fire' thrives in a moist spot where water is collected behind a mound.

bush gardens

Finding inspiration in the wild

For me, there is nothing more inspiring than exploring the Australian flora in the wild. Not only does this give you a good understanding of each plant's natural environment and how that might relate to its cultivation requirements, it also lets you see how Mother Nature fits the plants together in her 'wild gardens'. Whenever and wherever you venture into the bush, you will be learning more about Australian plants and how to grow them. Here are a few examples to stimulate your bushwalking appetite.

Fan flower (*Scaevola aemula*) is one of Australia's best bedding plants for its brilliant purple flowers, which remain right through the warmer months of the year. Walking one bright spring day at South West Rocks, on the New South Wales north coast, I was treated to a mass display of these stunning plants: thousands upon thousands of them, covering several kilometres of rugged terrain. Its origins lay in an intense bushfire that had swept across the area two years before. The fire had razed trees and shrubs to the ground, letting in much more light. This, combined with the nutrients released from the ash, was allowing the scaevolas to dominate the landscape. When I visited the area again a few years later, the spectacle had all but vanished. The lesson here is that while this species is very tolerant of coastal conditions, it needs full sun and a reasonably high level of nutrition to flower well.

Along the Western Australian coast, north and south of Perth, it is relatively common to find large drifts of red and green kangaroo paw (*Anigozanthos manglesii*) flowering in profusion in spring. I was delighted to discover a patch, near Lancelin, north of Perth, while on a wildflower 'crawl' one year. The display stretched over several hectares of an area that had clearly been burnt the previous year. Once again, the lesson is that profuse flowering like this requires full or near-full sun and high levels of nutrients (supplied in this case, as with the scaevolas, by ash from the fire). Another lesson is that this kangaroo paw is a short-lived plant in the wild. It has evolved to grow and flower rapidly after a fire, release copious amounts of seed, and then die a couple of years later as acacias, banksias and other shrubs grow back and smother it.

ABOVE The NSW north coast is home to many outstanding plants that have been adapted for gardens, such as the fan flower (*Scaevola aemula*).

FAR LEFT Observing the habitat of the cushion bush (*Leucophyta brownii*) near these tidal ocean pools gives us valuable information on how to use this species in the garden.

I have come across some mind-blowing displays of flowering grass trees over the decades. On the New South Wales north coast, I stumbled upon a swampy area where thousands of grass trees in flower were hosting huge numbers of native bees. I was amazed to see a plant I had always thought of as one for a well-drained soil growing so prolifically in a swamp. Subsequent experience in the garden has taught me that grass trees will grow much faster if supplied with lots of extra water and nutrients.

I have done a lot of walking through coastal heathlands around Australia. By definition, this vegetation type features low-growing shrubs from all sorts of families. In Western Australia's heathlands you will see some of the most spectacular arrays of wildflowers anywhere in the world. In these coastal habitats, the harsh environment and particularly the strong onshore winds have caused the plants to evolve dwarf forms that often stay true to type when they are brought into gardens. Breeders are using such plants as the basis for many of the compact cultivars that are so well suited to the smaller gardens of today.

I had no idea that wildflower watching could be a dangerous activity until I ventured to Mullewa, Western Australia, in search of the famous wreath lechenaultia. The local petrol station apparently knew something I didn't, for it warned that the plant grew in a 'hazardous area'. Taking my life in my hands, I finally discovered what all the fuss was about. The road in a nearby rural area was lined for several kilometres with thousands of plants in full flower. I am still mystified about the nature of the hazard, but my close encounter with the wreath lechenaultia taught me that it thrives where the soil has been disturbed—in this case by a road grader ploughing it up.

The diversity of the Western Australian flora is thought to be linked to its tough conditions. The soils of Western Australia are, without doubt, among the most impoverished in the world. According to evolutionary botanists, this is no coincidence. The harsh environment puts great pressure on all the area's species to evolve and adapt—or die out. What I have learned from observing these glorious plants is that many of the sand-plain species grow best with a mulch of coarse gravel around them. This lowers the humidity directly around the crown of the plant. I have found this a very useful technique to use when growing such plants in the more humid climate of coastal New South Wales. Gravel mulch around the base seems to help protect them from crown rot during the hot, humid periods that are relatively common in the Sydney summer.

I once saw gnarly old paperbark (*Melaleuca* species) growing in an inundated swamp in south-west Western Australia. The roots of the tree were clearly able to cope with very little oxygen for long periods whenever the swamp filled up after rain. This scene was made especially lovely by the reflections of the many magnificent melaleucas that were thriving there. The lesson here is that certain species will not just cope with conditions that would kill most other plants, they will actually thrive in them. So through clever plant selection, you can turn even the most difficult areas of your garden into fabulous features.

When I am not in the garden, I just love getting out and enjoying the bush. And when I'm in the bush, I observe everything closely. That way, I can take what I learn back to the garden—and recreate the magnificence of the Australian bush in my backyard.

An array of natural 'gardens' that have been the inspiration to create a similar style in my own garden.

kings park and botanic garden, perth

It is no wonder that Kings Park in Perth attracts over six million visitors each year. This is undoubtedly one of the finest gardens ever created with Australian plants. Nestled high above Perth and the picturesque Swan River, this amazing place not only presents a 400-hectare snapshot of the Perth area's flora more or less as it was before European settlement, it also contains a series of beautifully landscaped gardens that showcase the entire flora of the state of Western Australia.

For those who are unfamiliar with the Western Australian flora, these gardens are a sumptuous entrée that should inspire you to take the main course of a road trip through some of the state's more spectacular wildflower regions. At the very least, such a trip should run from Perth north to Kalbarri, then inland through the wheat belt and goldfields country, then south to Esperance, then west to the Stirling Ranges and Albany, before finally exploring the limestone coastal area in the south-west corner of the state, around Margaret River.

Between August and November, these areas are a kaleidoscope of almost psychedelic colours. My own experience tends to go like this: I'll be driving along an unmarked country road when I glimpse such a vivid flash of colour, movement or texture that I hit the brakes, scattering maps everywhere. I reverse, get out of the car, and drink in a stunning display of wildflowers. I grab my camera and start snapping. Half an hour later, having wandered from one amazing flower to another and then another, I look up and see the car way off in the distance. If you are interested in plants, you will find this journey mesmerising—the trip of a lifetime. But back to Kings Park …

THE FLORAL CLOCK

A reminder of the past is the floral clock created with the help of a bequest from F.F.B. Wittenoom, a Western Australian pastoralist. It was unveiled in 1962, and has the quaint quirk that each half hour is marked by the recorded call of the rufous whistler bird. Some might call the clock botanical kitsch, but it is an intriguing formal showcase for a variety of Western Australian plants. Dwarf agonis, for example, is clipped into tight hedges to form the numbers of the clock, while ostentatious colour is provided by plants such as *Pimelea ferruginea*, *Conostylis candicans* and *Scaevola aemula*.

ABOVE Kings Park abounds with thoughtfully designed display beds that highlight the vibrant colours of the Western Australian flora. In this case the blue of the Swan River daisy (*Brachyscome iberidifolia*) contrasts with the yellow of a feather flower (*Verticordia* species).
FAR LEFT The floral clock at Kings Park has been based on a 'cottage garden' look that has been created totally from Western Australian plants such as the pink *Pimelea ferruginea*, yellow *Verticordia* species and grey-leaved *Conostylis candicans*.

GENERAL DISPLAY GARDENS

As you enter Kings Park, you pass a number of formal and informal gardens around the Visitor Centre and Botanical Café area. Some are simply stunning show gardens, while others are designed to display particular groups of ornamental plants, such as kangaroo paws and Geraldton waxflowers. These latter gardens feature many of Western Australia's signature endemic plants, such as the black kangaroo paw (*Macropidia fuliginosa*), blue lechenaultia (*Lechenaultia biloba*) and scarlet feather flower (*Verticordia grandis*).

Other ornamental gardens are based on colour themes, such as combinations of yellow and blue or red, yellow and purple. Drifts of everlasting daisies simulate the amazing displays that often sweep across areas of the Western Australian landscape. You can see annuals such as *Rhodanthe chlorocephala* and *Xerochrysum bracteatum*.

NATURAL BUSHLAND AREAS

One of the outstanding features of Kings Park, and one that sets it apart from almost any other botanical garden in the world, is its hundreds of hectares of largely undisturbed bushland. The park is set on an escarpment overlooking Perth whose endemic plants make this a feature garden in its own right. Western Australia's floral emblem, the red and green kangaroo paw (*Anigozanthos manglesii*), is one of a host of delightful flowering plants in the bush understorey, along with cottonheads (*Conostylis candicans*), cowslip orchid (*Caladenia flava*) and fringe lily (*Thysanotus* species). Grass trees (*Xanthorrhoea* species) are ubiquitous, and a major fire along the escarpment in 2008 triggered a spectacular display of flowers in 2009.

The Kings Park website describes the plant life as follows:

> Within the Kings Park bushland, three major plant communities are supported—limestone heathland; Banksia woodland with *B. attenuata*, *B. grandis*, *B. menziesii* and *B. prionotes*; and low moist areas with *Banksia ilicifolia*. Prior to European settlement, the Kings Park bushland would have been dominated by tall Tuart (*Eucalyptus gomphocephala*), Jarrah (*Eucalyptus marginata*) and Marri (*Corymbia calophylla*), with Banksia species and *Allocasuarina fraseriana* sub-dominating. Today the woodlands are often dominated by *Banksia* species, *Allocasuarina fraseriana* and *Dryandra sessilis*. There are 324 species of local native plants growing in the bushland, which represents about 15 per cent of the native flora of the Perth Region.
>
> Of particular importance is the limestone escarpment. Only three relatively large areas of cliff-side vegetation, Kings Park, Blackwall Reach and Mt Henry, can now be found along the Swan River. The mixed closed heaths of the escarpment contain a diverse and unique assemblage of shrubs, herbs, sedges and grasses normally associated with limestone heaths of nearer coastal areas. The mixed closed heaths in Kings Park are one of the most inland occurrences of these estuarine cliff communities and are contiguous with adjacent bushland areas.

The remnant bushland at Kings Park is typical of many Australian towns and cities. Such areas provide priceless wildlife corridors in urban areas.

ABOVE Drifts of everlasting daisies such as this *Rhodanthe manglesii* have been created to mimic the mass displays that can be found naturally in spring in the wild in Western Australia.
FAR RIGHT A variety of display beds merge with remnant bushland in a setting that overlooks the majestic Swan River and cityscape of Perth.

royal botanic gardens, cranbourne

Set within the 363 hectares of native heathlands, wetlands and woodlands of the Royal Botanic Gardens, Cranbourne, this contemporary garden is the latest addition to the array of public gardens devoted to Australian plants. Presenting a huge variety of natives in a landscaped setting, the Australian Garden is designed as a 'concept' garden that takes the visitor on a unique journey through the Australian landscape and flora.

The main aims of the garden are to showcase a diversity of Australian plants; provide inspiration for garden designers; and teach visitors how best to care for native plants. But I think it achieves much more than this. The contemporary design, with its emphasis on colour, cleverly defined 'snapshot' gardens and brilliant blending of hard and soft landscaping, is a delight to wander through. Every section is clearly signposted, so you know what the designers were attempting to achieve, and everywhere you look is a visual feast.

It might seem paradoxical, but I believe one of the best reasons to visit the garden is its immaturity. Stage 1 of the Australian Garden opened in 2006, and in many sections the underlying structure is still apparent. This kind of information is invaluable when designing and building your own garden, because we usually have access only to mature landscapes. These may look splendid, but they don't tell us much about how the finished product was achieved. Stage 2 of the Australian Garden, which opens in 2011, is also an excellent source of information, and many areas in the building stages are visible from different parts of Stage 1. I suggest taking many photos!

RED SAND GARDEN

Upon exiting the visitor centre, you come face to face with the magnificent panorama of the Red Sand Garden. This majestic expanse encourages us to consider the role that water (or lack of it) has played in the evolution of the Australian landscape and the adaptations of its flora—considerations that are more relevant than ever today.

ABOVE Everlasting daisies (*Xerochrysum* species) can brighten the dullest day.
FAR LEFT The Red Sand Garden provides a breathtaking entrance to the Australian Garden (*TOP*); Choosing native plants for home is so much easier when you see them in a landscaped setting (*BOTTOM*).

EXHIBITION GARDENS

A series of innovative small gardens shows off impressive specimens of a wide range of ornamental native plants suitable for the home garden—including species and modern cultivars of ground-covers, shrubs and climbers. The exhibition gardens include the Home Garden, the Kids' Backyard, the Future Garden, the Water Saving Garden and the Diversity Garden, and each one floods the mind with creative ideas.

The Home Garden challenges visitors to think outside the square when using Australian plants. A series of 'period' suburban gardens looks at the way our gardens have traditionally been laid out and explores native alternatives for the exotic plants once used for hedging (buxus), informal screens (camellia) and borders (petunia).

Relax awhile in the exhibition gardens and contemplate the effect of mass plantings of your favourite native plants. As throughout the gardens, the display beds here present plant collections in creative and innovative ways. This is one of the things that makes Cranbourne so different from most botanic gardens I have visited around the world.

ARID GARDEN

Set on a small hill, the Arid Garden offers a great view over the whole site. In these dry times for much of Australia, it's encouraging to find such a diversity of colourful low-growing shrubs, grasses and ground covers, all adapted to survive in the arid Australian interior.

EUCALYPT WALK

Never before has it been such fun to discover Australia's iconic eucalypts. Separate sections for stringybarks, bloodwoods, peppermints, boxes and ironbarks are separated by white-pebble swales, united by massive boulders and decorated with grasses and shrubs.

SURROUNDING BUSHLAND

Cranbourne's extensive woodlands, heathlands and wetlands are an excellent remnant of the indigenous vegetation that once covered extensive areas around Westernport and Port Phillip bays. If you're quiet and patient, your walks here can bring you into contact with indigenous fauna such as koalas, bandicoots, wallabies and blue-tongue lizards.

CLOCKWISE FROM TOP LEFT Looking from the Dry River Bed walk to the Red Sand Garden; The Arid Garden proves how spectacular drought-tolerant plants can look when placed creatively; Gravel paths snake through the gardens, leading the visitor on a visual journey; Massive boulders create a variety of microclimates along the Eucalyptus Walk; *Xanthorrhoea* in flower; Flowering up to six months of the year, *Derwentia perfoliata* would be a welcome addition to any garden.

mount annan botanic garden, sydney

The 1988 bicentennial celebrations of European settlement in Australia were celebrated in New South Wales by the creation of an annexe of the Royal Botanic Gardens at Mount Annan, in Sydney's south-west. The 410-hectare site contains cycling and walking tracks as well as picnic areas, and was deliberately chosen to serve as a recreational setting for the burgeoning population of south-western Sydney. However, its primary purpose was to showcase vast numbers of native plants and cultivars to help preserve biodiversity, educate people generally about our flora, and explore the horticultural potential of Australian plants.

Mt Annan is a very young garden that is still developing and maturing. It is, however, well worth a visit from several points of view. A number of feature gardens are scattered throughout the site. Give yourself a whole day if you want to fully explore everything these developing gardens have to offer. The most visited area is a series of gardens and terraces near the Visitor Centre, which features some stunning ornamental gardens based on cultivars of Australian plants and is particularly impressive in spring. Extensive lawns and other amenities, such as an excellent children's playground and barbecue areas, make this a great place for a family excursion. There are also other interesting themes in this section of the gardens, including plantings of rare and endangered species as well as bush tucker plants (in the humorously named 'Fruit Loop' Garden).

The 'What's the Big Idea' garden is a novel concept designed to stimulate and inspire the visitor to think about sustainability in garden areas. There are numerous demonstrations of materials and methods that can be used to make your garden more environmentally friendly. This garden started out in 1988 as a *Callistemon* collection, and this genus still dominates. Spring is an ideal time to see the astonishing diversity in this adaptable group of Australian plants.

ABOVE Various feature gardens have a very contemporary feel which befits one of the country's youngest botanic gardens.
FAR LEFT Wildlife such as this water dragon have become permanent residents in the carefully designed garden habitats.

THE WOLLEMI WALK OF DISCOVERY

The Wollemi pine (*Wollemia nobilis*) caused a worldwide botanical sensation when it was discovered in the mid-1990s in the wilderness that is Wollemi National Park, north of the Blue Mountains. Not only was this a new species, it was an entirely new genus, whose closest relatives were known only from ancient fossils. The Wollemi Walk of Discovery is designed to show visitors the habitat that enabled this remarkable species to survive unchanged for tens of millions of years. This is a wonderful learning experience for young and old alike.

PLANT COLLECTIONS

Various gardens scattered throughout the Mount Annan site are designed to house collections of particular groups within the Australian flora. The Wattle Garden is particularly impressive in winter but is worth a look at any time, as there is a species of wattle in flower every month of the year. The Banksia and Grevillea Gardens are also must-sees, as there are good picnic facilities where you can park the family before walking through an impressive landscape that not only features some wonderful examples of Australian Proteaceae but also has extensive dry-stone walls built by staff and volunteers. Other gardens feature collections of *Callitris* (native conifers) and mallee eucalypts.

TOP LEFT Intricate dry-stone walls and steps are extensively used throughout a number of the feature gardens at Mount Annan.
LEFT The Wollemi pine was first brought into cultivation at Mount Annan and has a whole feature garden devoted to a 'Wollemi walk'.
RIGHT, CLOCKWISE FROM TOP The extensive gardens are a journey of discovery of the Australian flora; A series of terrace gardens has raised beds that create a microclimate suitable for plants from all over Australia; Large areas of lawn are interspersed with the gardens to create a family-friendly destination.

australian national botanic gardens, canberra

The first trees were planted at the Australian National Botanic Gardens in the late 1940s; one just inside the front gate was ceremonially planted in 1949 by Prime Minister Ben Chifley. The gardens were designed to display the ornamental beauty of the Australian flora as well as providing a scientific resource for those wishing to learn more about our native plants. This objective was reinforced by their proximity to the Australian National University and the headquarters of the Commonwealth Scientific and Industrial Research Organisation (CSIRO).

Today the gardens are a great resource for gardeners who want to see mature specimens of native plants from all over the continent, but they are particularly useful for plants from colder climates. Created in an area where the climate veers from chilling, frosty winters to harsh summer heat, the National Botanic Gardens are a truly remarkable horticultural achievement.

THE PLANT COLLECTION

After six decades of development, this site—on ninety hectares of the lower slopes of Black Mountain, overlooking Canberra—has many impressive gardens to explore. More than 6000 species have been successfully established, in a variety of distinct gardens based on themes like scientific classification, ethnobotanical use, horticultural use, rare and threatened species and geographical habitat. These themes have been cleverly woven through an overall 'bush garden' landscape style that unifies the gardens. It is easy to wander off and lose yourself as you discover all sorts of unexpected botanical delights.

ABOVE Mature specimens such as this grass tree are a feature of many areas of the gardens.
FAR LEFT Shady water features such as this provide habitat for dozens of bird species that are readily observed by visitors.

THE RAINFOREST GULLY

Once a dry creekbed dominated by eucalypts, this is perhaps the most remarkable area in the gardens. Various fast-growing species, such as cedar wattle (*Acacia elata*), were used to create shelter for rainforest species from the entire east coast—all the way from North Queensland to Tasmania. An irrigation system was installed at soil level to provide an intermittent mist of water, creating a humid microclimate throughout the gully. Several decades on, visitors are easily able to compare species from the tropics with those from the cool temperate rainforests of Tasmania and Victoria.

THE ROCKERY

Another favourite area of mine is the Rockery, where again various microclimates and soil environments have been created to enable the cultivation of species from areas as diverse as the semi-arid wildflower meadows of Western Australia and the Alpine areas around Mount Kosciuszko. High light levels and excellent drainage are the keys to this garden's diverse range of Australian plants.

OTHER AREAS

It is hard to convey the botanical wealth of the numerous garden beds scattered over this large site. The Sydney Sandstone Gully is a good example of the gems tucked away in various corners that may elude the casual visitor. Take a visitor's map and spend a whole day exploring these areas if you want to take in all the botanical diversity on offer.

THE EUCALYPT LAWN

A large expanse of lawn in the middle of the gardens is home to an extensive collection of eucalypts from all over the country. It also doubles as an excellent recreational area, with a small amphitheatre for outdoor performances of various kinds.

CLOCKWISE FROM TOP LEFT Naturalistic water features such as this provide planting sites for riparian plant species; This cascading fountain provides inspiration for those interested in garden art and aerates the water; An extensive rockery features species that require specialised soil types such as those from sub-alpine or semi-arid regions.

native plant cultivar list

LEGEND

↑   HEIGHT

↔   WIDTH

☼   TOLERATES FULL SUN

⚘   TOLERATES PART SUN

FROST TOLERANCE

❄   High

❄   Medium

❄   Low

Ⓢ   SALT TOLERANT

🐦   ATTRACTS BIRDS

🐞   ATTRACTS INSECTS

FLOWER COLOUR

✸   Blue

✸   Yellow

✸   Red

✸   Pink

✸   Purple

✸   Cream

✸   Brown

✸   Mauve

✸   Orange

✸   Black

✸   White

FLOWERING SEASONS

✸   Spring

✸   Summer

✸   Autumn

✸   Winter

✸   All year

✸   Combination

There are thousands of Australian plants worthy of garden space. The wild species are very well documented in various other books. What is not so readily available is an up-to-date list of the many selections that have been made over the years and named as cultivars. Compiling a comprehensive list of Australian plant cultivars is an impossible task, since it is changing all the time. My guiding principle in compiling the following list has been to present older cultivars that have stood the test of time and new ones about which information is hard to find. My other criterion was to list as far as possible cultivars that are available commercially.

I will endeavour to keep the cultivar list updated on my website: *www.angusstewart.com.au*

Pimelea 'Deep Dream' is a dramatic example of the types of new cultivars appearing from Australian plant breeders.

1 *Acacia acinacea* 'Pot o' Gold'

A low, dense-spreading mounded shrub. Soft rounded leaves on graceful stems that are covered in golden balls in spring and early summer. A handsome landscape accent; plant along path edges for a soft mounded hedge effect, among bold rockwork, or in large containers for a stunning long-flowering focus in patio or courtyard environment. **CLIMATE**: Cool, temperate or sub-tropical. **SOIL**: In loam, clay and sand, moist, well-drained or dry.

2 *Acacia baileyana* 'Prostrate'

Feathery silver-grey bipinnate foliage with masses of spherical flower heads 1cm in diameter. A great plant to use on embankments and as a general ground cover. Also worth considering as a weeping standard. **CLIMATE**: Cool or temperate. **SOIL**: In loam, clay and sand, moist, well-drained or dry.

Acacia baileyana 'Purpurea'

A contrast plant whose feathery silver-grey bipinnate foliage features striking purple new growth for most of the year with masses of spherical flower heads 1cm in diameter. **CLIMATE**: Cool or temperate. **SOIL**: In loam, clay and sand, moist, well-drained or dry.

3 *Acacia cognata* 'Bower Beauty'

A compact form of *A. cognata* with graceful weeping foliage that makes it a stunning foliage plant all year round. Small ball-shaped flowers are a secondary pleasure when they appear in spring. Prone to root rot in humid climates; at its best in southern states. **CLIMATE**: Cool or temperate. **SOIL**: In loam and sand, moist, well-drained or dry. Not clay.

4 *Acacia cognata* 'Curvaceous'

A compact form of *A. cognata* with graceful weeping foliage that makes it a stunning foliage plant all year round. Small ball-shaped flowers are a secondary pleasure when they appear in spring. Prone to root rot in humid climates; at its best in southern states. **CLIMATE**: Cool or temperate. **SOIL**: In loam and sand, moist, well-drained or dry. Not clay.

5 *Acacia cognata* 'Fettucine'

A compact form of *A. cognata* that makes a stunning foliage plant, with lovely 'rippled' weeping foliage and small ball-shaped flowers that appear in spring. Prone to root rot in humid climates; at its best in southern states. **CLIMATE**: Cool or temperate. **SOIL**: In loam and sand, moist, well-drained or dry. Not clay.

6 *Acacia cognata* 'Green Mist'

A relatively compact form of *A. cognata* with graceful weeping foliage that makes it a stunning foliage plant all year round. Somewhat taller and with a more open habit than other compact forms of *A. cognata*. Small ball-shaped flowers are a secondary pleasure when they appear in spring. Prone to root rot in humid climates; at its best in southern states. **CLIMATE**: Cool or temperate. **SOIL**: In loam and sand, moist, well-drained or dry. Not clay.

7 *Acacia cognata* 'Limelight'

A compact form of *A. cognata* with graceful weeping foliage that makes it a stunning foliage plant all year round. Small ball-shaped flowers are a secondary pleasure when they appear in spring. Prone to root rot in humid climates; at its best in southern states. **CLIMATE**: Cool or temperate. **SOIL**: In loam and sand, moist, well-drained or dry. Not clay.

8 *Acacia cognata* 'Lime Magik'

A medium to tall shrub with graceful weeping bright, lime-yellow foliage that makes it a stunning foliage plant all year round. Small ball-shaped flowers are a secondary pleasure when they appear in spring. Prone to root rot in humid climates; at its best in southern states. **CLIMATE**: Cool or temperate. **SOIL**: In loam and sand, moist, well-drained or dry. Not clay.

Acacia cognata 'Mini Cog'

A compact form of *A. cognata* with graceful weeping foliage that makes it a stunning foliage plant all year round. Small ball-shaped flowers are a secondary pleasure when they appear in spring. Prone to root rot in humid climates; at its best in southern states. **CLIMATE**: Cool or temperate. **SOIL**: In loam and sand, moist, well-drained or dry. Not clay.

9 *Acacia cognata* 'Mop Top'

A low-mounding dense shrub with aromatic foliage, plum-coloured new growth, and bright yellow perfumed flowers in spring, enticing small insect feeders such as wrens and thornbills. Use to create soft low hedging along pathways; plant in massed formation on banks or in wide garden beds where impact is required; use as dramatic accent container plant for courtyard or patio. **CLIMATE**: Cool or temperate. **SOIL**: In loam and sand, moist, well-drained or dry. Not clay.

10 *Acacia cognata* 'River Cascade'

A medium shrub with very dense weeping foliage that makes it a stunning foliage plant all year round. Small ball-shaped flowers are a secondary pleasure when they appear in spring. Prone to root rot in humid climates; at its best in southern states. **CLIMATE**: Cool or temperate. **SOIL**: In loam and sand, moist, well-drained or dry. Not clay.

11 Acacia cognata 'Waterfall'

20-30cm

100-200cm

A prostrate form of this very popular wattle that retains its foliage along the stem as it matures. The base from which the stems emerge will, over time, develop its own architectural character, adding to the intrigue of the plant. For dramatic impact, plant in tall containers or large pipes along walkways; beside waterfalls or cascades; or on sloping banks where landscape design calls for an especially strong note. **CLIMATE**: Cool or temperate. **SOIL**: In loam and sand, moist, well-drained or dry. Not clay.

Acacia cultriformis 'Cascade'

30cm

200-400cm

A dense ground cover or cascading plant with arching or weeping stems with neatly arranged silver-grey foliage covered in clusters of golden flowers in spring. Small insect-eating birds such as wrens and thornbills will probe among the flowers for food. Looks spectacular cascading from tall timber planter boxes, free-standing pipes, over walls and down banks; can also be planted as a dramatic ground cover. **CLIMATE**: Cool or temperate. **SOIL**: In loam and sand, moist, well-drained or dry. Not clay.

12 Acacia leprosa 'Scarlet Blaze'

400-500cm

200cm

A red flower in the genus Acacia is a real novelty. The weeping habit of this medium shrub is another attractive feature. The ball-shaped flowers appear in spring. **CLIMATE**: Cool or temperate. **SOIL**: In loam and sand, moist, well-drained or dry. Not clay.

Acmena 'Moonlight Flame'

100cm

50-70cm

Compact, low-branching shrub with pink new growth and miniature cream flowers. Perfect for hedging or containers. Use low phosphorous fertiliser. **CLIMATE**: Cool, temperate, sub-tropical or tropical. **SOIL**: In loam, clay and sand, moist.

13 Acmena smithii 'Allyn Magic'

50cm

100cm

A fantastic dwarf form of this species. Low-mounding shrub with cream flowers followed by fleshy pink berries. Ideal for hedging and borders or as a tub or patio specimen. **CLIMATE**: Temperate or sub-tropical. **SOIL**: In loam, clay and sand, wet, moist or dry.

Acmena smithii 'Dusky'

400cm

200cm

A tough lilly pilly with bronze new growth as the feature. Great for hedges and screens. **CLIMATE**: Temperate or sub-tropical. **SOIL**: In loam, clay and sand, wet, moist or dry.

Acmena smithii 'Minipilly'

200cm

200cm

A small bushy form of *Acmena smithii* with striking new colourful tips. Responds well to regular pruning and feeding. Fleshy pink berries follow cream flowers. Ideal for hedging and borders or as a tub or patio specimen. **CLIMATE**: Temperate or sub-tropical. **SOIL**: In loam, clay and sand, wet, moist or dry.

Agonis flexuosa 'Burgundy'

200-300cm

100-200cm

The very dark purple foliage makes this an outstanding contrast plant in the garden for its leaves alone. A reasonably tough and vigorous plant that makes a great feature or screen plant. **CLIMATE**: Cool or temperate. **SOIL**: In loam and sand, moist, well-drained or dry. Not clay.

Agonis flexuosa 'Jervis Bay Afterdark'

300cm

100cm

The very dark purple foliage makes this an outstanding contrast plant in the garden for its leaves alone. Has proven to be slow growing and somewhat prone to root rot, but makes a great feature or screen plant. **CLIMATE**: Cool or temperate. **SOIL**: In loam and sand, moist, well-drained or dry. Not clay.

14 Agonis flexuosa 'Nana'

150cm

200cm

A dwarf shrub with dense foliage, reddish new growth and naturally compact growth habit. An outstanding hedge or low-growing screen. **CLIMATE**: Cool or temperate. **SOIL**: In loam and sand, moist, well-drained or dry. Not clay.

Alyogyne hakeifolia 'Elle Marie'

200-250cm

200cm

Native hibiscus. Outstanding, long-flowering medium shrub. Prune after spring flowering. Beautiful creamy yellow flower with red centre. **CLIMATE**: Cool or temperate. **SOIL**: In loam and sand, moist, well-drained or dry. Not clay.

Alyogyne hakeifolia 'Melissa Anne'

200-250cm

200cm

Native hibiscus. Outstanding, long-flowering medium shrub. Prune after spring flowering. Beautiful pink flower with red centre. **CLIMATE**: Cool or temperate. **SOIL**: In loam and sand, moist, well-drained or dry. Not clay.

12 14

13

15 Alyogyne huegelii 'West Coast Gem'

200-250cm

200cm

Native hibiscus. Outstanding, long-flowering medium shrub. Prune after spring flowering. **CLIMATE**: Cool or temperate. **SOIL**: In loam and sand, moist, well-drained or dry. Not clay.

16 Anigozanthos 'Amber Velvet'

100cm

100cm

A medium-sized kangaroo paw with quite good vigour. Limited flowering season with branched stems. **CLIMATE**: Cool or temperate. **SOIL**: In loam, clay and sand, moist or well-drained.

17 Anigozanthos 'Big Red'

200cm

100cm

A tall kangaroo paw with large individual flowers. Strong grower that persists from year to year. Good cut flower. Strappy dark-green leaves. **CLIMATE**: Cool, temperate or sub-tropical. **SOIL**: In loam, clay and sand, moist or well-drained.

18 Anigozanthos 'Bush Ballad'

60cm

50cm

Dwarf habit with exceptionally high density of branched flower stems and prolific non-stop blooming performance. A reasonable garden plant but outstanding in a pot. **CLIMATE**: Cool or temperate. **SOIL**: In loam and sand, moist or well-drained. Not clay.

19 Anigozanthos 'Bush Blitz'

70cm

50cm

An incredibly prolific flowering kangaroo paw of small to medium stature with branched stems. Best grown in a container. **CLIMATE**: Cool or temperate. **SOIL**: In loam and sand, moist or well-drained. Not clay.

20 Anigozanthos 'Bush Bonanza'

60cm

50cm

Kangaroo paw of dwarf stature with lightly branched red stems and yellow flowers. Not as vigorous in humid climates, where it is disease-prone and best grown in a pot. **CLIMATE**: Cool or temperate. **SOIL**: In loam and sand, moist or well-drained. Not clay.

SpS

21 Anigozanthos 'Bush Bounty'

60cm

50cm

Kangaroo paw with unusual two-toned yellow flower with purple tips. Dwarf habit. Not as vigorous in humid climates, where it is disease-prone and best grown in a pot. **CLIMATE**: Cool or temperate. **SOIL**: In loam and sand, moist or well-drained. Not clay.

SpS

22 Anigozanthos 'Bush Dance'

60cm

50cm

Kangaroo paw with excellent colour definition. Dwarf habit with unbranched flowering stems. A short-lived garden plant but outstanding in a pot. **CLIMATE**: Cool or temperate. **SOIL**: In loam and sand, moist or well-drained. Not clay.

23 Anigozanthos 'Bush Dawn'

200cm

100cm

Tall habit. Very tough plant, great garden performance. Vibrant flower colour on highly branched stems. **CLIMATE**: Cool, temperate or sub-tropical. **SOIL**: In loam, clay and sand, moist or well-drained.

SpS

24 Anigozanthos 'Bush Diamond'

60cm

50cm

An unusually coloured flower for a kangaroo paw, varying from snow white when grown in warmer temperatures to white with a pink overtone in cooler conditions. Dwarf habit, with branched stems and prolific non-stop blooming performance. A reasonable garden plant but outstanding in a pot. **CLIMATE**: Cool or temperate. **SOIL**: In loam and sand, moist or well-drained. Not clay.

25 Anigozanthos 'Bush Elegance'

70cm

50cm

Kangaroo paw with dwarf habit, distinct burgundy-coloured flowers on branched stems. A relatively strong garden performer even in humid climates. **CLIMATE**: Cool or temperate. **SOIL**: In loam and sand, moist or well-drained. Not clay.

26 Anigozanthos 'Bush Endeavour'

200cm

100cm

Tall habit. Very tough kangaroo paw, great garden performance. Vibrant flower colour on highly branched stems. **CLIMATE**: Cool, temperate or sub-tropical. **SOIL**: In loam, clay and sand, moist or well-drained.

27 Anigozanthos 'Bush Fury'

150cm / 100cm

A medium-sized kangaroo paw that is a good garden performer with an extended flowering period. Dark red flowers on a well-branched stem. **CLIMATE**: Cool, temperate or sub-tropical. **SOIL**: In loam, clay and sand, moist or well-drained.

Anigozanthos 'Bush Games'

120cm / 50cm

Reasonably tough red and green kangaroo paw with good colour definition. Not as vigorous in humid climates where it is disease-prone and best grown in a pot. Flowering season limited to spring. **CLIMATE**: Cool or temperate. **SOIL**: In loam and sand, moist or well-drained. Not clay.

28 Anigozanthos 'Bush Gold'

80cm / 50cm

One of the toughest medium-sized kangaroo paws with branched flowering stems. An excellent long-lived garden plant. **CLIMATE**: Cool or temperate. **SOIL**: In loam and sand, moist or well-drained. Not clay.

29 Anigozanthos 'Bush Inferno'

60cm / 50cm

Kangaroo paw of dwarf habit. Not as vigorous in humid climates, where it is disease-prone and best grown in a pot. **CLIMATE**: Cool or temperate. **SOIL**: In loam and sand, moist or well-drained. Not clay.

30 Anigozanthos 'Bush Pearl'

60cm / 50cm

Kangaroo paw of dwarf habit with branched stems and prolific non-stop blooming performance. A reasonable garden plant but outstanding in a pot. **CLIMATE**: Cool or temperate. **SOIL**: In loam and sand, moist or well-drained. Not clay.

31 Anigozanthos 'Bush Pioneer'

200cm / 100cm

Kangaroo paw with unusual gold-coloured flowers on an extremely tough tall grower with a well-branched flower stem. **CLIMATE**: Cool, temperate or sub-tropical. **SOIL**: In loam, clay and sand, moist or well-drained.

32 Anigozanthos 'Bush Pizzaz'

60cm / 50cm

Kangaroo paw of dwarf habit with unusual cerise flowers in profusion on a well-branched flower stem. One of the better garden performers among the dwarf kangaroo paws. **CLIMATE**: Cool or temperate. **SOIL**: In loam and sand, moist or well-drained. Not clay.

33 Anigozanthos 'Bush Ranger'

60cm / 50cm

Kangaroo paw of dwarf habit with branched stems and prolific non-stop blooming performance. A reasonable garden plant but outstanding in a pot. **CLIMATE**: Cool or temperate. **SOIL**: In loam and sand, moist or well-drained. Not clay.

34 Anigozanthos 'Bush Rebel'

200cm / 100cm

Kangaroo paw of tall habit. Very tough plant, great garden performance. Relatively large individual flowers with vibrant colour on highly branched stems. **CLIMATE**: Cool, temperate or sub-tropical. **SOIL**: In loam, clay and sand, moist or well-drained.

35 Anigozanthos 'Bush Revolution'

200cm / 100cm

Kangaroo paw of tall habit. Vibrant flower colour on highly branched stems. Very tough plant, great garden performance. **CLIMATE**: Cool, temperate or sub-tropical. **SOIL**: In loam, clay and sand, moist or well-drained.

36 Anigozanthos 'Bush Spark'

60cm / 50cm

Kangaroo paw of dwarf habit. Not as vigorous in humid climates, where it is disease-prone and best grown in a pot. **CLIMATE**: Cool or temperate. **SOIL**: In loam and sand, moist or well-drained. Not clay.

Anigozanthos 'Bush Sundown'

60cm / 50cm

Kangaroo paw of dwarf habit. Not as vigorous in humid climates, where it is disease-prone and best grown in a pot. Light orange flower colour. **CLIMATE**: Cool or temperate. **SOIL**: In loam and sand, moist or well-drained. Not clay.

37 Anigozanthos 'Bush Sunset'

↑ 200cm
↔ 100cm

Kangaroo paw of tall habit. Very tough plant, great garden performance. Vibrant flower colour on highly branched stems. **CLIMATE:** Cool, temperate or sub-tropical. **SOIL:** In loam, clay and sand, moist or well-drained.

38 Anigozanthos 'Bush Volcano'

↑ 60cm
↔ 50cm

Kangaroo paw of dwarf habit. Not as vigorous in humid climates, where it is disease-prone and best grown in a pot. Vibrant dark orange flower colour. **CLIMATE:** Cool or temperate. **SOIL:** In loam and sand, moist or well-drained. Not clay.

Anigozanthos 'Cross of Gold'

↑ 90–120cm
↔ 40–60cm

A clumping kangaroo paw with clean strap leaves of medium dark green. A relatively tough medium-sized paw with quite good vigour. Limited flowering season with branched stems. **CLIMATE:** Cool or temperate. **SOIL:** In loam, clay and sand, moist or well-drained.

39 Anigozanthos 'Gold Velvet'

↑ 100cm
↔ 100cm

A relatively tough medium-sized kangaroo paw with quite good vigour. Limited flowering season with branched stems. Gold flower colour. **CLIMATE:** Cool or temperate. **SOIL:** In loam, clay and sand, moist or well-drained.

40 Anigozanthos 'Green Dragon'

↑ 60cm
↔ 50cm

Emerald green flower is the feature of this kangaroo paw cultivar. Dwarf habit with unbranched stems. A short-lived garden plant but outstanding in a pot. **CLIMATE:** Cool or temperate. **SOIL:** In loam and sand, moist or well-drained. Not clay.

41 Anigozanthos 'Kings Park Federation Flame'

↑ 200cm
↔ 100cm

Tall habit. Relatively tough plant, grey foliage is a feature. Vibrant flower colour on highly branched stems. **CLIMATE:** Cool, temperate or sub-tropical. **SOIL:** In loam, clay and sand, moist or well-drained.

42 Anigozanthos 'Orange Cross'

↑ 200cm
↔ 100cm

Kangaroo paw of tall habit. Very tough plant, great garden performance. Vibrant flower colour on highly branched stems. **CLIMATE:** Cool, temperate or sub-tropical. **SOIL:** In loam, clay and sand, moist or well-drained.

43 Anigozanthos 'Rampaging Roy Slaven'

↑ 150cm
↔ 100cm

A medium-sized kangaroo paw that is a good garden performer with an extended flowering period. Dark orange flowers on a well-branched stem. **CLIMATE:** Cool, temperate or sub-tropical. **SOIL:** In loam, clay and sand, moist or well-drained.

44 Anigozanthos 'Regal Velvet'

↑ 100cm
↔ 100cm

A medium-sized kangaroo paw with quite good vigour. Limited flowering season, with branched stems. Flower colour is not as bright as other red/green cultivars, but it is a tougher plant. **CLIMATE:** Cool or temperate. **SOIL:** In loam, clay and sand, moist or well-drained.

45 Anigozanthos 'Ruby Velvet'

↑ 100cm
↔ 100cm

A medium-sized kangaroo paw with quite good vigour. Limited flowering season, with branched stems. A relatively tough garden plant. **CLIMATE:** Cool or temperate. **SOIL:** In loam, clay and sand, moist or well-drained.

46 Anigozanthos 'Yellow Gem'

↑ 200cm
↔ 100cm

Kangaroo paw of tall habit. Very tough plant, great garden performance. Vibrant bicoloured red and yellow flower on highly branched stems. **CLIMATE:** Cool, temperate or sub-tropical. **SOIL:** In loam, clay and sand, moist or well-drained.

Austromyrtus 'Copper Tops'

↑ 50cm
↔ 100cm

A hardy spreading shrub with arching branches of green foliage and coppery new growth. The edible greyish white berries are delicious and are produced in autumn. **CLIMATE:** Cool, temperate or sub-tropical. **SOIL:** In loam, clay and sand, moist, well-drained or dry.

47 Babingtonia 'Howies Sweet Midget'

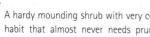

100cm · 100cm

A hardy mounding shrub with very compact habit that almost never needs pruning. A great low-maintenance plant for shrubberies that adapts well to a wide range of conditions. **CLIMATE:** Cool, temperate or sub-tropical. **SOIL:** In loam, clay and sand, moist, well-drained or dry.

Baloskion pallens 'Didgery Sticks'

100–150cm · 100cm

A type of native sedge that forms a clump of wiry upright stems, giving a grass-like appearance. Good for vertical accent in garden beds or pots. Tolerates waterlogged conditions and adapts well to heavy soils. **CLIMATE:** Cool, temperate or sub-tropical. **SOIL:** In loam, clay and sand, wet, moist, well-drained or dry.

48 Banksia ericifolia 'Little Eric'

150–200cm · 100cm

A more compact form of a very adaptable banksia. Great medium-sized screen plant with attractive flowers with maroon styles and whitish perianth. **CLIMATE:** Temperate or sub-tropical. **SOIL:** In loam, clay and sand, moist, well-drained or dry.

49 Banksia 'Giant Candles'

400cm · 200cm

The massive flower spikes up to 40cm long are the outstanding feature of this cultivar. A very adaptable plant that makes a fantastic medium-sized screen as well as a great cut flower. **CLIMATE:** Temperate or sub-tropical. **SOIL:** In loam, clay and sand, moist, well-drained or dry.

50 Banksia integrifolia 'Roller Coaster'

10–15cm · 400cm

Vigorous cascading ground cover suitable for banks, rockeries, and the borders of shrubberies. Very tough, especially for coastal areas with sandy soil. **CLIMATE:** Cool, temperate or sub-tropical. **SOIL:** In loam, clay and sand, moist, well-drained or dry.

Banksia marginata 'Minimarg'

50cm · 100cm

A very tough dwarf banksia that adapts well to a wide range of soil and climate types. Suitable for low hedges, rockeries and as a general low mounding garden shrub. **CLIMATE:** Cool, temperate or sub-tropical. **SOIL:** In loam, clay and sand, moist, well-drained or dry.

Banksia 'Sentinel'

2–2.5cm · 65–90cm

Multi-stemmed, narrow upright shrub with entire and toothed glossy leaves and upright yellow candle flowers to 15cm. Ideal for screening, containers or to use formally as pathway borders. **CLIMATE:** Cool, temperate, sub-tropical or tropical. **SOIL:** In loam and sand, moist, well-drained or dry. Not clay.

51 Banksia serrata 'Pygmy Possum'

60cm · 250cm

A prostrate form of Old Man banksia with lovely arching branches. A great rockery or bank plant. **CLIMATE:** Temperate or sub-tropical. **SOIL:** In loam and sand, moist, well-drained or dry. Not clay.

52 Banksia spinulosa 'Birthday Candles'

50cm · 50cm

A dense compact small shrub that is perfect for rockeries and smaller gardens, whether mass planted for dramatic effect, in small groups or in containers on the patio, veranda or deck. **CLIMATE:** Temperate or sub-tropical. **SOIL:** In loam and sand, moist, well-drained or dry. Not clay.

53 Banksia spinulosa 'Black Magic'

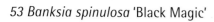

100–150cm · 100–120cm

A compact small shrub that is perfect for rockeries and smaller gardens, whether mass planted for dramatic effect, in small groups or in containers on the patio, veranda or deck. Lovely golden flower colour contrasting with almost black styles. **CLIMATE:** Temperate or sub-tropical. **SOIL:** In loam and sand, moist, well-drained or dry. Not clay.

54 Banksia spinulosa 'Cherry Candles'

50cm · 50cm

A dense compact small shrub that is perfect for rockeries and smaller gardens, whether mass planted for dramatic effect, in small groups or in containers on the patio, veranda or deck. Good strong flower colour. **CLIMATE:** Temperate or sub-tropical. **SOIL:** In loam and sand, well-drained or dry. Not clay.

Banksia spinulosa 'Honey Pots'

100cm · 100cm

A dense compact small shrub that is perfect for rockeries and smaller gardens, whether mass planted for dramatic effect, in small groups or in containers on the patio, veranda or deck. Lovely golden flower colour. **CLIMATE:** Temperate or sub-tropical. **SOIL:** In loam and sand, moist, well-drained or dry. Not clay.

55 Banksia spinulosa 'Stumpy Gold'

100cm
100cm

A dense, compact small shrub that is perfect for rockeries and smaller gardens, whether mass planted for dramatic effect, in small groups or in containers on the patio, veranda or deck. Lovely golden flower colour. **CLIMATE**: Temperate or sub-tropical. **SOIL**: In loam and sand, moist, well-drained or dry. Not clay.

AW

56 Banksia 'Yellow Wing'

150-180cm
150-180cm

A medium rounded shrub with fine dense foliage. The flower spikes are held well above the foliage as beacons for a range of honey-eating birds, and parrots love their seed. Particularly suitable for hedging, screening or specimen plantings; cut flowers last well in water, may also be dried. **CLIMATE**: Temperate or sub-tropical. **SOIL**: In loam and sand, moist, well-drained or dry. Not clay.

AW

57 Bauera 'Rose Carpet'

50cm
100cm

Hardy ground cover with dense layers of bronze-green slightly furry foliage with plentiful miniature rose-like flowers. Use for defining pathways, rockery plant, large containers, formal shaping. Feed and trim lightly in spring or summer. **CLIMATE**: Cool, temperate, sub-tropical or tropical. **SOIL**: In loam, clay and sand, well-drained.

Boronia megastigma 'Heaven Scent'

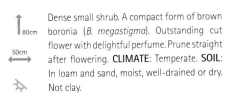

80cm
50cm

Dense small shrub. A compact form of brown boronia (*B. megastigma*). Outstanding cut flower with delightful perfume. Prune straight after flowering. **CLIMATE**: Temperate. **SOIL**: In loam and sand, moist, well-drained or dry. Not clay.

Boronia 'Purple Jared'

100cm
50cm

Dense small shrub. A deep purple-flowered hybrid of brown boronia (*B. megastigma*). Outstanding cut flower with delightful perfume. Prune straight after flowering. **CLIMATE**: Temperate. **SOIL**: In loam and sand, moist, well-drained or dry. Not clay.

Sp

Brachyscome 'Breakoday'

30cm
50cm

A compact mounding daisy that does not sucker. Vivid purple flowers are a feature. Great for rockeries, pots and borders. **CLIMATE**: Cool, temperate or sub-tropical. **SOIL**: In loam, clay and sand, moist, well-drained or dry.

58 Brachyscome 'Country Lights'

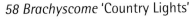

30cm
50cm

A compact mounding daisy that does not sucker. Dark purple colour is a feature of this tough, colourful plant. Great for rockeries, pots and borders. **CLIMATE**: Cool, temperate or sub-tropical. **SOIL**: In loam, clay and sand, moist, well-drained or dry.

Brachyscome 'Hot Candy'

30cm
50cm

The vibrant purple pink flower colour is a striking feature of this old favourite *Brachyscome*. Has a compact suckering growth habit and with masses of relatively small flowers. **CLIMATE**: Cool, temperate or sub-tropical. **SOIL**: In loam, clay and sand, moist, well-drained or dry.

Brachyscome 'Mauve Delight'

30cm
50cm

A proven performer over a number of years. This is the best mauve *Brachyscome* due to its long flowering time, compact suckering growth habit and nice divided foliage. Great for rockeries, pots and borders. **CLIMATE**: Cool, temperate or sub-tropical. **SOIL**: In loam, clay and sand, moist, well-drained or dry.

59 Brachyscome 'Pacific Breeze'

30cm
50cm

This is one of the best mauve-flowered *Brachyscomes* yet released, with larger flowers than similar varieties and a vigorous suckering growth habit and attractive divided foliage. Great for rockeries, pots and borders. **CLIMATE**: Cool, temperate or sub-tropical. **SOIL**: In loam, clay and sand, moist, well-drained or dry.

60 Brachyscome 'Pacific Cloud'

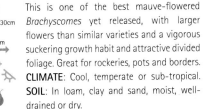

30cm
50cm

This is one of the best white-flowered *Brachyscomes* yet released, with compact growth habit and attractive divided foliage. Great for rockeries, pots and borders. **CLIMATE**: Cool, temperate or sub-tropical. **SOIL**: In loam, clay and sand, moist, well-drained or dry.

61 Brachyscome 'Pacific Island'

30cm
50cm

Masses of small bright pink flowers on a compact suckering plant. Great for rockeries, pots and borders. **CLIMATE**: Cool, temperate or sub-tropical. **SOIL**: In loam, clay and sand, moist, well-drained or dry.

62 Brachyscome 'Pacific Reef'

30cm · 50cm

The vibrant purple-pink flower colour is a striking feature of this new *Brachyscome*. Has a compact suckering growth habit and nice divided foliage. **CLIMATE**: Cool, temperate or sub-tropical. **SOIL**: In loam, clay and sand, moist, well-drained or dry.

63 Brachyscome 'Pacific Sun'

50cm · 50cm

An unusual bicolour of yellow with orange tinges in cooler weather. A rather leggy grower, so needs regular cutbacks through the warmer months to keep a compact shape. Does not sucker and therefore needs regular replacement. **CLIMATE**: Cool, temperate or sub-tropical. **SOIL**: In loam, clay and sand, moist, well-drained or dry.

64 Brachyscome 'Pacific Tide'

30cm · 50cm

A compact mounding daisy that does not sucker. Mauve flowers that fade to white are the feature of this tough plant. Great for rockeries, pots and borders. **CLIMATE**: Cool, temperate or sub-tropical. **SOIL**: In loam, clay and sand, moist, well-drained or dry.

65 Brachyscome 'Pacific Storm'

30cm · 50cm

A compact mounding daisy that does not sucker. Large mauve flowers with attractive divided foliage. Great for rockeries, pots and borders. **CLIMATE**: Cool, temperate or sub-tropical. **SOIL**: In loam, clay and sand, moist, well-drained or dry.

66 Brachyscome 'Pacific Wave'

30cm · 50cm

The soft mauve-pink flower colour is a striking feature of this new *Brachyscome*. Has a compact suckering growth habit and feathery greyish divided foliage. **CLIMATE**: Cool, temperate or sub-tropical. **SOIL**: In loam, clay and sand, moist, well-drained or dry.

Brachyscome 'Pilliga Posy'

30cm · 50cm

The vibrant pink flower colour is a striking feature of this old favourite *Brachyscome*. Has a compact suckering growth habit and nice divided foliage. **CLIMATE**: Cool, temperate or sub-tropical. **SOIL**: In loam, clay and sand, moist, well-drained or dry.

67 Callistemon 'Betka Beauty'

120–180cm · 120–150cm

A compact single- or multi-stemmed bottlebrush with papery bark and fresh light green foliage. Plant as a specimen or in groups, around pools or for screening; in streetscapes and open parkland. **CLIMATE**: Cool, temperate or sub-tropical. **SOIL**: In loam, clay and sand, wet, moist, well-drained or dry.

SpA

68 Callistemon 'Burgundy Jack'

300cm · 200cm

A relatively compact, free-flowering bottlebrush with deep burgundy flower heads. **CLIMATE**: Cool, temperate or sub-tropical. **SOIL**: In loam, clay and sand, wet, moist, well-drained or dry.

SpA

Callistemon 'Cameo Pink'

200–300cm · 200cm

A medium-sized bottlebrush, relatively dense with smallish deep pink flower heads. Good general garden shrub. **CLIMATE**: Cool, temperate or sub-tropical. **SOIL**: In loam, clay and sand, wet, moist, well-drained or dry.

Callistemon 'Candelabra'

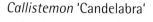

250–300cm · 100–200cm

An upright narrow dense shrub with masses of perfumed yellow flowers set above silver-grey foliage. Ideal for narrow garden areas such as driveways; as a screening or specimen plant; and suited to streetscapes and parklands. May also be hedged. **CLIMATE**: Cool, temperate or sub-tropical. **SOIL**: In loam, clay and sand, wet, moist, well-drained or dry.

SpA

Callistemon 'Candle Glow'

60–90cm · 200–350cm

A low arching shrub with elegant silvery new growth on the grey foliage. It bears perfumed, bright-lemon brushes in spring, summer and autumn, highly attractive to honeyeaters, and to small insect-feeding birds such as wrens and thornbills. Ideal for banks, open garden beds, median strips and broad landscape design where it performs reliably and always looks attractive. **CLIMATE**: Cool, temperate or sub-tropical. **SOIL**: In loam, clay and sand, wet, moist, well-drained or dry.

SpA

69 Callistemon 'Candy Pink'

400cm · 200cm

A medium bottlebrush that is incredibly adaptable. The large flower spikes are a lovely dark pink colour and are borne in flushes virtually all year round after a flush of new growth. **CLIMATE**: Cool, temperate or sub-tropical. **SOIL**: In loam, clay and sand, wet, moist, well-drained or dry.

70 Callistemon 'Captain Cook'

150cm
100cm

One of the best red bottlebrushes, on an erect but compact shrub. The small, narrow leaves make this a great hedge plant. **CLIMATE:** Cool, temperate or sub-tropical. **SOIL:** In loam, clay and sand, wet, moist, well-drained or dry.

71 Callistemon 'Cherry Time'

150-180cm
150cm

A medium weeping shrub with fine glossy leaves and bronze new growth. Colourful new growth makes it a good hedging plant or a shapely specimen, and spectacular in a large container. **CLIMATE:** Cool, temperate or sub-tropical. **SOIL:** In loam, clay and sand, wet, moist, well-drained or dry.

Callistemon 'Dawson River Weeper'

500-600cm
300-400cm

A large shrub to small tree with weeping habit. Profuse flowering in spring, with a follow-up in autumn, makes this a great screening plant for a variety of climates. **CLIMATE:** Cool, temperate or sub-tropical. **SOIL:** In loam, clay and sand, wet, moist, well-drained or dry.

72 Callistemon 'Edna Walling Scarlet Willow'

250-300cm
200cm

A graceful soft-foliaged large shrub with pinky-tan new growth and a weeping habit. A colourful shapely specimen or street tree, ideal for group planting in larger sites beside water features and for soft, graceful screening. **CLIMATE:** Cool, temperate or sub-tropical. **SOIL:** In loam, clay and sand, wet, moist, well-drained or dry.

Callistemon 'Endeavour'

200cm
200cm

One of the best red bottlebrushes, on an erect but compact shrub. Very large flower heads on a very adaptable plant. **CLIMATE:** Cool, temperate or sub-tropical. **SOIL:** In loam, clay and sand, wet, moist, well-drained or dry.

Callistemon 'Firebrand'

50-80cm
200-300cm

A low, spreading bottlebrush, dense and fast-growing. A great plant for rockeries and steep banks, median strips and for municipal plantings. Also good as a low hedge for screening. **CLIMATE:** Cool, temperate or sub-tropical. **SOIL:** In loam, clay and sand, wet, moist, well-drained or dry.

73 Callistemon 'Four Seasons'

180-200cm
150-180cm

A dense medium-sized shrub with a low branching habit and pendulous foliage. The distinguishing feature of this bottlebrush is its huge bunches of crimson-pink flowers throughout the year. Plant for compact hedging, screening or in a planting mixed with other shrubs or beneath taller screening plants. **CLIMATE:** Cool, temperate or sub-tropical. **SOIL:** In loam, clay and sand, wet, moist, well-drained or dry.

74 Callistemon 'Genoa Glory'

150-250cm
120-200cm

A compact shrub, single or multi-stemmed, with light papery bark and dense grey-green foliage. Plant as a showy specimen or in groups, around pools or for screening; in streetscapes and open parkland. **CLIMATE:** Cool, temperate or sub-tropical. **SOIL:** In loam, clay and sand, wet, moist, well-drained or dry.

75 Callistemon 'Great Balls of Fire'

100cm
100cm

This cultivar rarely flowers but should be grown for its wonderful, bright-red new growth, borne on a very compact, bun-shaped shrub. **CLIMATE:** Cool, temperate or sub-tropical. **SOIL:** In loam, clay and sand, wet, moist, well-drained or dry.

Callistemon 'Hannah Ray'

400-500cm
200-300cm

A large shrub with weeping habit. Profuse flowering in spring, with a follow-up in autumn, makes this a great screening plant for a variety of climates. **CLIMATE:** Cool, temperate or sub-tropical. **SOIL:** In loam, clay and sand, wet, moist, well-drained or dry.

Callistemon 'Happy Valley'

400cm
200cm

Unusual and rather stunning bicoloured flower heads are the feature of this little-known cultivar. A good feature or screen plant. **CLIMATE:** Cool, temperate or sub-tropical. **SOIL:** In loam, clay and sand, wet, moist, well-drained or dry.

76 Callistemon 'Hot Pink'

150-200cm
150-200cm

This is perhaps the brightest pink flower I have seen in a bottlebrush. Forms a very compact rounded shrub that flowers prolifically in late spring and more lightly again in autumn. Great rockery, container plant or general garden shrub. **CLIMATE:** Cool, temperate or sub-tropical. **SOIL:** In loam, clay and sand, wet, moist, well-drained or dry.

77 Callistemon 'Kings Park Special'

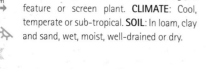

300-400cm
300cm

A relatively compact, free-flowering bottlebrush with bright-red flower heads. One of the best bottlebrushes ever. A good feature or screen plant. **CLIMATE:** Cool, temperate or sub-tropical. **SOIL:** In loam, clay and sand, wet, moist, well-drained or dry.

78 Callistemon 'Little John'

75cm
50cm

A dwarf bottlebrush with dark red flowers and attractive blue-grey foliage. Can be shy to flower but is worth growing for the foliage alone. Great rockery, container plant or general garden shrub. **CLIMATE:** Cool, temperate or sub-tropical. **SOIL:** In loam, clay and sand, wet, moist, well-drained or dry.

79 Callistemon 'Mary McKillop'

200-250cm
100-200cm

A dense, lightly weeping medium shrub with glossy leaves and lettuce-green new growth. Plant as specimens or groups in gardens or streetscapes, or as hedges. Also looks spectacular in a large tub. A dense plantation along a boundary or for screening will give a brilliant flowering display over many months and supply a continuous flush of nectar for honeyeaters. **CLIMATE:** Cool, temperate or sub-tropical. **SOIL:** In loam, clay and sand, wet, moist, well-drained or dry.

Callistemon 'Matthew Flinders'

75cm
50cm

Fantastic new dwarf bottlebrush with dark red flowers and attractive mid-green foliage. Great rockery, container plant or general garden shrub. **CLIMATE:** Cool, temperate or sub-tropical. **SOIL:** In loam, clay and sand, wet, moist, well-drained or dry.

80 Callistemon 'Mauve Mist'

200-300cm
200-300cm

An unusual colour for bottlebrush. A compact growing, free-flowering small to medium shrub. Great feature or screen plant. **CLIMATE:** Cool, temperate or sub-tropical. **SOIL:** In loam, clay and sand, wet, moist, well-drained or dry.

Callistemon 'Pink Alma'

150cm
150cm

This shade of mid-pink in the flower is unusual for *Callistemon*. It forms a well-branched compact shrub that flowers profusely in spring and again in less profusion in autumn. **CLIMATE:** Cool, temperate or sub-tropical. **SOIL:** In loam, clay and sand, wet, moist, well-drained or dry.

81 Callistemon 'Prolific'

300-400cm
300cm

A relatively compact, free-flowering bottlebrush with smallish bright-red flower heads. Upright growth habit. A good feature or screen plant. **CLIMATE:** Cool, temperate or sub-tropical. **SOIL:** In loam, clay and sand, wet, moist, well-drained or dry.

82 Callistemon 'Purple Splendour'

200cm
150cm

A relatively compact bottlebrush with brilliant purple flower heads in profusion in spring, with a follow-up flowering in autumn. **CLIMATE:** Cool, temperate or sub-tropical. **SOIL:** In loam, clay and sand, wet, moist, well-drained or dry.

Callistemon 'Rose Opal'

150-180cm
100-150cm

A dwarf compact shrub that is great for smaller gardens. This growth habit, coupled with the rosy red flowers, distinguishes it from most other bottlebrushes. It is an excellent garden or tub specimen and can also be used for hedging. **CLIMATE:** Cool, temperate or sub-tropical. **SOIL:** In loam, clay and sand, wet, moist, well-drained or dry.

83 Callistemon 'Rosy Morn'

60-100cm
100-120cm

A dense compact shrub with grey-green, purple-tinged foliage. Useful for low hedging requiring only minimal pruning, or specimen planting mixed with other shrubs or beneath taller screening plants. A strikingly handsome container plant. **CLIMATE:** Cool, temperate or sub-tropical. **SOIL:** In loam, clay and sand, wet, moist, well-drained or dry.

84 Callistemon 'Silver Cloud'

150-180cm
120-150cm

A small, dense shrub with striking silver-grey foliage and plum-coloured new growth. A lovely small specimen for narrow screening or hedging; plant in multiples as a background or edging for water areas. **CLIMATE:** Cool, temperate or sub-tropical. **SOIL:** In loam, clay and sand, wet, moist, well-drained or dry.

SpA

Callistemon 'Sugar Candy'

250-300cm
180-220cm

Shapely shrub or small tree with silvery foliage and candy pink brushes. Particularly ornamental when planted with contrasting foliage. **CLIMATE:** Cool, temperate, sub-tropical or tropical. **SOIL:** In loam, clay and sand, moist or dry.

Callistemon 'Summer Days'

A small, arching, free-flowering shrub with dense foliage and reddish new growth. The purple-red brushes open in late spring and continue through summer, flowering much later than other small bottlebrushes. Use as low hedging or specimen planting mixed with other shrubs or beneath taller screening plants. **CLIMATE**: Cool, temperate or sub-tropical. **SOIL**: In loam, clay and sand, wet, moist, well-drained or dry.

85 Callistemon 'Tango'

A dwarf compact shrub that is great for smaller gardens. This growth habit, coupled with the unusual orange flowers, distinguishes this from other bottlebrushes. It is an excellent garden or tub specimen and can also be used for hedging. **CLIMATE**: Cool, temperate or sub-tropical. **SOIL**: In loam, clay and sand, wet, moist, well-drained or dry.

86 Callistemon 'Taree Pink'

The bright pink new growth adds further interest to the profuse mid-pink flower heads on a relatively compact medium shrub. Good general garden shrub or screen plant. **CLIMATE**: Cool, temperate or sub-tropical. **SOIL**: In loam, clay and sand, wet, moist, well-drained or dry.

87 Callistemon 'White Anzac' ('Anzac')

One of the best white-flowered bottlebrushes. Can become straggly unless pruned every year after flowering. Good general garden shrub. **CLIMATE**: Cool, temperate or sub-tropical. **SOIL**: In loam, clay and sand, wet, moist, well-drained or dry.

88 Casuarina glauca 'Cousin It'

A prostrate form of a very adaptable coastal plant. Flowers are insignificant but the foliage more than makes up for it. Great for rockeries or spilling down embankments. **CLIMATE**: Cool, temperate or sub-tropical. **SOIL**: In loam, clay and sand, moist, well-drained or dry.

89 Ceratopetalum gummiferum 'Albery's Red'

An outstanding form of NSW Christmas Bush with very bright red flowers on a compact large shrub/small tree. Prune off about 30 per cent straight after flowering for best results. Great feature plant and cut flower. **CLIMATE**: Temperate or sub-tropical. **SOIL**: In loam and sand, moist, well-drained or dry. Not clay.

90 Chamelaucium 'Dancing Queen'

A medium-sized upright shrub featuring a profusion of dark reddish-purple buds that open to medium-sized ruffled double lilac-pink flowers. Stunning double flowers make this a great feature plant and cut flower. **CLIMATE**: Temperate. **SOIL**: In sand, moist, well-drained or dry. Not loam or clay.

91 Chamelaucium 'Lady Stephanie'

Compact, very floriferous rounded shrub. Great feature plant, good for cut flowers. **CLIMATE**: Temperate. **SOIL**: In sand, moist, well-drained or dry. Not loam or clay.

92 Chamelaucium 'Revelation'

An upright somewhat open small shrub. The distinctive feature is the way the flower colour changes from white to mauve-purple as it ages. Great feature plant, good for cut flowers. **CLIMATE**: Temperate. **SOIL**: In sand, moist, well-drained or dry. Not loam or clay.

Chamelaucium uncinatum 'Purple Pride'

An old favourite spreading, floriferous shrub. Great feature plant, good for cut flowers. **CLIMATE**: Temperate. **SOIL**: In sand, moist, well-drained or dry. Not loam or clay.

93 Chrysocephalum apiculatum 'Desert Flame'

A ground-covering herbaceous perennial whose silvery grey foliage contrasts beautifully with bright yellow/orange flowers. Use as a border or pot plant. **CLIMATE**: Cool or temperate. **SOIL**: In loam and sand, moist, well-drained or dry. Not clay.

94 Chrysocephalum apiculatum 'Silver and Gold'

A ground-covering herbaceous perennial whose silvery grey foliage contrasts beautifully with bright yellow flowers. Use as a border or pot plant. **CLIMATE**: Cool or temperate. **SOIL**: In loam and sand, moist, well-drained or dry. Not clay.

95 Chrysocephalum apiculatum 'Silver Sunburst'

A ground-covering herbaceous perennial whose silvery grey foliage contrasts beautifully with bright yellow-orange flowers. Use as a border or pot plant. **CLIMATE**: Cool or temperate. **SOIL**: In loam and sand, moist, well-drained or dry. Not clay.

96 Coronidium 'Sunny Side Up'

A compact sub-shrub that features lovely grey foliage and masses of white everlasting daisy flowers in spring. A wonderful feature plant for smaller and larger gardens alike. Relatively tough. **CLIMATE**: Temperate or sub-tropical. **SOIL**: In loam and sand, moist, well-drained or dry. Not clay.

97 Correa 'Catie Bec'

A small shrub that becomes covered in pale pink star-shaped flowers. A tough shrub particularly good for coastal areas. Feature plant for a shrubbery. **CLIMATE**: Cool, temperate or sub-tropical. **SOIL**: In loam and sand, moist, well-drained or dry. Not clay.

98 Correa 'Dusky Bells'

An old favourite dense-mounding shrub with profuse flowering. Great shrubbery plant that is a great bird attractor. Prune straight after flowering. **CLIMATE**: Cool, temperate or sub-tropical. **SOIL**: In loam and sand, moist, well-drained or dry. Not clay.

Correa 'Federation Belle'

Small rounded shrub with excellent, bright flower colour. A tough shrub, particularly good for coastal areas. Feature plant for a shrubbery. **CLIMATE**: Cool or temperate. **SOIL**: In loam and sand, moist, well-drained or dry. Not clay.

Correa 'Firebird'

Low mounded shrub with distinctive flower colour. A tough shrub particularly good for coastal areas. Feature plant for a shrubbery. **CLIMATE**: Cool or temperate. **SOIL**: In loam and sand, moist, well-drained or dry. Not clay.

Correa glabra 'Barossa Gold'

Low mounded shrub with attractive golden foliage for year-round interest. Feature plant for a shrubbery but also fantastic for pots. **CLIMATE**: Cool or temperate. **SOIL**: In loam and sand, moist, well-drained or dry. Not clay.

99 Correa 'Green Dream'

Low mounded shrub with distinctive green flower colour. A tough shrub particularly good for coastal areas. Feature plant for a shrubbery. **CLIMATE**: Cool or temperate. **SOIL**: In loam and sand, moist, well-drained or dry. Not clay.

100 Correa 'Isabell'

Mounded ground-covering shrub with distinctive flower colour. A tough shrub particularly good for coastal areas. Feature plant for a shrubbery but also fantastic for pots. **CLIMATE**: Cool or temperate. **SOIL**: In loam and sand, moist, well-drained or dry. Not clay.

101 Correa 'Jezabell'

Low mounded shrub with distinctive flower colour. A tough shrub, particularly good for coastal areas. Feature plant for a shrubbery. **CLIMATE**: Cool or temperate. **SOIL**: In loam and sand, moist, well-drained or dry. Not clay.

102 Correa 'Tucker Time Dawn Bells'

A low-spreading dense shrub with bright variegated foliage. Good for a low hedge in gardens of all sizes. Plant in shady corners to impart a brightening effect; use among mixed plantings for additional bird habitat. **CLIMATE**: Cool or temperate. **SOIL**: In loam and sand, moist, well-drained or dry. Not clay.

103 Correa 'Tucker Time Dinner Bells'

A dense mounding shrub with glossy dark green foliage and a profusion of green-tipped, red bell flowers from mid-summer to winter. The nectar-rich tubular flowers are highly attractive to honeyeaters, and other small birds will feed upon visiting insects. A good feature plant for a shrubbery. **CLIMATE**: Cool or temperate. **SOIL**: In loam and sand, moist, well-drained or dry. Not clay.

104 Correa 'Tucker Time Multi Bella'

40-60cm

30-40cm

A dense mounding shrub with clusters of nectar-rich pink and green-tipped bell flowers. These are displayed en masse both outside and inside the canopy of soft grey-green leaves, and are irresistible to honey-eating birds. Great feature or pot plant. **CLIMATE:** Cool or temperate. **SOIL:** In loam and sand, moist, well-drained or dry. Not clay.

105 Corymbia 'Baby Orange'

300cm

200cm

Large shrub/small tree with large glossy dark-green leaves with a light-green reverse and reddish new foliage during the warmer months of the year. Outstanding terminal display of large flowers. **CLIMATE:** Temperate. **SOIL:** In loam and sand, moist, well-drained or dry. Not clay.

106 Corymbia 'Baby Scarlet'

300cm

200cm

Large shrub/small tree with large glossy dark-green leaves with a light-green reverse and reddish new foliage during the warmer months of the year. Outstanding terminal display of large flowers. **CLIMATE:** Temperate. **SOIL:** In loam and sand, moist, well-drained or dry. Not clay.

107 Corymbia 'Fairy Floss'

300cm

200cm

Large shrub/small tree with large glossy dark-green leaves with a light-green reverse . Very unusual bicoloured pink and white flowers displayed on the ends of the branches. **CLIMATE:** Temperate. **SOIL:** In loam and sand, moist, well-drained or dry. Not clay.

108 Corymbia ficifolia 'Wildfire'

600cm

300cm

Large shrub/small tree with large glossy dark-green leaves with a light-green reverse and reddish new foliage during the warmer months of the year. Outstanding terminal display of large flowers. **CLIMATE:** Temperate. **SOIL:** In loam and sand, moist, well-drained or dry. Not clay.

109 Corymbia 'Summer Red'

300-500cm

300cm

Large shrub/small tree with large glossy dark-green leaves with a light-green reverse and reddish new foliage during the warmer months of the year. Outstanding terminal display of large flowers. **CLIMATE:** Temperate. **SOIL:** In loam and sand, moist, well-drained or dry. Not clay.

110 Corymbia 'Summer Beauty'

300-500cm

300cm

Large shrub/small tree with large glossy dark-green leaves with a light-green reverse and reddish new foliage during the warmer months of the year. Outstanding terminal display of large flowers. **CLIMATE:** Temperate. **SOIL:** In loam and sand, moist, well-drained or dry. Not clay.

111 Crowea exalata 'Edna Walling Crowea'

30-45cm

80-120cm

A dainty, low-arching shrub with aromatic foliage festooned with multi-hued pink star flowers sought by native bees and butterflies. Use as a mounding ground cover in beds, cascading over banks or walls, or as a pot plant for balconies, courtyards and patios. **CLIMATE:** Temperate. **SOIL:** In loam and sand, moist, well-drained or dry. Not clay.

112 Crowea exalata 'Green Cape Crowea'

15-20cm

50-80cm

A compact, prostrate dwarf shrub with short, thick aromatic foliage and masses of multi-hued pink waxy star flowers. Butterflies, moths and native bees love the flowers. Use as a mounding ground cover in beds, cascading over banks or walls, or as a pot plant for balconies, courtyards and patios. **CLIMATE:** Temperate. **SOIL:** In loam and sand, moist, well-drained or dry. Not clay.

113 Crowea hybrid 'Festival'

100-150cm

100-150cm

Small shrub that flowers over a long period in autumn. Good rockery or container plant that is useful as a cut flower as well. **CLIMATE:** Temperate. **SOIL:** In loam and sand, moist, well-drained or dry. Not clay.

Crowea exalata 'Rhapsody'

50-75cm

50-75cm

A small rounded shrub with dark-green leaves. Attracts many nectar-feeding insects including butterflies and native bees. Use as a feature shrub, or as a pot plant for balconies, courtyards and patios. **CLIMATE:** Temperate. **SOIL:** In loam and sand, moist, well-drained or dry. Not clay.

Crowea exalata 'Symphony'

50-75cm

50-75cm

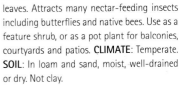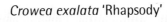

A small rounded shrub with dark-green leaves. Attracts many nectar-feeding insects including butterflies and native bees. Use as a feature shrub, or as a pot plant for balconies, courtyards and patios. **CLIMATE:** Temperate. **SOIL:** In loam and sand, moist, well-drained or dry. Not clay.

Dampiera stricta 'Glasshouse Glory'

30-50cm
30-100cm

A beautiful ground-covering perennial that suckers to fill an area. Can be short-lived if the soil is too wet. Cut back after flowering. **CLIMATE:** Temperate. **SOIL:** In loam and sand, moist, well-drained or dry. Not clay.

114 Darwinia citriodora 'Seaspray'

10-20cm
50-100cm

A low mounding shrub with silvery-green aromatic foliage, dense and very attractively set on fine stems. Vivid orange-red bracted flowers attract honeyeaters, butterflies and native bees. A fast and effective ground cover in small or large gardens. Also great in rockeries or in containers on patio or deck. **CLIMATE:** Temperate. **SOIL:** In loam and sand, moist, well-drained or dry. Not clay.

115 Dianella 'Australiana'

60cm
50cm

Strappy-leaved clumping perennial with bright-green foliage. Tough, drought-tolerant low-maintenance plant for borders, pots or as an accent plant. **CLIMATE:** Cool or temperate. **SOIL:** In loam, clay and sand, moist, well-drained or dry.

116 Dianella caerulea 'Breeze'

70cm
70cm

Strappy-leaved clumping perennial with bright-green foliage. Tough, drought-tolerant low-maintenance plant for borders, pots or as an accent plant. Attractive purple berries in summer. **CLIMATE:** Cool or temperate. **SOIL:** In loam, clay and sand, moist, well-drained or dry.

117 Dianella caerulea 'Cassa Blue'

40cm
40cm

Compact strappy-leaved clumping perennial with attractive blue-grey foliage. Tough, drought-tolerant low-maintenance plant for borders, pots or as an accent plant. Attractive purple berries in summer. **CLIMATE:** Cool or temperate. **SOIL:** In loam, clay and sand, moist, well-drained or dry.

118 Dianella caerulea 'Little Jess'

40cm
40cm

Compact strappy-leaved clumping perennial with green foliage. Tough, drought-tolerant low-maintenance plant for borders, pots or as an accent plant. Attractive purple berries in summer. **CLIMATE:** Cool or temperate. **SOIL:** In loam, clay and sand, moist, well-drained or dry.

Dianella caerulea 'Little Russ'

25-50cm
25-50cm

Compact strappy-leaved clumping perennial with green foliage. Tough, drought-tolerant low-maintenance plant for borders, pots or as an accent plant. Attractive purple berries in summer. **CLIMATE:** Cool or temperate. **SOIL:** In loam, clay and sand, moist, well-drained or dry.

Dianella caerulea 'Paroo Petite'

10-20cm
20-30cm

Compact strappy-leaved clumping perennial with green foliage. Tough, drought-tolerant low-maintenance plant for borders, pots or as an accent plant. Attractive purple berries in summer. **CLIMATE:** Cool or temperate. **SOIL:** In loam, clay and sand, moist, well-drained or dry.

Dianella caerulea 'Stampede'

25cm
40cm

Very compact strappy-leaved clumping perennial with attractive blue-grey foliage. Tough, drought-tolerant low-maintenance plant for borders, pots or as an accent plant. Attractive purple berries in summer. **CLIMATE:** Cool or temperate. **SOIL:** In loam, clay and sand, moist, well-drained or dry.

119 Dianella 'Goddess'

100cm
100cm

Strappy-leaved clumping perennial with dark-green foliage. Tough, drought-tolerant low-maintenance plant for borders, pots or as an accent plant. Attractive purple berries in summer. **CLIMATE:** Cool or temperate. **SOIL:** In loam, clay and sand, moist, well-drained or dry.

120 Dianella 'Kentlyn'

80cm
50cm

Strappy-leaved clumping perennial with bright-green foliage. Tough, drought-tolerant low-maintenance plant for borders, pots or as an accent plant. **CLIMATE:** Cool or temperate. **SOIL:** In loam, clay and sand, moist, well-drained or dry.

Dianella prunina 'Somersby'

40cm
40cm

Strappy-leaved clumping perennial with beautiful blue-grey foliage. Tough, drought-tolerant low-maintenance plant for borders, pots or as an accent plant. Not as tough as other *Dianellas*. **CLIMATE:** Temperate. **SOIL:** In loam and sand, moist, well-drained or dry. Not clay.

Dianella prunina 'Utopia'

50cm | 50cm

Strappy-leaved clumping perennial with beautiful blue-grey foliage. Tough, drought-tolerant low-maintenance plant for borders, pots or as an accent plant. Not as tough as other *Dianellas*. **CLIMATE:** Temperate. **SOIL:** In loam and sand, moist, well-drained or dry. Not clay.

Dianella tasmanica 'Little Devil'

60cm | 60cm

Compact *Dianella* that is distinguished by an attractive red tinge to the base of the leaves. Flowers are not a prominent feature when they appear in spring. Good plant for borders, pots or as an accent plant. Attractive purple berries in summer. **CLIMATE:** Cool or temperate. **SOIL:** In loam and sand, well-drained or dry. Not clay.

121 Dianella revoluta 'Baby Bliss'

25-30cm | 30-40cm

Very compact strappy-leaved clumping perennial with attractive blue-grey foliage. Tough, drought-tolerant low-maintenance plant for borders, pots or as an accent plant. Attractive purple berries in summer. **CLIMATE:** Cool or temperate. **SOIL:** In loam, clay and sand, moist, well-drained or dry.

122 Dianella revoluta 'Little Rev'

30cm | 30cm

Very compact strappy-leaved clumping perennial with attractive blue-grey foliage. Tough, drought-tolerant low-maintenance plant for borders, pots or as an accent plant. Attractive purple berries in summer. **CLIMATE:** Cool or temperate. **SOIL:** In loam, clay and sand, moist, well-drained or dry.

Dianella revoluta 'Petite Marie'

25-30cm | 30-40cm

Very compact strappy-leaved clumping perennial with attractive blue-grey foliage. Tough, drought-tolerant low-maintenance plant for borders, pots or as an accent plant. Attractive purple berries in summer. **CLIMATE:** Cool or temperate. **SOIL:** In loam, clay and sand, moist, well-drained or dry.

123 Dianella 'Silver Streak'

50cm | 40cm

Compact strappy-leaved clumping perennial with attractive green and white variegated foliage. A tough, drought-tolerant low-maintenance plant for borders, pots or as an accent plant. Attractive purple berries in summer. **CLIMATE:** Cool or temperate. **SOIL:** In loam, clay and sand, moist, well-drained or dry.

124 Dianella tasmanica 'Emerald Arch'

40cm | 40cm

Very compact strappy-leaved clumping perennial with attractive arching foliage that is the distinctive feature of this cultivar. Tough drought-tolerant low-maintenance plant for borders, pots or as an accent plant. Blue flowers in spring and purple berries in summer. **CLIMATE:** Cool or temperate. **SOIL:** In loam and sand, moist, well-drained or dry. Not clay.

125 Dianella tasmanica 'Splice'

60cm | 60cm

Compact strappy-leaved clumping perennial with attractive variegated green and white foliage that has an attractive red tinge as the new leaves are forming. As the leaves mature, lime and yellow vertical streaks intensify along the leaf. Tough, low-maintenance plant for borders, pots or as an accent plant. **CLIMATE:** Cool or temperate. **SOIL:** In loam and sand, moist, well-drained or dry. Not clay.

126 Dianella tasmanica 'Tasred'

40cm | 40cm

Very compact strappy-leaved clumping perennial with attractive foliage and stem bases that develop a distinct red colouring during winter. Tough, low-maintenance plant for borders as an accent plant. Blue flowers in spring and purple berries in summer. **CLIMATE:** Cool or temperate. **SOIL:** In loam and sand, moist, well-drained or dry. Not clay.

127 Elaeocarpus reticulatus 'Prima Donna'

8-10m | 3-5m

Wonderful small tree. The pink flowers distinguish this from the normal form of blueberry ash. It has beautiful blue berries through summer. Very adaptable plant that will suit most gardens. **CLIMATE:** Cool, temperate or sub-tropical. **SOIL:** In loam and sand, moist, well-drained or dry. Not clay.

128 Goodenia 'Gold Trail'

10cm | 200cm

Very adaptable ground cover that features interesting divided foliage and massed, showy golden-yellow flowers throughout the warmer months. It tolerates drought conditions and uses include banks, retaining walls, ground covering and container planting for patios and courtyards. **CLIMATE:** Cool, temperate or sub-tropical. **SOIL:** In loam, clay and sand, moist, well-drained or dry.

SpS

129 Goodenia ovata 'Edna Walling Coverup'

10cm | 200cm

Very adaptable ground cover that features lush green, toothed foliage and massed, showy golden-yellow flowers throughout the warmer months. Tolerates drought conditions. Uses include banks, retaining walls, ground covering and container planting for patios and courtyards. **CLIMATE:** Cool, temperate or sub-tropical. **SOIL:** In loam, clay and sand, moist, well-drained or dry.

SpSA

130 *Goodenia ovata* 'Gold Cover'

Very adaptable ground cover that features lush green foliage and massed, showy golden yellow flowers throughout the warmer months. Tolerates drought conditions. Uses include banks, retaining walls, ground covering and container planting for patios and courtyards. **CLIMATE:** Cool, temperate or sub-tropical. **SOIL:** In loam, clay and sand, moist, well-drained or dry.

131 *Goodenia ovata* 'Lightenup'

A small soft bright shrub. Striking variegated foliage creates year-round interest so it may be used as a foliage highlight among darker shrubs; attractive cut foliage for indoor decoration. Will attract fauna, especially butterflies. **CLIMATE:** Cool, temperate or sub-tropical. **SOIL:** In loam, clay and sand, moist, well-drained or dry.

Grevillea 'Abracadabra'

A dense shrub with bunches of red and gold waxy flowers across the canopy through the year. Lovely for screening, bordering pathways or as a colourful specimen. Prune after flowering in late summer if formal shape required. **CLIMATE:** Cool, temperate, sub-tropical or tropical. **SOIL:** In loam, clay and sand, well-drained.

Grevillea 'Apricot Charm'

A very hardy medium-sized dense shrub with glossy green leaves and pendulous apricot-coloured flowers. Great general garden plant or can be clipped into a low-growing hedge. **CLIMATE:** Cool or temperate. **SOIL:** In loam, clay and sand, moist, well-drained or dry.

132 *Grevillea* 'Autumn Waterfall'

A spreading small shrub. Somewhat similar to 'Robyn Gordon' in habit but the subtle bicoloured flower head distinguishes it from most other grevilleas. A great feature shrub or screen plant. **CLIMATE:** Temperate or sub-tropical. **SOIL:** In loam, clay or sand, moist, well-drained or dry.

133 *Grevillea* 'Bedspread'

Fast-growing ground cover ideal for covering large areas such as embankments and driveways. **CLIMATE:** Cool or temperate. **SOIL:** In loam, clay and sand, moist, well-drained or dry.

134 *Grevillea* 'Billy Bonkers'

A fantastic ever-blooming low-growing shrub. A great feature or pot plant. **CLIMATE:** Cool or temperate. **SOIL:** In loam and sand, moist, well-drained or dry. Not clay.

135 *Grevillea* 'Blood Orange'

Fast-growing medium shrub with deeply divided dark green foliage. The intensity of the dark-orange flowers distinguishes this from other large flowering grevilleas. **CLIMATE:** Temperate or sub-tropical. **SOIL:** In loam and sand, moist, well-drained or dry. Not clay.

136 *Grevillea* 'Bon Accord'

A medium grevillea with fine, dark green leaves and relatively large, showy flower heads. A good screen plant or general garden shrub. **CLIMATE:** Cool or temperate. **SOIL:** In loam, clay and sand, moist, well-drained or dry.

137 *Grevillea* 'Bonfire'

A medium grevillea with fine, dark green leaves. A good screen plant or general garden shrub. **CLIMATE:** Cool or temperate. **SOIL:** In loam, clay and sand, moist, well-drained or dry.

138 *Grevillea* 'Bonnie Prince Charlie'

A compact, dwarf shrub with red and yellow bicoloured flowers. Great pot plant for courtyards and patios, and is excellent for massed planting in garden beds or to provide dramatic accent in rockeries. **CLIMATE:** Cool or temperate. **SOIL:** In loam and sand, moist, well-drained or dry. Not clay.

Grevillea 'Boongala Spinebill'

A spreading medium-sized shrub with attractive toothed foliage that has a red tinge when new. Red, toothbrush-like flowers. A great feature shrub or screen plant. **CLIMATE:** Temperate or sub-tropical. **SOIL:** In loam, clay and sand, moist, well-drained or dry.

130 131 132 134 133 137 135 136 138

139 *Grevillea* 'Border Red'

100cm
200cm

A low-spreading shrub, which flowers for most of the year. Great as a feature plant for rockeries and shrubberies as well as pots. **CLIMATE:** Cool or temperate. **SOIL:** In loam, clay and sand, moist, well-drained or dry.

140 *Grevillea* 'Bronze Rambler'

40-65cm
300-500cm

A spreading ground cover with bronze-red deeply divided foliage. Nectar-rich toothbrush flowers of deep purple-red appear throughout the year. Good for banks and as a ground cover in large gardens. Also makes a great weeping standard. **CLIMATE:** Cool, temperate or sub-tropical. **SOIL:** In loam, clay and sand, moist, well-drained or dry.

141 *Grevillea* 'Bulli Beauty'

300-500cm
200-400cm

A fast-growing medium shrub with deeply divided dark-green foliage. Exceptionally long soft pink flower heads distinguish this cultivar from other large-flowered grevilleas. A good feature or screening plant. **CLIMATE:** Temperate, sub-tropical or tropical. **SOIL:** In loam and sand, moist, well-drained or dry. Not clay.

142 *Grevillea* 'Bush Lemons'

300cm
300cm

A fast-growing medium shrub with deeply divided dark green foliage. One of the few large yellow-flowered grevilleas on the market. Makes a great feature or screen plant. **CLIMATE:** Temperate or sub-tropical. **SOIL:** In loam and sand, moist, well-drained or dry. Not clay.

Grevillea 'Butterscotch'

300cm
300cm

A fast-growing medium shrub with deeply divided dark green foliage. A very unusual dark orange-bronze flower colour distinguishes this little-known cultivar. Makes a great feature or screen plant. **CLIMATE:** Temperate or sub-tropical. **SOIL:** In loam and sand, moist, well-drained or dry. Not clay.

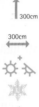

143 *Grevillea* 'Canterbury Gold'

100-150cm
200-300cm

A dense, low-spreading shrub with soft grey-green leaves, and bunches of gold flowers most of the year. Use in mass plantings to define paths or driveways, and among dark shrubs, where its soft grey-green foliage has a lightening effect. An outstanding bird attracter. Frequently used for low ground cover or low to medium hedging. **CLIMATE:** Cool or temperate. **SOIL:** In loam and sand, moist, well-drained or dry. Not clay.

144 *Grevillea* 'Carpet Crawl'

40-65cm
200-300cm

A spreading ground cover with bronze-red deeply divided foliage. Nectar-rich toothbrush flowers of deep purple-red with pink styles appear throughout the year. The combination of foliage and flower provide safe habitat and feeding for wrens, honeyeaters and other small birds. Good for banks and as a ground cover in large gardens. Also makes a great weeping standard. **CLIMATE:** Cool, temperate, sub-tropical. **SOIL:** In loam, sand and clay, moist, well-drained or dry.

145 *Grevillea* 'Carpet Layer'

10cm
300-800cm

A spreading dense ground cover with attractive toothed leaves. Pink toothbrush-like flowers. Fantastic for banks and as a ground cover in large gardens. Also makes a great weeping standard. **CLIMATE:** Cool, temperate, sub-tropical. **SOIL:** In loam, sand and clay, moist, well-drained or dry.

Grevillea 'Cherry Pie'

150-180cm
180cm

A dense shrub with finely divided foliage and large bunches of waxy red-pink flowers. A spectacular specimen or background plant. Prune to shape if required. **CLIMATE:** Cool, temperate, sub-tropical or tropical. **SOIL:** In loam, clay and sand, well-drained.

Grevillea 'Coastal Dawn'

300-400cm
200-300cm

A fast-growing medium shrub with deeply divided dark-green foliage. The intensity of the dark-pink flowers is the unique feature of this cultivar. A good feature or screening plant. **CLIMATE:** Temperate or sub-tropical. **SOIL:** In loam and sand, moist, well-drained or dry. Not clay.

Grevillea 'Coastal Sunset'

300-400cm
200-300cm

A fast-growing medium shrub with deeply divided dark-green foliage. The intensity of the bright-orange flowers is the unique feature of this cultivar. A good feature or screening plant. **CLIMATE:** Temperate or sub-tropical. **SOIL:** In loam and sand, moist, well-drained or dry. Not clay.

Grevillea 'Coastal Twilight'

300-400cm
200-300cm

A fast-growing medium shrub with deeply divided dark-green foliage. The intensity of the dark-orange flowers is the unique feature of this cultivar. A good feature or screening plant. **CLIMATE:** Temperate or sub-tropical. **SOIL:** In loam and sand, moist, well-drained or dry. Not clay.

Grevillea 'Coconut Ice'

150-200cm
200cm

A spreading medium-sized shrub. Very similar to 'Robyn Gordon' but has red-pink flowers rather than pure red. A great feature shrub or screen plant. **CLIMATE**: Temperate or sub-tropical. **SOIL**: In loam, clay and sand, moist, well-drained or dry.

146 Grevillea 'Cooroora Cascade'

40cm
300cm

A low-growing shrub with cascading branches that feature masses of stunning flower heads 20–25cm long and attractive grey-green fern-like foliage. A great feature or pot plant. **CLIMATE**: Temperate or sub-tropical. **SOIL**: In loam and sand, moist, well-drained or dry. Not clay.

147 Grevillea 'Copper Crest'

10cm
200-300cm

A prostrate dense ground cover with copper-coloured divided foliage and bronze new growth. Pink toothbrush-like flowers. Fantastic for banks and as a ground cover in large gardens. Also makes a great weeping standard. **CLIMATE**: Cool, temperate or sub-tropical. **SOIL**: In loam, clay and sand, moist, well-drained or dry.

Grevillea 'Coral Baby'

30-40cm
50-80cm

A dense shapely mounding shrub with massed soft pink and cream flowers covering the foliage. Use in the rockery, container or mass planted along pathways. Trim lightly after flowering. **CLIMATE**: Cool, temperate or sub-tropical. **SOIL**: In loam and sand, moist, well-drained or dry. Not clay.

148 Grevillea 'Droopy Drawers'

30cm
100-150cm

A stunning low-growing shrub with cascading branches that feature masses of long pink flower heads. **CLIMATE**: Temperate or sub-tropical. **SOIL**: In loam and sand, moist, well-drained or dry. Not clay.

149 Grevillea 'Edna Walling Softly Softly'

30-40cm
35-55cm

A compact little shrub with soft grey-green foliage and showy bunches of pink and cream flowers. Great as a feature plant for rockeries and shrubberies as well as for pots. **CLIMATE**: Cool or temperate. **SOIL**: In loam, clay and sand, moist, well-drained or dry.

150 Grevillea 'Ember Glow'

100cm
200cm

A low-spreading shrub, which flowers for most of the year. Great as a feature plant for rockeries and shrubberies as well as pots. **CLIMATE**: Cool or temperate. **SOIL**: In loam, clay and sand, moist, well-drained or dry.

151 Grevillea 'Fanfare'

10cm
200-300cm

A prostrate dense ground cover with attractive toothed leaves. Delicate red-pink toothbrush-like flowers. Fantastic for banks and as a ground cover in large gardens. Also makes a great weeping standard. **CLIMATE**: Cool or temperate. **SOIL**: In loam and sand, moist, well-drained or dry. Not clay.

Grevillea 'Firesprite'

250-300cm
400-500cm

A fast-growing medium shrub with deeply divided dark-green foliage. Ball-shaped bright red flower heads are the distinctive feature of this beautiful cultivar. A great feature or screening plant. **CLIMATE**: Temperate or sub-tropical. **SOIL**: In loam and sand, moist, well-drained or dry. Not clay.

152 Grevillea 'Fireworks'

100cm
100cm

A small shrub, with bright red and yellow flowers and soft blue-green foliage. Flowers occur on the ends of short branches, making this a great feature or pot plant. **CLIMATE**: Cool or temperate. **SOIL**: In loam and sand, moist, well-drained or dry. Not clay.

153 Grevillea 'Flamingo'

300-400cm
200-300cm

A fast-growing medium shrub with deeply divided dark-green foliage. The profusion of flowers makes this an outstanding feature or screening plant. **CLIMATE**: Temperate or sub-tropical. **SOIL**: In loam and sand, moist, well-drained or dry. Not clay.

154 Grevillea 'Golden Lyre'

150cm
300-500cm

A stunning low-growing shrub with cascading branches that feature masses of flower heads 20–25cm long as well as beautiful grey-green divided foliage. One of the showiest native plants I have ever seen when in full flower. **CLIMATE**: Temperate or sub-tropical. **SOIL**: In loam and sand, moist, well-drained or dry. Not clay.

Grevillea 'Golden Yul-lo'

300cm / 200cm

A fast-growing medium shrub with deeply divided dark-green foliage. One of the few large yellow-flowered grevilleas on the market. **CLIMATE**: Temperate or sub-tropical. **SOIL**: In loam and sand, moist, well-drained or dry. Not clay.

WSp

155 Grevillea 'Goldfever'

30cm / 150cm

A low spreading shrub, which flowers for most of the year. Great as a feature ground-cover plant for rockeries and shrubberies as well as for pots. **CLIMATE**: Cool or temperate. **SOIL**: In loam, clay and sand, moist, well-drained or dry.

All year

156 Grevillea 'Honey Gem'

300-400cm / 200-300cm

A fast-growing medium shrub with deeply divided dark-green foliage. An old favourite cultivar, the first orange large-flowered grevillea. A good feature or screening plant. **CLIMATE**: Temperate, sub-tropical or tropical. **SOIL**: In loam and sand, moist, well-drained or dry. Not clay.

Grevillea 'Honey Wonder'

300-400cm / 150-200cm

A fast-growing medium shrub with deeply divided green and white variegated foliage. A good feature or screening plant. **CLIMATE**: Temperate, sub-tropical or tropical. **SOIL**: In loam and sand, moist, well-drained or dry. Not clay.

WSp

Grevillea 'Ivanhoe'

200-500cm / 300-500cm

A spreading medium shrub with very attractive toothed leaves and red toothbrush-like flowers. Good general garden shrub for larger areas or as a screen plant that is regularly pruned. Makes good cut foliage. **CLIMATE**: Cool, temperate or sub-tropical. **SOIL**: In loam, clay and sand, moist, well-drained or dry.

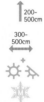

157 Grevillea 'Ivory Whip'

200cm / 200cm

A medium-sized spreading shrub that flowers for most of the year. The white flower colour on a spreading shrub distinguishes this cultivar from other large-flowered grevilleas. Great as a feature ground-cover plant for rockeries and shrubberies; also for pots. **CLIMATE**: Temperate or sub-tropical. **SOIL**: In loam and sand, moist, well-drained or dry. Not clay.

All year

Grevillea 'Jelly Baby'

30-40cm / 80cm-1m

A dense low mounding ground cover with massed jelly-pink flowers covering the soft grey foliage. Use in rockery, mass planted along pathways, in containers, or as a contrast with dark foliage. Trim lightly after flowering. **CLIMATE**: Cool, temperate or sub-tropical. **SOIL**: In loam and sand, moist, well-drained or dry. Not clay.

WSp

158 Grevillea 'Jester'

200-250cm / 300-400cm

A moderately dense spreading shrub. The fern-like leaves are green above and much paler below. Great as a feature ground-cover plant for rockeries and shrubberies. **CLIMATE**: Temperate or sub-tropical. **SOIL**: In loam and sand, moist, well-drained or dry. Not clay.

159 Grevillea 'Jubilee'

80-100cm / 80-100cm

A compact upright fine-foliaged shrub with bunches of waxy golden-red flowers. Ideal for low, neat hedging in narrow areas, or attractive as massed plantings in broader landscapes. Stunning as a patio plant in a decorative large container, and a posy of small sprigs will last well in water. **CLIMATE**: Cool or temperate. **SOIL**: In loam and sand, moist, well-drained or dry. Not clay.

WSp

160 Grevillea 'Lady O'

100-150cm / 200cm

A medium-sized spreading shrub, which flowers for most of the year. Great as a feature ground-cover plant for rockeries and shrubberies as well as for pots. **CLIMATE**: Cool or temperate. **SOIL**: In loam and sand, moist, well-drained or dry. Not clay.

161 Grevillea 'Lana Maree'

150cm / 200cm

A medium-sized spreading shrub, with bright-pink metallic flowers for most of the year. Great as a feature ground-cover plant for rockeries and shrubberies as well as for pots. **CLIMATE**: Temperate or sub-tropical. **SOIL**: In loam and sand, moist, well-drained or dry. Not clay.

All year

162 Grevillea 'Lemon Daze'

100-150cm / 100cm

A low spreading shrub, which flowers for most of the year. Great as a feature ground-cover plant for rockeries and shrubberies as well as for pots. **CLIMATE**: Cool or temperate. **SOIL**: In loam, clay and sand, moist, well-drained or dry.

163 Grevillea 'Lime Spider'

A fast-growing medium shrub with deeply divided dark-green and white variegated foliage. The variegated leaf makes this a good contrast plant that has year-round interest. A good feature or screening plant. **CLIMATE:** Temperate, sub-tropical or tropical. **SOIL:** In loam and sand, moist, well-drained or dry. Not clay.

164 Grevillea 'Lollypops!'

A medium-sized spreading shrub, with raspberry-coloured flowers for most of the year. Great as a feature ground-cover plant for rockeries and shrubberies as well as for pots. **CLIMATE:** Temperate or sub-tropical. **SOIL:** In loam and sand, moist, well-drained or dry. Not clay.

Grevillea 'Long John' synonym 'Elegance'

A fast-growing medium shrub with deeply divided dark-green foliage. Ball-shaped bright-red flower heads are the distinctive feature of this beautiful cultivar. A great feature or screening plant. **CLIMATE:** Temperate or sub-tropical. **SOIL:** In loam and sand, moist, well-drained or dry. Not clay.

165 Grevillea 'Loopy Lou'

A small spreading shrub, with amazing multi-coloured flowers for most of the year. Great as a feature ground-cover plant for rockeries and shrubberies as well as for pots. **CLIMATE:** Temperate or sub-tropical. **SOIL:** In loam and sand, moist, well-drained or dry. Not clay.

166 Grevillea 'Majestic'

A fast-growing medium shrub with deeply divided dark-green foliage. The large flower heads have a good colour contrast of pink and white. A good feature or screening plant. **CLIMATE:** Temperate, sub-tropical or tropical. **SOIL:** In loam and sand, moist, well-drained or dry. Not clay.

Grevillea 'Metallica Supanova'

Striking marked silver-grey foliage and a profusion of vivid orange-red flowers. Use as a highlight shrub among mixed plantings; contrast against dark foliage, a stunning silver hedge or as a standard in a formal setting. Prune lightly after flowering. **CLIMATE:** Temperate or sub-tropical. **SOIL:** In loam, clay and sand, well-drained.

167 Grevillea 'Miami Pink'

A fast-growing medium shrub with deeply divided dark-green foliage. Beautiful soft pink flower. A good feature or screening plant. **CLIMATE:** Temperate, sub-tropical or tropical. **SOIL:** In loam and sand, moist, well-drained or dry. Not clay.

168 Grevillea 'Misty Pink'

A fast-growing medium shrub with deeply divided dark-green foliage. One of the original and best large-flowered grevilleas. A good feature or screening plant. **CLIMATE:** Temperate, sub-tropical or tropical. **SOIL:** In loam and sand, moist, well-drained or dry. Not clay.

Grevillea 'Molly'

A spreading medium-sized shrub. Very similar to 'Robyn Gordon', but has greyish foliage with broader lobes. A great feature shrub or screen plant. **CLIMATE:** Temperate or sub-tropical. **SOIL:** In loam, clay and sand, moist, well-drained or dry.

Grevillea 'Moonlight'

A fast-growing medium shrub with deeply divided dark-green foliage. One of the original and best large-flowered grevilleas. A good feature or screening plant. **CLIMATE:** Temperate, sub-tropical or tropical. **SOIL:** In loam and sand, moist, well-drained or dry. Not clay.

169 Grevillea 'Ned Kelly' ('Mason's Hybrid')

A spreading medium-sized shrub. Very similar to 'Robyn Gordon' but has greyish foliage and apricot-orange flowers. A great feature shrub or screen plant. **CLIMATE:** Temperate or sub-tropical. **SOIL:** In loam, clay and sand, moist, well-drained or dry.

170 Grevillea 'New Blood'

A low spreading shrub, which flowers for most of the year. Great as a feature ground-cover plant for rockeries and shrubberies as well as for pots. **CLIMATE:** Cool or temperate. **SOIL:** In loam, clay and sand, moist, well-drained or dry.

171 Grevillea 'Orange Box'

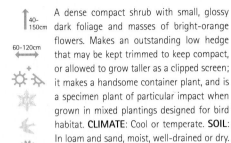

A dense compact shrub with small, glossy dark foliage and masses of bright-orange flowers. Makes an outstanding low hedge that may be kept trimmed to keep compact, or allowed to grow taller as a clipped screen; it makes a handsome container plant, and is a specimen plant of particular impact when grown in mixed plantings designed for bird habitat. **CLIMATE**: Cool or temperate. **SOIL**: In loam and sand, moist, well-drained or dry. Not clay.

172 Grevillea 'Old Gold'

A low mounding dense shrub with golden-green foliage highlighted by golden new growth. Either in bud or displaying a profusion of coral pink–orange flowers throughout the year. Great for banks or bare areas—plant at 75cm centres; may also be planted as a hardy, long-flowering container plant in hot, dry regions. **CLIMATE**: Cool or temperate. **SOIL**: In loam and sand, moist, well-drained or dry. Not clay.

173 Grevillea 'Orange Marmalade'

Vigorous medium-sized spreading shrub with long entire leaves. Unusual erect clusters of orange flowers with brown styles during most of the year. An excellent screen plant. **CLIMATE**: Temperate or sub-tropical. **SOIL**: In loam and sand, moist, well-drained or dry. Not clay.

174 Grevillea 'Peaches and Cream'

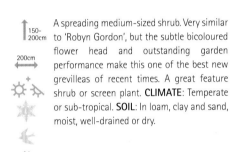

A spreading medium-sized shrub. Very similar to 'Robyn Gordon', but the subtle bicoloured flower head and outstanding garden performance make this one of the best new grevilleas of recent times. A great feature shrub or screen plant. **CLIMATE**: Temperate or sub-tropical. **SOIL**: In loam, clay and sand, moist, well-drained or dry.

Grevillea 'Pick o' the Crop'

A low, arching intricately foliaged ground cover or screen for retaining walls. Large flower bunches constantly attract honeyeaters. Low-maintenance container plant, pathways or rockeries. Prune lightly after flowering. **CLIMATE**: Cool, temperate or sub-tropical. **SOIL**: In loam and sand, moist, well-drained or dry. Not clay.

175 Grevillea 'Pink Candelabra'

An interesting new plant habit for a large-flowered grevillea. This cultivar is a narrow, pencil-shaped shrub with pinkish-red flowers. A useful screen or feature plant for narrow areas such as driveways or general garden beds. **CLIMATE**: Temperate or sub-tropical. **SOIL**: In loam and sand, moist, well-drained or dry. Not clay.

176 Grevillea 'Pink Midget'

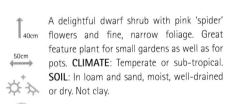

A delightful dwarf shrub with pink 'spider' flowers and fine, narrow foliage. Great feature plant for small gardens as well as for pots. **CLIMATE**: Temperate or sub-tropical. **SOIL**: In loam and sand, moist, well-drained or dry. Not clay.

Grevillea 'Pink Parfait'

A fast-growing medium shrub with deeply divided dark-green foliage. Beautiful rosy-pink flower. A good feature or screen plant. **CLIMATE**: Temperate, sub-tropical or tropical. **SOIL**: In loam and sand, moist, well-drained or dry. Not clay.

177 Grevillea 'Poorinda Blondie'

A spreading medium shrub with very attractive toothed leaves and yellow toothbrush-like flowers. Good general garden shrub for larger areas or as a screen plant that is regularly pruned. Makes good cut foliage. **CLIMATE**: Cool, temperate or sub-tropical. **SOIL**: In loam, clay and sand, moist, well-drained or dry.

178 Grevillea 'Poorinda Constance'

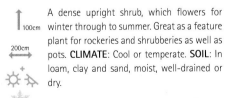

A dense upright shrub, which flowers for winter through to summer. Great as a feature plant for rockeries and shrubberies as well as pots. **CLIMATE**: Cool or temperate. **SOIL**: In loam, clay and sand, moist, well-drained or dry.

179 Grevillea 'Poorinda Peter'

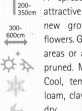

A spreading medium shrub with very attractive dark-green toothed leaves, bronze new growth and purple toothbrush-like flowers. Good general garden shrub for larger areas or as a screen plant that is regularly pruned. Makes good cut foliage. **CLIMATE**: Cool, temperate or sub-tropical. **SOIL**: In loam, clay and sand, moist, well-drained or dry.

Grevillea 'Poorinda Queen'

A dense medium-sized shrub with attractive dark-green foliage. Good general garden shrub or screen plant. **CLIMATE**: Cool or temperate. **SOIL**: In loam and sand, moist, well-drained or dry. Not clay.

180 *Grevillea* 'Poorinda Royal Mantle'

10cm
300-800cm

A prostrate dense ground cover with attractive toothed leaves. One of the original grevillea cultivars, and one of the best ever released. Fantastic for banks and as a ground cover in large gardens. Also makes a great weeping standard. **CLIMATE**: Cool, temperate or sub-tropical. **SOIL**: In loam, clay and sand, moist, well-drained or dry.

Grevillea 'Pretty Polly'

120-150cm
150-180cm

A medium shrub with a soft, semi-weeping habit and light-green foliage. Excellent for low hedges; plant as specimen or in groups for outstanding bird habitat. **CLIMATE**: Cool or temperate. **SOIL**: In loam and sand, moist, well-drained or dry. Not clay.

Grevillea 'Quick Silver'

20-30cm
40-70cm

A dwarf lightly suckering plant, with fine silver-grey foliage. Good border plant, or can be used as a lightly suckering undershrub. It performs beautifully as a soft dense cascading specimen in a container for patio or balcony, and honeyeaters will readily find its flowers in such situations. **CLIMATE**: Cool or temperate. **SOIL**: In loam and sand, moist, well-drained or dry. Not clay.

181 *Grevillea* 'Raptor'

30cm
150cm

A fast-growing hardy ground cover. The toothbrush-like flowers complement the new growth, which is also a deep red colour. During cold winters plants develop a bronzed appearance. Ideal for covering large areas such as embankments and driveways. **CLIMATE**: Cool or temperate. **SOIL**: In loam, clay and sand, moist, well-drained or dry.

Grevillea 'Robyn Gordon'

150-200cm
200cm

A spreading medium-sized shrub. One of the most successful Australian plants of all times—enough said. A great feature shrub or screen plant. **CLIMATE**: Temperate or sub-tropical. **SOIL**: In loam, clay and sand, moist, well-drained or dry.

Grevillea rosmarinifolia 'Scarlet Sprite'

100cm
100cm

A small shrub with needle-like foliage. A very adaptable cultivar, good for hedging or shrubberies. **CLIMATE**: Cool or temperate. **SOIL**: In loam and sand, moist, well-drained or dry. Not clay.

182 *Grevillea* 'Rosy Posy'

100-120cm
100-120cm

A small compact shrub with dense needle foliage that provides safe nesting habitat for small birds such as Scrub Wrens. Good as a feature shrub, or plant at 1.5m centres and trim as a flowering hedge. **CLIMATE**: Cool or temperate. **SOIL**: In loam and sand, moist, well-drained or dry. Not clay.

183 *Grevillea* 'Rosy's Baby'

80-100cm
60-80cm

A small shrub with an upright to lightly spreading habit; soft grey-green leaves with striking bronze new growth. Use to create a charming hedge or as a border plant, or grow among other bird habitat plantings. Especially stunning when grown in a tub and placed on a deck, patio or in a courtyard, so the visiting honeyeaters can be seen up close and personal. **CLIMATE**: Cool or temperate. **SOIL**: In loam and sand, moist, well-drained or dry. Not clay.

Grevillea 'Sandra Gordon'

300-800cm
200-500cm

A fast-growing large shrub/small tree with deeply divided dark-green foliage. Beautiful yellow flower. A good feature or screening plant, but needs to be pruned annually to keep a reasonably compact shape. **CLIMATE**: Temperate, sub-tropical or tropical. **SOIL**: In loam and sand, moist, well-drained or dry. Not clay.

184 *Grevillea* 'Silvereye Cream'

150-200cm
100-150cm

A fast-growing small shrub with deeply divided dark-green foliage. A good feature or screening plant. **CLIMATE**: Temperate, sub-tropical or tropical. **SOIL**: In loam and sand, moist, well-drained or dry. Not clay.

Grevillea 'Soft Touch'

40-60cm
100-150cm

A soft, densely silver-grey mounding plant with finely divided leaves and bunches of bright waxy red flowers. **CLIMATE**: Cool, temperate or sub-tropical. **SOIL**: In loam, clay and sand, well-drained.

185 *Grevillea* 'Soopa Doopa'

150-200cm
200cm

A spreading medium-sized shrub. Somewhat similar to 'Robyn Gordon' but with much larger bright pink-orange flower heads. A great feature shrub or screen plant. **CLIMATE**: Temperate and sub-tropical. **SOIL**: In loam, clay and sand, moist, well-drained or dry.

180 181

182 183

184 185

Grevillea 'Strawberry Blonde'

A spreading medium shrub with very attractive toothed leaves and large yellow toothbrush-like flowers. Good general garden shrub for larger areas, or as a screen plant that is regularly pruned. Makes good cut foliage. **CLIMATE:** Cool, temperate or sub-tropical. **SOIL:** In loam, clay and sand, moist, well-drained or dry.

200-300cm
300-400cm

Grevillea 'Strawberry Topping'

Upright spreading shrub with soft divided foliage with large white heads of white flowers. Mature flowers are bright strawberry pink providing a beautiful two-toned effect. **CLIMATE:** Cool, temperate or sub-tropical. **SOIL:** In loam, clay and sand, well-drained.

50-100cm
100-150cm

Grevillea 'Sunset Bronze'

A fast-growing medium shrub with deeply divided dark-green foliage. The unusual bronze-orange flowers distinguish this from other large flowering grevilleas. **CLIMATE:** Temperate or sub-tropical. **SOIL:** In loam and sand, moist, well-drained or dry. Not clay.

300cm
200cm

Grevillea 'Superb'

A spreading medium-sized shrub. Very similar to 'Robyn Gordon' but more vigorous and has a bright red-orange flower. A great feature shrub or screen plant. **CLIMATE:** Temperate or subtropical. **SOIL:** In loam, clay and sand, moist, well-drained or dry.

150-200cm
200cm

186 Grevillea 'Sylvia'

A fast-growing medium shrub with deeply divided dark-green foliage. Beautiful rosy-pink flower. A good feature or screening plant. **CLIMATE:** Temperate, sub-tropical or tropical. **SOIL:** In loam and sand, moist, well-drained or dry. Not clay.

300-500cm
200-400cm

187 Grevillea 'Tangerine'

A low-spreading dense shrub with attractive small dark-green leaves. Good as a spreading feature shrub to attract birds. **CLIMATE:** Cool or temperate. **SOIL:** In loam and sand, moist, well-drained or dry. Not clay.

30-60cm
100-150cm

188 Grevillea 'Tucker Time Cherry Ripe'

An upright compact small shrub with soft grey-green leaves. An ideal plant for small gardens, mixed with other small shrubs, or mass planted for special bird attraction. Eye-catching when repeat planted in containers for deck or patio. **CLIMATE:** Cool or temperate. **SOIL:** In loam and sand, moist, well-drained or dry. Not clay.

30-50cm
40-50cm

189 Grevillea 'Tucker Time Entree'

A compact, free-flowering small shrub with soft narrow foliage and delicate tricoloured flowers. A great source of nectar for honey-eating birds during colder months. A versatile, colourful low shrub for garden beds, or a long-flowering container plant for deck, patio or balcony. **CLIMATE:** Cool or temperate. **SOIL:** In loam and sand, moist, well-drained or dry. Not clay.

35-50cm
30-40cm

Grevillea 'Tucker Time New Day'

An upright compact small shrub with narrow erect leaves of mid green, with silvery overtones especially noticeable in bright light. An ideal plant for small gardens, mixed with other small shrubs, or mass planted for special bird attraction. Eye-catching when repeat planted in containers for deck or patio. **CLIMATE:** Cool or temperate. **SOIL:** In loam and sand, moist, well-drained or dry. Not clay.

40-60cm
30-45cm

Grevillea 'Tucker Time Winter Feast'

A gently arching or ground-covering plant with neat bluish-green foliage and soft-pink new growth. A versatile, long-flowering low shrub or ground cover in open garden beds, on slopes and banks. **CLIMATE:** Cool or temperate. **SOIL:** In loam and sand, moist, well-drained or dry. Not clay.

50-100cm
120-200cm

190 Grevillea 'Wakiti Sunrise'

A small spreading shrub with greyish foliage and soft-orange flowers. A good plant for small gardens, mixed with other small shrubs, or mass planted for bird attraction. **CLIMATE:** Cool or temperate. **SOIL:** In loam and sand, moist, well-drained or dry. Not clay.

60-150cm
100-250cm

191 Grevillea 'Wattlebird Yellow'

A fast-growing small shrub with deeply divided dark-green foliage. A good feature or screening plant. **CLIMATE:** Temperate, sub-tropical or tropical. **SOIL:** In loam and sand, moist, well-drained or dry. Not clay.

150-200cm
100-150cm

192 Grevillea 'White Candelabra'

↑ 300cm
↔ 100cm

An interesting new plant habit for a large-flowered grevillea. This cultivar is a narrow, pencil-shaped shrub with white flowers. A useful screen or feature plant for narrow areas such as driveways or general garden beds. **CLIMATE:** Temperate or sub-tropical. **SOIL:** In loam and sand, moist, well-drained or dry. Not clay.

Grevillea 'Woolly Bear Hero'

↑ 10–30cm
↔ 150cm

A dense mounding shrub with arching branchlets bedecked with shell pink and white flowers. Massed bud set provides added attraction. An outstanding living mulch, path edging or rockery plant. Easily maintained in containers. Royalties directed to Free The Bears Fund Inc. **CLIMATE:** Cool, temperate or sub-tropical. **SOIL:** In loam, clay and sand, well-drained.

Grevillea 'Woolly Bear Mian'

↑ 100–150cm
↔ 100–150cm

Soft, dense shrub with purple-blushed new leaf growth and large clusters of burnt-orange woolly flowers which remain in bud for many months. Outstanding specimen shrub, strong hedge when clipped into shape, or hardy container plant. **CLIMATE:** Cool, temperate or sub-tropical. **SOIL:** In loam, clay and sand, well-drained.

193 Hakea 'Burrendong Beauty'

↑ 50–80cm
↔ 150cm

A low-spreading shrub that is absolutely spectacular when in flower. Great feature plant in a shrubbery or pot. **CLIMATE:** Cool or temperate. **SOIL:** In loam and sand, moist, well-drained or dry. Not clay.

194 Hakea laurina 'Mini Pini'

↑ 50cm
↔ 50cm

A dwarf selection of the pincushion hakea with beautiful spherical flower heads. Great feature or pot plant. **CLIMATE:** Temperate. **SOIL:** In loam and sand, moist, well-drained or dry. Not clay.

195 Hakea 'Pink Lace'

↑ 180–220cm
↔ 150–200cm

A medium-sized shrub with a graceful weeping habit and sweetly perfumed multi-hued pink flowers. It provides a perfect habitat for many small native birds, including honeyeaters, wrens and thornbills. **CLIMATE:** Cool, temperate or sub-tropical. **SOIL:** In loam and sand, moist, well-drained or dry. Not clay.

196 Hardenbergia 'Bliss'

↑ 70cm
↔ 40cm

A self-supporting small shrub with dark-green foliage and unusual lilac colour for a hardenbergia. Mass plant in your garden to create a feature or low hedge. Suitable also as a pot specimen. **CLIMATE:** Cool, temperate or sub-tropical. **SOIL:** In loam, clay and sand, moist, well-drained or dry.

Hardenbergia 'Bushy Blue'

↑ 60cm
↔ 60cm

A shrubby form of what is normally a climbing species. The plant may be hedged or shaped as required. It has interesting blue-grey leaves that create year round interest in the garden. Mass plant to create a feature or low hedge. Also suitable as a pot specimen. **CLIMATE:** Cool, temperate or sub-tropical. **SOIL:** In loam, clay and sand, moist, well-drained or dry.

197 Hardenbergia 'Edna Walling Wild Wisteria'

↑ 10cm or climber
↔ 100–200cm

A vigorous climbing form of this wonderful pioneer plant with large dark-green leaves. This plant makes a great ground cover but will also climb when given something to support it. **CLIMATE:** Cool, temperate or sub-tropical. **SOIL:** In loam, clay and sand, moist, well-drained or dry.

198 Hardenbergia 'Edna Walling Snow White'

↑ 10cm or climber
↔ 100–200cm

A vigorous climbing form of this wonderful pioneer plant with light-green leaves. This plant makes a great ground cover but will also climb when given something to support it. **CLIMATE:** Cool, temperate or sub-tropical. **SOIL:** In loam, clay and sand, moist, well-drained or dry.

199 Hardenbergia 'Free'n'Easy'

↑ 10cm or climber
↔ 100–200cm

A vigorous climbing form of this wonderful pioneer plant with light-green leaves. The very subtle mauve flowers are sensational. This plant makes a great ground cover but will also climb when given something to support it. **CLIMATE:** Cool, temperate or sub-tropical. **SOIL:** In loam, clay and sand, moist, well-drained or dry.

Hardenbergia 'Happy Wanderer'

↑ 10cm or climber
↔ 100–200cm

A vigorous climbing form of this wonderful pioneer plant with dark-green leaves. This plant makes a great ground cover but will also climb when given something to support it. **CLIMATE:** Cool, temperate or sub-tropical. **SOIL:** In loam, clay and sand, moist, well-drained or dry.

Hardenbergia 'Mini Ha Ha'

15-30cm / 100cm

A shrubby form of what is normally a climbing species with smaller leaves than other hardenbergia cultivars. The plant may be hedged or shaped as required. Mass plant in your garden to create a feature or low hedge. Also suitable as a pot specimen. **CLIMATE:** Cool, temperate or sub-tropical. **SOIL:** In loam, clay and sand, moist, well-drained or dry.

200 Hardenbergia 'Pink Spray'

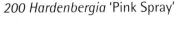

50-80cm / 100cm

A shrubby form of what is normally a climbing species with smaller leaves than other hardenbergia cultivars. The plant may be hedged or shaped as required. Mass plant in your garden to create a feature or low hedge. Also suitable as a pot specimen. **CLIMATE:** Cool, temperate or sub-tropical. **SOIL:** In loam, clay and sand, moist, well-drained or dry.

201 Hardenbergia 'Purple Spray'

80-100cm / 100cm

A self supporting small shrub with dark-green foliage. Mass plant in your garden to create a feature or low hedge. Also suitable as a pot specimen. **CLIMATE:** Cool, temperate or sub-tropical. **SOIL:** In loam, clay and sand, moist, well-drained or dry.

202 Hardenbergia violacea 'Regent'

100cm / 75cm

A hardy, upright shrub with large leathery leaves that stand out from the stems. A great pioneer plant for the new garden. Mass plant in your garden to create a feature or low hedge. Also suitable as a pot specimen. **CLIMATE:** Cool, temperate or sub-tropical. **SOIL:** In loam, clay and sand, moist, well-drained or dry.

203 Hardenbergia 'Sweet Heart'

10cm or climber / 250cm

A vigorous climber with attractive heart-shaped leaves that are useful for cut foliage in floral arrangements. Ideal to provide a quick screen covering fences or pergolas. Planted in open areas, it forms a dense ground cover. Can be grown spilling down banks or over walls. **CLIMATE:** Cool, temperate or sub-tropical. **SOIL:** In loam, clay and sand, moist, well-drained or dry.

Hardenbergia 'White Out'

10cm or climber / 250cm

A vigorous climbing form of this wonderful pioneer plant with dark-green leaves that contrast beautifully with the snow-white flowers. This plant makes a great ground cover but will also climb when given something to support it. **CLIMATE:** Cool, temperate or sub-tropical. **SOIL:** In loam, clay and sand, moist, well-drained or dry.

204 Hibbertia 'Sun Drops'

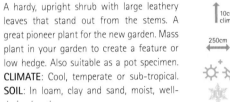

15-20cm / 40-50cm

A tiny compact shrub with neat dark foliage and bright-yellow guinea flowers in spring-early summer, pollinated by insects. Plant as edging for pathways or paving; dotted among other dainty-foliaged plants in rocky outcrops and raised beds; as a dainty container plant for small gardens, patios or balconies. **CLIMATE:** Cool, temperate or sub-tropical. **SOIL:** In loam and sand, moist, well-drained or dry. Not clay.

205 Hibbertia 'Sunny Daze'

15-20cm / 40-50cm

A compact ground cover with dark foliage and bright-yellow guinea flowers in spring-early summer, pollinated by insects. Good for rockeries and container plantings. **CLIMATE:** Cool or temperate. **SOIL:** In loam and sand, moist, well-drained or dry. Not clay.

206 Hibiscus geranioides 'La Belle'

50-80cm / 60-70cm

A small free-flowering shrub with interesting divided foliage; profuse pink flowers are much visited by butterflies. Plant *en masse* for a showy display in open landscapes, or as a long flowering container plant for deck, patio or balcony; may also be regularly pruned for an unusual and attractive low hedge. **CLIMATE:** Temperate, sub-tropical or tropical. **SOIL:** In loam and sand, moist, well-drained or dry. Not clay.

207 Hymenosporum flavum 'Gold Nugget'

50-75cm / 50-75cm

A dwarf shrub with large glossy leaves and yellow perfumed flowers. Great feature or pot plant that can be used indoors as well as outdoors. **CLIMATE:** Temperate, sub-tropical or tropical. **SOIL:** In loam and sand, moist, well-drained or dry. Not clay.

Isopogon anemonifolius 'Little Drumsticks'

30-65cm / 45-80cm

A small compact upright shrub with intricate lobed foliage. Multitudes of buds develop in summer, opening to golden mini 'protea' flowers in winter and spring, attractive to honeyeaters and insect-eating birds such as scrub and blue wrens. Makes a showy display when grouped in small garden beds and rockeries; or mass plant in containers for dramatic effect on a patio or deck, or to decorate a sunny courtyard. **CLIMATE:** Temperate. **SOIL:** In loam and sand, moist, well-drained or dry. Not clay.

208 Isopogon anemonifolius 'Woorikee 2000'

50cm / 50cm

A dwarf compact shrub with attractive divided bronze-tipped foliage. Intriguing buds develop in summer, opening to golden mini 'protea' flowers in winter and spring, attractive to honeyeaters and butterflies. Plant in cottage gardens for borders or in mixed plantings; in rock gardens for landscape impact, especially when mass planted; a perfect year-round container plant for both foliage and flower interest. **CLIMATE:** Temperate. **SOIL:** In loam and sand, moist, well-drained or dry. Not clay.

Isopogon 'Candy Cones'

120cm · 100cm

A small shrub with attractive foliage and stunning purple flower heads that are great as cut flowers. Great feature plant but needs low phosphorus levels. Good as a potted specimen. **CLIMATE**: Temperate. **SOIL**: In loam and sand, moist, well-drained or dry. Not clay.

Isopogon 'Pink Profusion'

30-50cm · 50cm

A small shrub with somewhat spiky foliage and stunning bright-pink flower heads that are great as cut flowers. Great feature plant but needs low phosphorus levels. Good as a potted specimen. **CLIMATE**: Temperate. **SOIL**: In loam and sand, moist, well-drained or dry. Not clay.

Kennedia 'Combo'

10cm or climber · 120-180cm

A small, matting plant with attractive trifoliate grey-green leaves covered in multi-hued pea flowers in spring and early summer, an unusual combination of pink, red and orange. Multi-purpose plant for pathway edging, retaining walls, hanging baskets or containers. Snip off stem ends if shaping required. **CLIMATE**: Cool, temperate or sub-tropical. **SOIL**: In loam, clay and sand, well-drained.

Kunzea ericoides 'Snowman'

50cm · 30cm

A dense compact dwarf shrub with attractive dark-green foliage. This cultivar is very hardy and suited to gardens with limited space and could be planted as a low formal hedge or as a rockery plant. **CLIMATE**: Cool or temperate. **SOIL**: In loam, clay and sand, moist, well-drained or dry.

209 Leionema 'Green Screen'

150-200cm · 100cm

A dense compact medium shrub with attractive dark-green foliage. This cultivar is very hardy and suited to gardens with limited space and could be planted as a formal hedge or screening plant. **CLIMATE**: Cool or temperate. **SOIL**: In loam, clay and sand, moist, well-drained or dry.

210 Leptospermum 'Aphrodite'

250cm · 200cm

A medium to tall tea-tree shrub with lush green foliage that contrasts well with the bright-pink flowers. Bushy habit makes it an ideal screening plant; tolerates damp as well as dry soils. **CLIMATE**: Cool or temperate. **SOIL**: In loam, clay and sand, all moisture levels.

Leptospermum 'Cherish'

200-300cm · 200cm

A medium shrub with large white flowers on long branches that can be also used as cut flowers. Bushy habit makes it an ideal screening plant; tolerates damp as well as dry soils. **CLIMATE**: Cool or temperate. **SOIL**: In loam, clay and sand, all moisture levels.

211 Leptospermum 'Daydream'

200cm · 150cm

A medium upright and tea-tree shrub with light-green foliage and vibrant bright-purple flower colour. An ideal screening plant; tolerates damp as well as dry soils. **CLIMATE**: Cool or temperate. **SOIL**: In loam, clay and sand, all moisture levels.

212 Leptospermum 'Freya'

100-150cm · 100cm

A small to medium upright shrub that is relatively narrow and therefore suitable for confined spaces such as driveways. It adapts well to a range of soil types and moisture levels. **CLIMATE**: Cool or temperate. **SOIL**: In loam, clay and sand, all moisture levels.

213 Leptospermum 'Lipstick'

150cm · 150cm

An upright shrub that features a very bright pink flower. It is a tough plant that will grow in a wide range of soil types and climates as either a feature or screen plant. **CLIMATE**: Cool or temperate. **SOIL**: In loam, clay and sand, all moisture levels.

Leptospermum 'Little Lemon Scents'

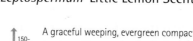

150-200cm · 150cm

A graceful weeping, evergreen compact tea-tree with a spectacular display of snow-white flowers in spring. The foliage has a delightful fresh lemon scent when crushed. It is a tough plant that will grow in a wide range of soil types and climates as either a feature or screen plant. **CLIMATE**: Cool, temperate or sub-tropical. **SOIL**: In loam, clay and sand, all moisture levels.

214 Leptospermum liversidgei 'Mozzie Blocker'

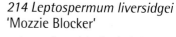

150-180cm · 100-120cm

An upright fine leafed ornamental tea-tree with soft-pink flowers. Grows well in tropical to cool temperate climates, will tolerate light frosts. Plant as hedging or screening around decks, pools, barbecue areas, or indoors as needed. The citronella oil perfumes the air and is said to repel mosquitoes. **CLIMATE**: Temperate, sub-tropical or tropical. **SOIL**: In loam and sand, wet or moist. Not clay.

209 210

211 213

214 212

Leptospermum morrisonii 'Burgundy'

300cm | **150cm**

A tall shrub with striking burgundy-coloured new growth and white flowers. It is great for a fast-growing screen or hedge. The boldly coloured leaves are useful for cut foliage in flower arrangements. **CLIMATE:** Cool, temperate or sub-tropical. **SOIL:** In loam, clay and sand, all moisture levels.

215 Leptospermum obovatum 'Lemon Bun'

50-100cm | **100-120cm**

A small dense mounding shrub with soft lemon-scented foliage and a profusion of lime-cream flowers that attract butterflies and provide food for insect-foraging small birds such as scrub wrens. It is perfect for low hedging, with minimal shaping required; may be planted beside pools and bog gardens; and can be clipped regularly to create a formal-looking ball in a decorative container. **CLIMATE:** Cool, temperate or sub-tropical. **SOIL:** In loam, clay and sand, all moisture levels.

216 Leptospermum obovatum 'Starry Night'

200-250cm | **150-180cm**

Graceful and pendulous with soft, fine, dark-purple foliage and purple-pink young stems. The flowers attract butterflies, wrens and thornbills. It may be planted as an eye-catching specimen in a paved courtyard, an informal screen against wall or fence line, or as a medium-sized hedge. **CLIMATE:** Cool, temperate or sub-tropical. **SOIL:** In loam, clay and sand, all moisture levels.

217 Leptospermum 'Merinda'

80-100cm | **100-150cm**

A low-spreading tea-tree with small mid-green leaves and stunning magenta flowers. Perfect for pot culture or as a feature plant in the garden. **CLIMATE:** Cool, temperate or sub-tropical. **SOIL:** In loam, clay and sand, all moisture levels.

218 Leptospermum 'Mesmer Eyes'

100-150cm | **100-150cm**

A low-spreading shrub with small mid-green leaves and stunning large white flowers that age to pink. Perfect for pot culture or as a feature plant in the garden. **CLIMATE:** Cool, temperate or sub-tropical. **SOIL:** In loam, clay and sand, all moisture levels.

Leptospermum 'Outrageous'

150-200cm | **100-150cm**

A low-spreading tea-tree with small mid-green leaves and showy large red flowers that age to pink. Perfect as a feature or screen plant in the garden. **CLIMATE:** Cool, temperate or sub-tropical. **SOIL:** In loam, clay and sand, all moisture levels.

219 Leptospermum 'Pageant'

100-150cm | **150-200cm**

A low-spreading shrub with small mid-green leaves. Perfect for pot culture or as a feature plant in the garden. **CLIMATE:** Cool, temperate or sub-tropical. **SOIL:** In loam, clay and sand, all moisture levels.

Leptospermum 'Rhiannon'

200cm | **100cm**

A small to medium upright tea-tree with brightly coloured flowers and dark, glossy foliage. It is relatively narrow and therefore suitable for confined spaces such as driveways or can be used as a screen or feature plant. **CLIMATE:** Cool, temperate or sub-tropical. **SOIL:** In loam, clay and sand, all moisture levels.

220 Leptospermum 'Rudolph'

200-300cm | **150-200cm**

A fast growing medium shrub that features purplish new growth and large red flowers in summer rather than spring as for most tea-trees. Great feature or screen plant. **CLIMATE:** Cool, temperate or sub-tropical. **SOIL:** In loam, clay and sand, all moisture levels.

221 Leptospermum 'Tickled Pink'

200cm | **150cm**

An upright medium shrub with small mid-green leaves and showy large pink flowers. Great feature or screen plant. **CLIMATE:** Cool, temperate or sub-tropical. **SOIL:** In loam, clay and sand, all moisture levels.

222 Leptospermum 'White Wave'

50cm | **100cm**

A lovely dwarf, cascading tea-tree with small mid-green leaves and masses of white flowers. A perfect plant for small gardens and large tubs; ideal for use on banks and cascading over retaining walls. **CLIMATE:** Cool, temperate or sub-tropical. **SOIL:** In loam, clay and sand, all moisture levels.

Leucophyta 'Tuffet'

25-35cm | **80-120cm**

A dense rounded mound of silver-grey, tightly arranged foliage with yellow button flowers. Contrasting border to path edges, rockeries and for soil binding on exposed sites, particularly coastal. Minimal maintenance. Trim if required. **CLIMATE:** Cool, temperate, sub-tropical or tropical. **SOIL:** In loam, clay and sand, well-drained.

Lomandra confertifolia 'Frosty Top'

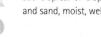

A dense, stylish decorator plant with graceful lightly weeping fine grey-green foliage and silver-frosted new growth. Yellow flowers are set among purple-grey stems. Low-maintenance container plant, along pathways or in rockeries. **CLIMATE**: Cool, temperate, sub-tropical or tropical. **SOIL**: In loam, clay and sand, moist, well-drained and dry.

223 Lomandra confertifolia 'Little Con'

A clumping grass-like perennial with bright-green narrow foliage. Great as a border or pot plant. **CLIMATE**: Cool, temperate or sub-tropical. **SOIL**: In loam, clay and sand, moist, well-drained and dry.

Lomandra confertifolia 'Little Pal'

A clumping grass-like perennial with bright-green narrow foliage. Great as a border or pot plant. **CLIMATE**: Cool, temperate or sub-tropical. **SOIL**: In loam, clay and sand, moist, well-drained and dry.

Lomandra confertifolia 'Seascape'

A clumping grass-like perennial with beautiful blue-grey narrow foliage. Great as a border or pot plant. **CLIMATE**: Cool or temperate. **SOIL**: In loam, clay and sand, moist, well-drained or dry.

224 Lomandra confertifolia 'Wingarra'

A clumping grass-like perennial with beautiful blue-grey narrow foliage. Great as a border or pot plant. **CLIMATE**: Cool or temperate. **SOIL**: In loam, clay and sand, moist, well-drained or dry.

225 Lomandra filiformis 'Savanna Blue'

A clumping grass-like perennial with sky-blue narrow foliage. Great as a border or pot plant. **CLIMATE**: Cool or temperate. **SOIL**: In loam, clay and sand, moist, well-drained or dry.

226 Lomandra fluviatilis 'Shara'

A clumping grass-like perennial with narrow leaves that have a slight blue-grey tinge. Great as a border or pot plant. **CLIMATE**: Cool, temperate or sub-tropical. **SOIL**: In loam, clay and sand, moist, well-drained and dry.

227 Lomandra hystrix 'Katie Belles'

A clumping grass-like perennial with broad shiny green foliage and masses of yellow flowers in spring. Great as a background or mass planting in the garden. **CLIMATE**: Cool, temperate or sub-tropical. **SOIL**: In loam, clay and sand, moist and dry.

228 Lomandra hystrix 'Tropic Belle'

A clumping grass-like perennial with broad shiny green foliage and masses of yellow flowers in spring. A much more compact form of *Lomandra hystrix* than normal. Great as a background or mass planting in the garden. **CLIMATE**: Cool, temperate or sub-tropical. **SOIL**: In loam, clay and sand, moist and dry.

229 Lomandra 'Lime Tuff'

A clumping grass-like perennial with attractive bright-green narrow foliage. Great as a border or pot plant. **CLIMATE**: Cool or temperate. **SOIL**: In loam, clay and sand, moist, well-drained or dry.

Lomandra longifolia 'Cassica'

A clumping grass-like perennial with broad bluish-green foliage and masses of perfumed yellow flowers in spring. Great as a background or mass planting in the garden. **CLIMATE**: Cool or temperate. **SOIL**: In loam and sand, moist or dry. Not clay.

230 Lomandra longifolia 'Katrinus'

A clumping grass-like perennial with broad green foliage and masses of perfumed yellow flowers in spring. Great as a background or mass planting in the garden. **CLIMATE**: Cool or temperate. **SOIL**: In loam, clay and sand, moist, well-drained or dry.

231 *Lomandra longifolia* 'Katrinus Deluxe'

A clumping grass-like perennial with broad green foliage and masses of perfumed yellow flowers in spring. Great as a background or mass planting in the garden. **CLIMATE**: Cool or temperate. **SOIL**: In loam, clay and sand, moist, well-drained or dry.

232 *Lomandra longifolia* 'Nyalla'

A clumping grass-like perennial with attractive narrow bluish-green foliage and masses of perfumed yellow flowers in spring. Great as a background or mass planting in the garden. **CLIMATE**: Cool or temperate. **SOIL**: In loam, clay and sand, moist, well-drained or dry.

233 *Lomandra longifolia* 'Tanika'

A clumping grass-like perennial with attractive narrow bluish-green foliage and masses of perfumed yellow flowers in spring. Great as a background or mass planting in the garden. This cultivar has proven to be very adaptable and is arguably the best lomandra on the market for appearance and all round performance. **CLIMATE**: Cool or temperate. **SOIL**: In loam, clay and sand, moist, well-drained or dry.

234 *Lomandra* 'Silver Grace'

A clumping grass-like perennial with beautiful blue-grey narrow foliage. Great as a border or pot plant. **CLIMATE**: Cool or temperate. **SOIL**: In loam, clay and sand, moist, well-drained or dry.

235 *Macropidia fuliginosa* 'Bush Eclipse'

A clumping grass-like perennial with broad bluish-green foliage and stunning black-and-green flowers in spring. A touchy plant with root rot, best grown in a rockery, raised bed or large pot. **CLIMATE**: Temperate. **SOIL**: In sand, moist or well-drained. Not loam or clay.

Mallophora globiflora 'Cotton Balls'

A soft, silvery-white small mounding or cascading shrub with small tight foliage and numerous 'cotton ball' flower heads. Wonderful contrast plant among greener neighbours, on path edges and in containers. **CLIMATE**: Cool or temperate. **SOIL**: In loam, clay and sand, well-drained.

236 *Melaleuca hypericifolia* 'Ulladulla Beacon'

A dense, fast-growing ground-cover, carpeting or mounding shrub. Bright-green foliage is highlighted in spring and summer with brilliant, bird-attracting orange-red brushes. Plant as an undershrub, or to cascade down walls or steep slopes. Excellent for coastal gardens, where it will provide protection for small plants just being established. **CLIMATE**: Cool, temperate or sub-tropical. **SOIL**: In loam, clay and sand, wet, all moisture levels.

237 *Melaleuca linariifolia* 'Claret Tops'

A dense compact shrub with small leaves and attractive claret-coloured new growth. A great foliage plant that has the form of a conifer but flowers as well. Great for shrubberies or pots. **CLIMATE**: Cool, temperate or sub-tropical. **SOIL**: In loam, clay and sand, all moisture levels.

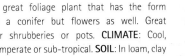

Melaleuca bracteata 'Revolution Gold'

A dense, upright medium shrub with attractive golden foliage, which is the distinguishing feature of this cultivar. It can be used as a colour-contrasted screening shrub or windbreak, or as a feature specimen in gardens and parklands. **CLIMATE**: Temperate or sub-tropical. **SOIL**: In loam, clay and sand, all moisture levels.

Melaleuca bracteata 'Revolution Green'

A dense upright medium shrub with dark-green foliage. It can be used as a colour-contrasted screening shrub or windbreak, or as a feature specimen in gardens and parklands. **CLIMATE**: Temperate or sub-tropical. **SOIL**: In loam, clay and sand, all moisture levels.

238 *Melaleuca* 'Little Red'

A dense compact shrub with small leaves and bright-red new growth throughout the warmer months. A great foliage plant that has the form of a conifer but flowers as well. Great for shrubberies or pots. **CLIMATE**: Cool, temperate or sub-tropical. **SOIL**: In loam, clay and sand, all moisture levels.

Melaleuca 'Little Nessie'

A dense mounded shrub with small bright-green leaves. The small leaf makes it useful as a low-growing hedge. Great for shrubberies or pots. **CLIMATE**: Temperate. **SOIL**: In loam, clay and sand, moist, well-drained or dry.

Melaleuca thymifolia 'Cotton Candy'

100-120cm / 100-200cm

A dense mounded shrub with small leaves and mauve bottlebrush flowers that are produced sporadically all year. The small leaf makes it useful as a low-growing hedge. Great for shrubberies or pots. **CLIMATE:** Cool, temperate or sub-tropical. **SOIL:** In loam, clay and sand, all moisture levels.

Melaleuca thymifolia 'Pink Lace'

100-120cm / 100-200cm

A dense mounded shrub with small leaves and pink bottlebrush flowers that are produced sporadically all year. The small leaf makes it useful as a low-growing hedge. Great for shrubberies or pots. **CLIMATE:** Cool, temperate or sub-tropical. **SOIL:** In loam, clay and sand, all moisture levels.

Melaleuca thymifolia 'White Lace'

100-120cm / 100-200cm

A dense mounded shrub with small leaves and white bottlebrush flowers that are produced sporadically all year. The small leaf makes it useful as a low-growing hedge. Great for shrubberies or pots. **CLIMATE:** Cool, temperate or sub-tropical. **SOIL:** In loam, clay and sand, all moisture levels.

239 Myoporum parvifolium 'Purpurea'

30cm / 200cm

Fast-growing ground cover ideal for covering large areas such as embankments and driveways. Attractive purplish new foliage. **CLIMATE:** Cool or temperate. **SOIL:** In loam, clay and sand, moist, well-drained or dry.

Olearia phlogopappa 'Pink Gem'

120-150cm / 80-100cm

A dense small shrub with small leaves and masses of soft-pink daisies in spring. Good for massed displays in shrubberies, as a low hedge or as a pot plant. **CLIMATE:** Temperate. **SOIL:** In loam and sand, moist, well-drained or dry. Not clay.

Olearia phlogopappa 'White Gem'

120-150cm / 80-100cm

A dense small shrub with small leaves and masses of soft-white daisies in spring. Good for massed displays in shrubberies, as a low hedge or as a pot plant. **CLIMATE:** Temperate. **SOIL:** In loam and sand, moist, well-drained or dry. Not clay.

240 Ozothamnus diosmifolius 'Coral Flush'

150-200cm / 100cm

A compact small shrub that has aromatic curry-scented leaves and clusters of coral-pink flowers in spring. Trim back after each flower flush to trigger a new burst of blooms. Great feature or pot plant that is also a great cut flower. **CLIMATE:** Cool, temperate or sub-tropical. **SOIL:** In loam and sand, moist, well-drained or dry. Not clay.

241 Ozothamnus diosmifolius 'Just Blush'

150-200cm / 100cm

A compact small shrub that has aromatic curry-scented leaves and clusters of mauve pink flowers in spring. Trim back after each flower flush to trigger a new burst of blooms. Great feature or pot plant that is also a great cut flower. **CLIMATE:** Cool, temperate or sub-tropical. **SOIL:** In loam and sand, moist, well-drained or dry. Not clay.

242 Ozothamnus diosmifolius 'Radiance'

150-200cm / 100cm

A compact small shrub that has aromatic curry-scented leaves and clusters of white flowers all year round that are pink in bud. Trim back after each flower flush to trigger a new burst of blooms. Great feature or pot plant that is also a great cut flower. **CLIMATE:** Cool, temperate or sub-tropical. **SOIL:** In loam and sand, moist, well-drained or dry. Not clay.

243 Ozothamnus diosmifolius 'Winter White'

150-200cm / 100cm

A compact small shrub that has aromatic curry-scented leaves and clusters of snow white flowers in winter and spring. Trim back after each flower flush to trigger a new burst of blooms. Great feature or pot plant that is also a great cut flower. **CLIMATE:** Cool, temperate or sub-tropical. **SOIL:** In loam and sand, moist, well-drained or dry. Not clay.

244 Pandorea jasminoides 'Charisma'

10cm or climber / 100-200cm

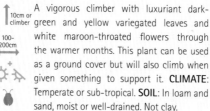

A vigorous climber with luxuriant dark-green and yellow variegated leaves and white maroon-throated flowers through the warmer months. This plant can be used as a ground cover but will also climb when given something to support it. **CLIMATE:** Temperate or sub-tropical. **SOIL:** In loam and sand, moist or well-drained. Not clay.

245 Pandorea jasminoides 'Flirty Bellz'

10cm or climber / 100-200cm

A vigorous climber with luxuriant dark-green leaves and dark-pink flowers with maroon throat produced in clusters through the warmer months. This plant can be used as a ground cover but will also climb when given something to support it. **CLIMATE:** Temperate or sub-tropical. **SOIL:** In loam and sand, moist or well-drained. Not clay.

242 240 243

241

244

239

245

246 Pandorea jasminoides 'Jazzy Bellz'

A vigorous climber with luxuriant dark-green leaves and white maroon-throated flowers through the warmer months. This plant can be used as a ground cover but will also climb when given something to support it. **CLIMATE:** Temperate or sub-tropical. **SOIL:** In loam and sand, moist or well-drained. Not clay.

Pandorea jasminoides 'Lady Di'

A vigorous climber with luxuriant dark-green leaves and snow-white flowers through the warmer months. This plant can be used as a ground cover but will also climb when given something to support it. **CLIMATE:** Temperate or sub-tropical. **SOIL:** In loam and sand, moist or well-drained. Not clay.

247 Pandorea jasminoides 'Southern Belle'

Either a climber or self-supporting shrub with luxuriant dark-green leaves and dark-pink flowers with maroon throats in clusters through the warmer months. This plant can be used as a ground cover but will also climb when given something to support it. **CLIMATE:** Temperate or sub-tropical. **SOIL:** In loam and sand, moist or well-drained. Not clay.

Pandorea pandorana 'Golden Showers'

A vigorous climber with dark-green leaves and golden flowers in a rush in spring. This plant can be used as a ground cover but will also climb when given something to support it. **CLIMATE:** Temperate or sub-tropical. **SOIL:** In loam and sand, moist or well-drained. Not clay.

Pandorea pandorana 'Snowbells'

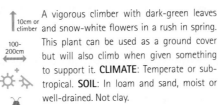

A vigorous climber with dark-green leaves and snow-white flowers in a rush in spring. This plant can be used as a ground cover but will also climb when given something to support it. **CLIMATE:** Temperate or sub-tropical. **SOIL:** In loam and sand, moist or well-drained. Not clay.

248 Pandorea pandorana 'Tiffany'

A vigorous climber with dark-green leaves and white flowers with burgundy throat in spring. This plant can be used as a ground cover but will also climb when given something to support it. **CLIMATE:** Temperate or sub-tropical. **SOIL:** In loam and sand, moist or well-drained. Not clay.

249 Pandorea pandorana 'Wonga Gold'

A vigorous climber with dark-green leaves and golden flowers in a rush in spring. This plant can be used as a ground cover but will also climb when given something to support it. **CLIMATE:** Temperate or sub-tropical. **SOIL:** In loam and sand, moist or well-drained. Not clay.

250 Pandorea pandorana 'Wonga Gold Sunset'

A dense, glossy-leafed screening climber of medium vigour, covered in multi-hued clusters of flowers (apricot, deep rose pink, purple and gold). Stunning display for fence or wall screening or as a central display on a tall frame. Prune heavily following flowering to shape as required. **CLIMATE:** Cool, temperate, sub-tropical or tropical. **SOIL:** In loam, clay and sand, well-drained.

251 Patersonia occidentalis 'Little Pat'

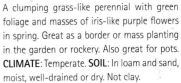

A clumping grass-like perennial with green foliage and masses of iris-like purple flowers in spring. Great as a border or mass planting in the garden or rockery. Also great for pots. **CLIMATE:** Temperate. **SOIL:** In loam and sand, moist, well-drained or dry. Not clay.

252 Pelargonium 'Applause'

A herbaceous perennial with attractive divided foliage and pink flowers over a long period. Can be pruned back to ground level after flowering. Ideal for planting in small gardens to attract butterflies, or in rockeries or hanging baskets. **CLIMATE:** Cool or temperate. **SOIL:** In loam and sand, moist, well-drained or dry. Not clay.

253 Pennisetum alopecuroides 'Black Lea'

A compact, clumping perennial grass with broad arching leaves and showy, black feathery flowers through the warmer months. Great for mass planting, accent planting for rockeries, and borders. Plumes suitable for dried arrangements. **CLIMATE:** Cool or temperate. **SOIL:** In loam, clay and sand, moist, well-drained or dry.
Note: This species can seed readily, so remove the flower heads before they go to seed to prevent self-seeding.

254 Pennisetum alopecuroides 'Nafray'

A compact, clumping perennial grass with broad arching leaves and showy, mauve-purple feathery flowers through the warmer months. Great for mass planting, accent planting for rockeries, and borders. Plumes suitable for dried arrangements. **CLIMATE:** Cool or temperate. **SOIL:** In loam, clay and sand, moist, well-drained or dry.
Note: This species can seed readily so remove the flower heads before they go to seed to prevent it self-seeding.

255 Pennisetum alopecuroides 'Pennstripe'

40-50cm
50-80cm

A compact, clumping perennial grass with broad arching variegated white and green leaves and showy, mauve-purple feathery flowers through the warmer months. Great for mass planting, accent planting for rockeries, and borders. Plumes suitable for dried arrangements. **CLIMATE:** Cool or temperate. **SOIL:** In loam, clay and sand, moist, well-drained or dry.
Note: This species can seed readily, so remove the flower heads before they go to seed to prevent self-seeding.

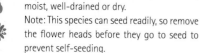

256 Pennisetum alopecuroides 'Purple Lea'

60-70cm
50-80cm

A compact, clumping perennial grass with broad arching leaves and showy purple feathery flowers through the warmer months. Great for mass planting, accent planting for rockeries, and borders. Plumes suitable for dried arrangements. **CLIMATE:** Cool or temperate. **SOIL:** In loam, clay and sand, moist, well-drained or dry.
Note: This species can seed readily, so remove the flower heads before they go to seed to prevent self-seeding.

Philotheca 'Bournda Beauty'

100-150cm
100-150cm

A hardy small shrub that adapts well to a wide range of environments. Profuse flowering is a feature. Great plant for a shrubbery or pot. Good cut flower as well. **CLIMATE:** Cool or temperate. **SOIL:** In loam, clay and sand, moist, well-drained or dry.

Philotheca 'Flower Girl'

100-150cm
100-150cm

A hardy small shrub that adapts well to a wide range of environments. The pinkish tinge to the open flowers is a feature. Great plant for a shrubbery or pot. Good cut flower as well. **CLIMATE:** Cool or temperate. **SOIL:** In loam, clay and sand, moist, well-drained or dry.

Philotheca myoporoides 'Moon Shadow'

100cm
100cm

A hardy small shrub with boldly variegated leaves. Adapts to a wide range of climates and soil types to create year-round interest in the garden. Good cut flower as well. **CLIMATE:** Cool, temperate or sub-tropical. **SOIL:** In loam, clay and sand, moist, well-drained or dry.

Philotheca myoporoides 'Profusion'

80cm
80cm

A hardy small shrub that adapts well to a wide range of environments. The smallish leaves have a wonderful apple-like fragrance when crushed. Spectacular plant when in flower. Great plant for a shrubbery or pot. Good cut flower as well. **CLIMATE:** Cool, temperate or sub-tropical. **SOIL:** In loam, clay and sand, moist, well-drained or dry.

Philotheca myoporoides 'Winter Rouge'

80cm
80cm

A hardy small shrub that adapts well to a wide range of environments. The reddish-pink flower buds are a feature. Great plant for a shrubbery or pot. Good cut flower as well. **CLIMATE:** Cool, temperate or sub-tropical. **SOIL:** In loam, clay and sand, moist, well-drained or dry.

Pimelea ferruginea 'Bonne Petite'

100-120cm
70-100cm

A small shrub with small dark-green glossy leaves and masses of magenta-pink tubular flowers in spring. A great feature plant for rockeries, borders or pots. Attracts butterflies. **CLIMATE:** Temperate. **SOIL:** In loam and sand, moist, well-drained or dry. Not clay.

257 Pimelea ferruginea 'Magenta Mist'

100-120cm
70-100cm

A small shrub with small dark-green glossy leaves and masses of magenta-pink tubular flowers in spring. A great feature plant for rockeries, borders or pots. Attracts butterflies. **CLIMATE:** Temperate. **SOIL:** In loam and sand, moist, well-drained or dry. Not clay.

258 Pimelea 'White Jewel'

30-40cm
50-80cm

A low mounding shrub with small mid-green leaves and masses of white tubular flowers all year round. A great feature plant for rockeries, borders or pots. Attracts butterflies. **CLIMATE:** Temperate or sub-tropical. **SOIL:** In loam, clay and sand, moist, well-drained or dry.

259 Pimelea rosea 'Deep Dream'

100-120cm
70-100cm

A small shrub with small light-green leaves and masses of purple-pink tubular flowers in spring. A great feature plant for rockeries, borders or pots. Attracts butterflies. **CLIMATE:** Temperate. **SOIL:** In loam and sand, moist, well-drained or dry. Not clay.

Pimelea 'Sunset Blush'

20-30cm
65-90cm

A dense, glossy-leaved ground cover. Gorgeous low-maintenance container plant, or outstanding along pathways or in rockeries. Prune lightly after flowering. **CLIMATE:** Cool, temperate or sub-tropical. **SOIL:** In loam and sand, moist, well-drained or dry. Not clay.

257

259

258

260 *Pimelea sylvestris* 'Edna Walling Rice Flower'

40-60cm
20-30cm

A multi-stemmed small shrub with light-green leaves, and massed terminal heads of perfumed pink-and-white flowers, highly attractive to butterflies and moths. Use as a feature for rockeries or borders and pots. **CLIMATE**: Temperate. **SOIL**: In loam and sand, moist, well-drained or dry. Not clay.

261 *Platysace* 'Edna Walling Flower Girl'

15-25cm
25-40cm

A compact, lightly suckering small shrub with tightly set tiny rounded leaves. Creamy flower heads open from pink buds, making a lovely combination of colour from spring to summer. Flowers attract butterflies and native bees. Use as a border, in mass plantings, or in pots. **CLIMATE**: Cool, temperate or sub-tropical. **SOIL**: In loam and sand, moist, well-drained or dry. Not clay.

SpS

262 *Platysace* 'Edna Walling Pom Pom'

40-65cm
50-75cm

An aromatic bushy small shrub with small leaves and white flower heads that are soft-pink when in bud and are displayed well above the foliage. Flowers attract butterflies and native bees. Use as a border, in mass plantings, or in pots. **CLIMATE**: Cool, temperate or sub-tropical. **SOIL**: In loam and sand, moist, well-drained or dry. Not clay.

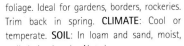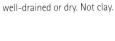

263 *Plectranthus* 'Blue Spires'

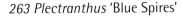

40-50cm
30-40cm

A low compact herbaceous sub-shrub with aromatic green-and-white variegated foliage. Intense blue-lilac, strongly perfumed flowers extend along leafy stems in spires 30-60cm long and attract butterflies and native bees. Use as a border and mixed among other cottage-garden plants. Beautiful in container or hanging basket. **CLIMATE**: Temperate or sub-tropical. **SOIL**: In loam and sand, moist, well-drained or dry. Not clay.

Plectranthus 'Edna Walling Spur Flower'

10-20cm
45-75cm

A low compact herbaceous sub-shrub with aromatic lobed foliage. Intense blue-lilac, strongly perfumed flowers extend along leafy stems in spires 30-60cm long and attract butterflies and native bees. Use as a border and mixed among other cottage-garden plants. Beautiful in container or hanging basket. **CLIMATE**: Temperate or sub-tropical. **SOIL**: In loam and sand, moist, well-drained or dry. Not clay.

264 *Poa labillardieri* 'Eskdale'

50-60cm
40-50cm

A tussock-forming perennial grass with highly ornamental needle-like blue-grey foliage. Ideal for gardens, borders, rockeries. Trim back in spring. **CLIMATE**: Cool or temperate. **SOIL**: In loam and sand, moist, well-drained or dry. Not clay.

265 *Poa poiformis* 'Kingsdale'

40-50cm
40-50cm

A tussock-forming perennial grass with weeping needle-like dark-green foliage. Ideal for gardens, borders, rockeries. Trim back in spring. **CLIMATE**: Cool or temperate. **SOIL**: In loam and sand, moist, well-drained or dry. Not clay.

266 *Prostanthera* 'Minty'

100-180cm
100-120cm

A small to medium dense shrub. Highly aromatic foliage continuously releases a mint essence into the atmosphere, so plant close to windows where you can enjoy the fragrance. A lavish display of violet flowers almost conceals the soft leaves throughout spring and early summer, attracting butterflies and small insect-eating birds. Great for hedging or as a pot plant. **CLIMATE**: Cool or temperate. **SOIL**: In loam and sand, moist, well-drained or dry. Not clay.

267 *Prostanthera* 'Poorinda Ballerina'

150-200cm
100cm

A small to medium dense shrub with small leaves and masses of white flowers in spring. Much tougher than other prostantheras. Can be clipped as a hedge or used as a feature shrub or pot plant. **CLIMATE**: Cool or temperate. **SOIL**: In loam and sand, moist, well-drained or dry. Not clay.

268 *Ptilotus exaltatus* 'Joey'

50-60cm
40-50cm

A short-lived herbaceous perennial with dark-green leaves and unusual mauve feathery flower heads in spring. Good for sunny rockeries and borders or in a decorative pot. **CLIMATE**: Temperate. **SOIL**: In loam and sand, moist, well-drained or dry. Not clay.

Ptilotus exaltatus 'Phoenix'

50-60cm
40-50cm

A short-lived herbaceous perennial with dark-green leaves and unusual mauve feathery flower heads in spring. Good for sunny rockeries and borders or in a decorative pot. **CLIMATE**: Temperate. **SOIL**: In loam and sand, moist, well-drained or dry. Not clay.

Ptilotus nobilis 'Outback Princess Poise'

60-70cm
40-50cm

A short-lived herbaceous perennial with dark-green leaves and unusual pink feathery flower heads reputedly produced all year round. Good for sunny rockeries and borders or in a decorative pot. **CLIMATE**: Temperate. **SOIL**: In loam and sand, moist, well-drained or dry. Not clay.

Ptilotus nobilis 'Outback Princess Passion'

60-70cm
40-50cm

A short-lived herbaceous perennial with dark-green leaves and unusual purple feathery flower heads reputedly produced all year round. Good for sunny rockeries and borders or in a decorative pot. **CLIMATE:** Temperate. **SOIL:** In loam and sand, moist, well-drained or dry. Not clay.

Ptilotus nobilis 'Outback Princess Purity'

60-70cm
40-50cm

A short-lived herbaceous perennial with dark-green leaves and unusual white feathery flower heads reputedly produced all year round. Good for sunny rockeries and borders or in a decorative pot. **CLIMATE:** Temperate. **SOIL:** In loam and sand, moist, well-drained or dry. Not clay.

Rhodanthe anthemoides 'Paper Baby'

30-40cm
40-50cm

Dwarf perennial herbaceous plant with attractive narrow grey-green foliage with masses of purple-budded white everlasting daisies in spring. A great border, rockery or potted plant. **CLIMATE:** Cool or temperate. **SOIL:** In loam and sand, moist, well-drained or dry. Not clay.

Rhodanthe anthemoides 'Paper Cascade'

30-40cm
40-50cm

Dwarf mounding, perennial herbaceous plant with attractive narrow grey-green foliage with masses of purple-budded white everlasting daisies in spring. This cultivar has a spreading habit and is great in hanging baskets or spilling over walls and rockeries. **CLIMATE:** Cool or temperate. **SOIL:** In loam and sand, moist, well-drained or dry. Not clay.

269 Rhodanthe anthemoides 'Paper Moon'

30-40cm
40-50cm

Dwarf mounding, perennial herbaceous plant with attractive narrow grey-green foliage with masses of purple-budded white everlasting daisies in spring. This cultivar has a spreading habit and is great in hanging baskets or spilling over walls and rockeries. **CLIMATE:** Cool or temperate. **SOIL:** In loam and sand, moist, well-drained or dry. Not clay.

Rhodanthe anthemoides 'Paper Star'

30-40cm
40-50cm

Dwarf upright perennial herbaceous plant with attractive narrow grey-green foliage with masses of white-budded white everlasting daisies in spring. The pure white flower distinguishes this cultivar. A great border, rockery or potted plant. **CLIMATE:** Cool or temperate. **SOIL:** In loam and sand, moist, well-drained or dry. Not clay.

270 Rhodanthe anthemoides 'Paper Trail'

30-40cm
40-50cm

Dwarf mounding, perennial herbaceous plant with attractive narrow grey-green foliage with masses of purple-budded white everlasting daisies in spring. This cultivar has a spreading habit and is great in hanging baskets or spilling over walls and rockeries. **CLIMATE:** Cool or temperate. **SOIL:** In loam and sand, moist, well-drained or dry. Not clay.

Rhodanthe anthemoides 'Sunray Snow'

30-40cm
40-50cm

Dwarf upright perennial herbaceous plant with attractive narrow grey-green foliage with masses of purple-budded white everlasting daisies in spring. This cultivar has a more upright habit than others and is a great border, rockery or potted plant. **CLIMATE:** Cool or temperate. **SOIL:** In loam and sand, moist, well-drained or dry. Not clay.

271 Scaevola aemula 'Aussie Crawl'

5cm
100-200cm

A vigorous but relatively short-lived soft-wooded ground cover with toothed mid-green foliage. Extremely floriferous and showy for many months of the year. A great feature, border, pot or hanging-basket plant. **CLIMATE:** Temperate. **SOIL:** In loam and sand, moist, well-drained or dry. Not clay.

272 Scaevola aemula 'Aussie Salute'

20-30cm
100-200cm

A vigorous but relatively short-lived soft-wooded perennial that forms a low mound. The distinguishing feature of this cultivar is its more upright habit than most forms of *Scaevola aemula* on the market. A great feature or pot plant. **CLIMATE:** Temperate. **SOIL:** In loam and sand, moist, well-drained or dry. Not clay.

Scaevola aemula 'Bombay Blue'

5cm
100-200cm

A vigorous but relatively short-lived soft-wooded ground cover with toothed mid-green foliage. Extremely floriferous and showy for many months of the year. A great feature, border, pot or hanging-basket plant. **CLIMATE:** Temperate. **SOIL:** In loam and sand, moist, well-drained or dry. Not clay.

273 Scaevola aemula 'Bombay Pink'

5cm
100-200cm

A vigorous but relatively short-lived soft-wooded ground cover with toothed mid-green foliage. Extremely floriferous and showy for many months of the year. The best true pink *Scaevola aemula* on the market. A great feature, border, pot or hanging-basket plant. **CLIMATE:** Temperate. **SOIL:** In loam and sand, moist, well-drained or dry. Not clay.

274 *Scaevola aemula* 'Lilac Fanfare'

A vigorous but relatively short-lived soft-wooded ground cover with toothed mid-green foliage. Extremely floriferous and showy for many months of the year. A great feature, border, pot or hanging-basket plant. **CLIMATE**: Temperate. **SOIL**: In loam and sand, moist, well-drained or dry. Not clay.

275 *Scaevola aemula* 'Purple Fanfare'

A vigorous but relatively short-lived soft-wooded ground cover with toothed mid-green foliage. Extremely floriferous and showy for many months of the year. A great feature, border, pot or hanging-basket plant. **CLIMATE**: Temperate. **SOIL**: In loam and sand, moist, well-drained or dry. Not clay.

276 *Scaevola aemula* 'Zig Zag'

A vigorous but relatively short-lived soft-wooded ground cover with toothed mid-green foliage. Extremely floriferous and showy for many months of the year. The bicoloured white and purple flowers distinguish this cultivar from other scaevolas. A great feature, border, pot or hanging-basket plant. **CLIMATE**: Temperate. **SOIL**: In loam and sand, moist, well-drained or dry. Not clay.

Scaevola albida 'Karwarra Pink'

A vigorous and relatively long-lived soft-wooded ground cover with small leaves and true pink flowers. Small flower size is compensated for by the extremely floriferous habit. A great feature, border, pot or hanging-basket plant. **CLIMATE**: Temperate. **SOIL**: In loam and sand, moist, well-drained or dry. Not clay.

277 *Scaevola albida* 'Mauve Carpet'

A vigorous and relatively long-lived soft-wooded ground cover with small leaves. Small flower size is compensated for by the extremely floriferous habit. A great feature, border, pot or hanging-basket plant. **CLIMATE**: Temperate. **SOIL**: In loam and sand, moist, well-drained or dry. Not clay.

Scaevola albida 'Mauve Clusters'

A vigorous and relatively long-lived soft-wooded ground cover with small leaves. Small flower size is compensated for by the extremely floriferous habit. A great feature, border, pot or hanging-basket plant. **CLIMATE**: Temperate. **SOIL**: In loam and sand, moist, well-drained or dry. Not clay.

278 *Scaevola albida* 'White Carpet'

A vigorous and relatively long-lived soft-wooded ground cover with small leaves. Small flower size is compensated for by the extremely floriferous habit. A great feature, border, pot or hanging-basket plant. **CLIMATE**: Temperate. **SOIL**: In loam and sand, moist, well-drained or dry. Not clay.

279 *Scaevola* 'Edna Walling Fan Tastic'

A vigorous but relatively short-lived soft-wooded ground cover with toothed mid-green foliage. Extremely floriferous and showy for many months of the year. A great feature, border, pot or hanging-basket plant. **CLIMATE**: Temperate. **SOIL**: In loam and sand, moist, well-drained or dry. Not clay.

Scaevola 'Fan Magic Spellbinder'

A dense low carpeting shrub with lush foliage and a lightly layering habit. Plentiful spires of large purple-blue fan flowers arise continuously in massed display amid the foliage during spring, summer and autumn. Attractive to butterflies. Plant as edging for pathways or paving; clustered among rocky outcrops and in raised beds; as a spectacular container plant for small gardens, patios or balconies; and as a highly decorative basket plant. **CLIMATE**: Temperate. **SOIL**: In loam and sand, moist, well-drained or dry. Not clay.

280 *Scaevola* 'Fandango Erect Early Blue'

A vigorous but relatively short-lived soft-wooded perennial that forms a low mound. The distinguishing feature of this cultivar is its more upright habit than most forms of *Scaevola aemula* on the market. A great feature or pot plant. **CLIMATE**: Temperate. **SOIL**: In loam and sand, moist, well-drained or dry. Not clay.

281 *Scaevola* 'Fandango White Wonder'

A vigorous but relatively short-lived soft-wooded ground cover with toothed mid-green foliage. Extremely floriferous and showy for many months of the year. The pure white flowers distinguish this cultivar from other scaevolas. A great feature, border, pot or hanging-basket plant. **CLIMATE**: Temperate. **SOIL**: In loam and sand, moist, well-drained or dry. Not clay.

282 *Scaevola nitida* 'Aussie Spirit'

A small dense shrub with glossy mid-green foliage and royal blue flowers. A great feature plant for a shrubbery or pot plant. Attracts butterflies. **CLIMATE**: Temperate. **SOIL**: In loam and sand, moist, well-drained or dry. Not clay.

Scaevola nitida 'Sapphire Skies'

50-60cm
50-60cm

A small dense shrub with glossy mid-green foliage and royal blue flowers. A great feature plant for a shrubbery or pot plant. Attracts butterflies. **CLIMATE**: Temperate. **SOIL**: In loam and sand, moist, well-drained or dry. Not clay.

283 Scaevola 'Super Clusters'

5cm
200-400cm

A vigorous and very long-lived soft-wooded ground cover with small leaves. Its good longevity distinguishes it from other herbaceous scaevolas. Small flower size is compensated for by the extremely floriferous habit. A great feature, border, pot or hanging-basket plant. **CLIMATE**: Temperate. **SOIL**: In loam and sand, moist, well-drained or dry. Not clay.

284 Sollya 'Edna Walling Blue Bells'

100-120cm or climber
100-150cm
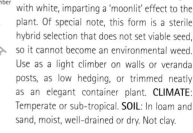

A small dense shrub or very light twining plant. The variegated leaves are finely edged with white, imparting a 'moonlit' effect to the plant. Of special note, this form is a sterile hybrid selection that does not set viable seed, so it cannot become an environmental weed. Use as a light climber on walls or veranda posts, as low hedging, or trimmed neatly as an elegant container plant. **CLIMATE**: Temperate or sub-tropical. **SOIL**: In loam and sand, moist, well-drained or dry. Not clay.

285 Spyridium 'Edna Walling Nimbus'

10-15cm
60-100cm

A dense ground-covering shrub with shiny dark-green foliage of intricate shape with contrasting silver floral bracts and perfumed white flowers. Often visited by butterflies. A startling contrasting ground cover well suited to path edges, rockeries, or as a very beautiful and easy-to-grow container plant. **CLIMATE**: Temperate or sub-tropical. **SOIL**: In loam and sand, moist, well-drained or dry. Not clay.

286 Stenanthemum 'White Mischief'

30-145cm
80-120cm

A compact small shrub with a dense mounding habit and dark green foliage. Massed bronze buds open to decorative silvery white cottonball flowers. Butterflies and small moths are attracted to the flowers, and wrens visit the plants to feed on small insects. **CLIMATE**: Cool, temperate or sub-tropical. **SOIL**: In loam and sand, moist, well-drained or dry. Not clay.

287 Stylidium graminifolium 'Little Sapphire'

30-50cm
30-40cm

A dwarf tufting perennial herb with striking blue foliage topped by deep pink 'trigger' flowers, which have a fascinating explosive action loved by kids. Great for rockeries, borders and mass plantings as well as for pots. **CLIMATE**: Temperate or sub-tropical. **SOIL**: In loam and sand, moist, well-drained or dry. Not clay.

288 Stylidium graminifolium 'Tiny Trina'

30-50cm
30-40cm

A dwarf tufting perennial herb with dark-green foliage topped by deep pink 'trigger' flowers, which have a fascinating explosive action loved by kids. Great for rockeries, borders and mass plantings as well as for pots. **CLIMATE**: Temperate or sub-tropical. **SOIL**: In loam and sand, moist, well-drained or dry. Not clay.

Syzygium australe 'Aussie Boomer'

150-250cm
120-150cm

A small dense shrub with mid-sized glossy green leaves, with bright-red new growth that is a distinguishing feature of this cultivar and white powder-puff flowers followed by pinkish fruits that attract birds. A great feature, screen, hedge or topiary plant that is also good for pots. **CLIMATE**: Temperate, sub-tropical or tropical. **SOIL**: In loam, clay and sand, moist or well-drained.

Syzygium australe 'Blaze'

150-250cm
120-150cm

A small dense shrub with mid-sized glossy green leaves, with bright-red new growth that is a distinguishing feature of this cultivar and white powder-puff flowers followed by pinkish fruits that attract birds. A great feature, screen, hedge or topiary plant that is also good for pots. **CLIMATE**: Temperate, sub-tropical or tropical. **SOIL**: In loam, clay and sand, moist or well-drained.

Syzygium australe 'Bush Christmas'

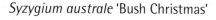

400-600cm
200-300cm

A medium-sized, dense shrub with mid-sized glossy green leaves and white powder-puff flowers followed by pinkish fruits that attract birds. A great feature, screen, hedge or topiary plant that is also good for pots. **CLIMATE**: Temperate, sub-tropical or tropical. **SOIL**: In loam, clay and sand, moist or well-drained.

Syzygium australe 'Hinterland Gold'

200-400cm
150-200cm

A small dense shrub with mid-sized glossy golden leaves that are a distinguishing feature of this cultivar and white powder-puff flowers followed by pinkish fruits that attract birds. A great feature, screen, hedge or topiary plant that is also good for pots. **CLIMATE**: Temperate, sub-tropical or tropical. **SOIL**: In loam, clay and sand, moist or well-drained.

Syzygium australe 'Oranges and Lemons'

120-150cm
80-100cm

A small dense shrub with mid-sized glossy green leaves, with bright-red new growth that is a distinguishing feature of this cultivar and white powder-puff flowers followed by pinkish fruits that attract birds. A great feature, screen, hedge or topiary plant that is also good for pots. **CLIMATE**: Temperate, sub-tropical or tropical. **SOIL**: In loam, clay and sand, moist or well-drained.

Syzygium australe 'Tayla Made'

200–250cm · 150cm

A small dense shrub with mid-sized glossy green leaves, with bronze-coloured new growth that is a distinguishing feature of this cultivar and white powder-puff flowers followed by pinkish fruits that attract birds. A great feature, screen, hedge or topiary plant that is also good for pots. **CLIMATE:** Temperate, sub-tropical or tropical. **SOIL:** In loam, clay and sand, moist or well-drained.

289 *Syzygium australe* 'Tiny Trev'

50cm · 75cm

A very dwarf, dense shrub with mid-sized glossy green leaves and white powder-puff flowers followed by pinkish fruits that attract birds. A great feature, screen, hedge or topiary plant that is also good for pots. **CLIMATE:** Temperate or sub-tropical. **SOIL:** In loam, clay and sand, moist or well-drained.

290 *Syzygium* 'Big Red'

400cm · 250cm

A medium-sized dense shrub with large, glossy leaves, with dark crimson new growth. A great feature, screen, hedge or topiary plant that is also good for pots. **CLIMATE:** Temperate, sub-tropical or tropical. **SOIL:** In loam, clay and sand, moist or well-drained.

291 *Syzygium* 'Cascade'

200–300cm · 100–200cm

A small shrub with mid-sized glossy green leaves, with attractive pink new growth and spectacular pink powder-puff flowers that are the distinguishing features of this cultivar followed by pinkish fruits that attract birds. A great feature, screen, hedge or topiary plant that is also good for pots. **CLIMATE:** Temperate or sub-tropical. **SOIL:** In loam, clay and sand, moist or well-drained.

Syzygium francisii 'Glossy Gem'

100–150cm · 100–150cm

A dwarf shrub with large glossy green leaves, with attractive pink new growth that is a distinguishing feature of this cultivar and white powder-puff flowers followed by mauve fruits that attract birds. A great feature, screen, hedge or topiary plant that is also good for pots. **CLIMATE:** Temperate or sub-tropical. **SOIL:** In loam, clay and sand, moist or well-drained.

292 *Syzygium francisii* 'Little Gem'

200–250cm · 150–200cm

A small shrub with mid-sized glossy green leaves, with attractive pink new growth that is a distinguishing feature of this cultivar and white powder-puff flowers followed by mauve fruits that attract birds. A great feature, screen, hedge or topiary plant that is also good for pots. **CLIMATE:** Temperate or sub-tropical. **SOIL:** In loam, clay and sand, moist or well-drained.

Syzygium luehmannii 'Little Lucy'

200–400cm · 100–200cm

A small to medium shrub with narrow, medium-sized glossy foliage and dark-red new growth that is a distinguishing feature of this cultivar. Small white flowers are followed by pinkish fruits. A great feature, screen, hedge or topiary plant that is also good for pots. **CLIMATE:** Temperate or sub-tropical. **SOIL:** In loam, clay and sand, moist or well-drained.

293 *Syzygium luehmannii* 'Lulu'

200–400cm · 100–200cm

A small to medium shrub with narrow, medium-sized glossy foliage and hot-pink new growth that is a distinguishing feature of this cultivar. Small white flowers are followed by reddish fruits. A great feature, screen, hedge or topiary plant that is also good for pots. **CLIMATE:** Temperate or sub-tropical. **SOIL:** In loam, clay and sand, moist or well-drained.

Syzygium luehmannii 'Petite Blush'

200–300cm · 100–150cm

A small shrub with narrow, medium-sized glossy foliage and mid-pink new growth. Small white flowers are followed by pinkish fruits. A great feature, screen, hedge or topiary plant that is also good for pots. **CLIMATE:** Temperate or sub-tropical. **SOIL:** In loam, clay and sand, moist or well-drained.

Syzygium luehmannii 'Sunset Mist'

200–300cm · 100–150cm

A small shrub with narrow, medium-sized white-and-green variegated glossy foliage and purplish new growth that is a distinguishing feature of this cultivar. Small white flowers are followed by pinkish fruits. A great feature, screen, hedge or topiary plant that is also good for pots. **CLIMATE:** Temperate or sub-tropical. **SOIL:** In loam, clay and sand, moist or well-drained.

Syzygium paniculatum 'Beachball'

100–150cm · 100–150cm

A small shrub with medium-sized glossy dark-green foliage and pink new growth that is a distinguishing feature of this cultivar. Medium-sized white flowers are followed by magenta fruits. A great feature, screen, hedge or topiary plant that is also good for pots. **CLIMATE:** Temperate or sub-tropical. **SOIL:** In loam, clay and sand, moist or well-drained.

294 *Syzygium paniculatum* 'Lillyput'

150–200cm · 150–200cm

A small to medium shrub with medium-sized glossy dark-green foliage and pink to red new growth that is a distinguishing feature of this cultivar. Medium-sized white flowers are followed by magenta fruits. A great feature, screen, hedge or topiary plant that is also good for pots. **CLIMATE:** Temperate or sub-tropical. **SOIL:** In loam, clay and sand, moist or well-drained.

Syzygium paniculatum 'Little Lil'

100-150cm
100-150cm

A small shrub with medium-sized glossy dark-green foliage and bronze to yellow or pink new growth that is a distinguishing feature of this cultivar. Medium-sized white flowers are followed by magenta fruits. A great feature, screen, hedge or topiary plant that is also good for pots. **CLIMATE:** Temperate or sub-tropical. **SOIL:** In loam, clay and sand, moist or well-drained.

295 Tecomanthe hillii 'Edna Walling Island Belle'

10cm or climber
100-200cm

A climber of moderate density and vigour, with glossy pinnate foliage and spectacular clusters of large waxy pink bells from spring through summer, pollinated by native bees, moths and insects, and honeyeaters. Performs beautifully as an elegant courtyard plant, on a wall or pergola, fence or veranda or in a container. If grown in a suitable pot, it can be brought inside when in flower. **CLIMATE:** Temperate, sub-tropical or tropical. **SOIL:** In loam and sand, moist or well-drained. Not clay.

296 Telopea 'Bridal Gown' marketed as 'Shady Lady White'

250-300cm
200-300cm

A dense medium to large shrub with broad deep-green foliage and beautiful snow-white medium-sized flower heads providing nectar for eager honeyeaters. Fantastic new waratah that is a cross between *T. speciosissima* and *T. oreades*. Needs a protected position, as the flower bracts burn in full sun or wind. A great feature shrub for general garden beds or rockeries. Also suitable for a large container, and is a great cut flower. **CLIMATE:** Cool or temperate. **SOIL:** In loam, clay and sand, moist, well-drained or dry.

Telopea 'Braidwood Brilliant'

150-200cm
150-200cm

A dense small shrub with broad deep-green foliage and medium-sized flat flower heads. A great feature shrub for general garden beds or rockeries. Also suitable for a large container, and is a great cut flower. **CLIMATE:** Cool or temperate. **SOIL:** In loam, clay and sand, moist, well-drained or dry.

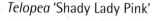

297 Telopea 'Corroboree Waratah'

250-300cm
200-300cm

A dense medium to large shrub with broad grey-green foliage and large flat flower heads providing nectar for eager honeyeaters. A great feature shrub for general garden beds or rockeries. Also suitable for a large container, and is a great cut flower. **CLIMATE:** Cool or temperate. **SOIL:** In loam, clay and sand, moist, well-drained or dry.

298 Telopea 'Golden Globe' marketed as 'Shady Lady Yellow'

250-300cm
200-300cm

A dense medium to large shrub with grey-green foliage and large flat flower heads. Fantastic new waratah that is a cross between *Telopea speciosissima x truncata* and *T. oreades*. The yellow flowers are a new colour in waratah cultivars. A great feature shrub for general garden beds or rockeries. Also suitable for a large container, and is a great cut flower. **CLIMATE:** Cool or temperate. **SOIL:** In loam, clay and sand, moist, well-drained or dry.

Telopea 'Shady Lady Pink'

250-300cm
3200-300cm

A dense medium to large shrub with grey-green foliage and large flat flower heads. A cross between *T. speciosissima* and *T. oreades*. A great feature shrub for general garden beds or rockeries. Also suitable for a large container, and is a great cut flower. **CLIMATE:** Cool or temperate. **SOIL:** In loam, clay and sand, moist, well-drained or dry.

299 Telopea 'Shady Lady Red'

250-300cm
200-300cm

A dense medium to large shrub with grey-green foliage and large flat flower heads. A cross between *T. speciosissima* and *T. oreades*. A great feature shrub for general garden beds or rockeries. Also suitable for a large container, and is a great cut flower. **CLIMATE:** Cool or temperate. **SOIL:** In loam, clay and sand, moist, well-drained or dry.

Telopea speciosissima 'Ballerina'

250-300cm
100-150cm

A dense medium to large shrub with deep-green foliage and cone-shaped bright-red blooms. A great feature shrub for general garden beds or rockeries. Also suitable for a large container, and is a great cut flower. **CLIMATE:** Cool or temperate. **SOIL:** In loam, clay and sand, moist, well-drained or dry.

Telopea speciosissima 'Cardinal'

250-300cm
100-150cm

A dense medium to large shrub with deep-green foliage and large red dome-shaped flowers. Needs a protected position, as the flower bracts tend to burn in full sun or wind. A great feature shrub for general garden beds or rockeries. Also suitable for a large container, and is a great cut flower. **CLIMATE:** Cool or temperate. **SOIL:** In loam, clay and sand, moist, well-drained or dry.

300 Telopea speciosissima 'Fire and Brimstone'

250-300cm
100-150cm

A dense medium to large shrub with deep-green foliage and large red flowers with white tips to the stigmas. Needs a protected position, as the flower bracts tend to burn in full sun or wind. A great feature shrub for general garden beds or rockeries. Also suitable for a large container, and is a great cut flower. **CLIMATE:** Cool or temperate. **SOIL:** In loam, clay and sand, moist, well-drained or dry.

Telopea speciosissima 'Pink Passion'

250-300cm
100-150cm

A dense medium to large shrub with broad pale-green foliage and large pink flowers. A great feature shrub for general garden beds or rockeries. Also suitable for a large container, and is a great cut flower. **CLIMATE:** Cool or temperate. **SOIL:** In loam, clay and sand, moist, well-drained or dry.

297

299

300

298

301

304

305

303

Thryptomene saxicola

'F.C. Payne'

302

306

Telopea speciosissima 'Shade of Pale'

250-300cm
100-150cm

A dense medium to large shrub with broad pale-green foliage and large white flowers suffused with pink. A great feature shrub for general garden beds or rockeries. Also suitable for a large container, and is a great cut flower. **CLIMATE:** Cool or temperate. **SOIL:** In loam, clay and sand, moist, well-drained or dry.

Telopea speciosissima 'Wirrimbirra White'

250-300cm
100-150cm

A dense medium to large shrub with broad pale-green foliage and large white flowers. Needs a protected position, as the flower bracts tend to burn in full sun or wind. A great feature shrub for general garden beds or rockeries. Also suitable for a large container, and is a great cut flower. **CLIMATE:** Cool or temperate. **SOIL:** In loam, clay and sand, moist, well-drained or dry.

301 Tetratheca 'Bicentennial Belle'

30-60cm
50-100cm

A dwarf, lightly suckering shrub with compact foliage covered in clusters of perfumed bright pink-mauve bells most of the year, especially in spring and autumn. The massed flowers are especially attractive to butterflies. Blends beautifully with other small shrubs in cottage-garden settings, and makes a particularly striking container plant. **CLIMATE:** Cool or temperate. **SOIL:** In loam and sand, moist, well-drained or dry. Not clay.

302 Themeda triandra 'Mingo'

15-30cm
50-60cm

A low spreading, tufting grass with attractive blue-green foliage and unusual flowers. An intriguing ground cover alternative or border plant. **CLIMATE:** Cool or temperate. **SOIL:** In loam and sand, moist, well-drained or dry. Not clay.

303 Thryptomene saxicola 'FC Payne' synonym 'Payne's Selection'

40-80cm
100-150cm

A small spreading shrub with horizontal branching habit, tiny aromatic leaves with soft pink flowers. A good background shrub and cut flower. **CLIMATE:** Cool or temperate. **SOIL:** In loam and sand, moist, well-drained or dry. Not clay.

Thryptomene saxicola 'Supernova'

40-80cm
100-150cm

A small spreading shrub with horizontal branching habit, tiny aromatic leaves and white flowers. A good background shrub and cut flower. **CLIMATE:** Cool or temperate. **SOIL:** In loam and sand, moist, well-drained or dry. Not clay.

304 Thysanotus multiflorus 'Frilly Nickers'

40-50cm
40-50cm

A clumping grass-like perennial with attractive narrow bluish-green foliage and masses of delicately fringed flowers. Good for a sunny rockery, raised bed or border, or in a pot. **CLIMATE:** Temperate. **SOIL:** In loam and sand, moist, well-drained or dry. Not clay.

Tristaniopsis laurina 'Hot Tips'

400-600cm
100-200cm

A large shrub with attractive broad, variegated red, yellow and green foliage that is particularly vivid in the new growth and yellow flowers in summer. A feature plant for year-round interest. **CLIMATE:** Cool, temperate or sub-tropical. **SOIL:** In loam and sand, moist, well-drained or dry. Not clay.

Tristaniopsis laurina 'Luscious'

7-12m
300-500cm

A small tree with attractive, broad deep-green foliage with copper-coloured new growth and yellow flowers in summer. A dense habit, larger leaves and brightly coloured new growth distinguish this cultivar from other forms of this species. A great specimen or shade tree. **CLIMATE:** Cool, temperate or sub-tropical. **SOIL:** In loam and sand, moist, well-drained or dry. Not clay.

305 Tristaniopsis laurina 'Winter Red'

150-200cm
100-150cm

A small, dense shrub with attractive deep-green foliage with bronze-red new growth and yellow flowers in summer. A great plant for shrubberies, low hedges, topiary and pot culture. **CLIMATE:** Cool, temperate or sub-tropical. **SOIL:** In loam and sand, moist, well-drained or dry. Not clay.

Viola hederacea 'Baby Blue'

10cm
30-60cm

A spreading herbaceous perennial with attractive deep-green foliage and delicate blue-violet flowers most of the year. An outstanding ground cover that flowers well in deep shade. Also makes a great pot plant. **CLIMATE:** Cool, temperate or sub-tropical. **SOIL:** In loam and sand, moist, well-drained or dry. Not clay.

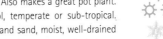

306 Wahlenbergia stricta 'Blue Mist'

30-40cm
30-40cm

Dwarf, tufted herbaceous perennial with small leaves and stunning double royal blue flowers. A great rockery or border plant that is also good for hanging baskets and pots as well. **CLIMATE:** Cool, temperate or sub-tropical. **SOIL:** In loam and sand, moist, well-drained or dry. Not clay.

307 *Westringia* 'Blue Heaven'

150-200cm
150-200cm

A small shrub with soft green foliage and white flowers. Attractive as a specimen or flowering container plant; ideal for formal hedging and screening. **CLIMATE:** Cool, temperate or sub-tropical. **SOIL:** In loam, clay and sand, moist, well-drained or dry.

308 *Westringia* 'Edna Walling Rosemary'

80-120cm
100-120cm

A small shrub with soft grey-green foliage to complement the dainty violet-lilac flowers that are attractive to butterflies and native bees. Attractive as a specimen or flowering container plant; ideal for formal hedging and for mid-level screening. **CLIMATE:** Cool, temperate or sub-tropical. **SOIL:** In loam and sand, moist, well-drained or dry. Not clay.

Westringia fruticosa 'Morning Light'

100-120cm
100-150cm

A small shrub with soft grey-green and yellow variegated foliage with small white flowers that are attractive to butterflies and native bees. Attractive as a specimen or flowering container plant; ideal for formal hedging and for mid-level screening. **CLIMATE:** Cool, temperate or sub-tropical. **SOIL:** In loam and sand, moist, well-drained or dry. Not clay.

Westringia fruticosa 'Mundi'

10-15cm
100-150cm

A prostrate shrub with soft grey-green foliage and small white flowers that are attractive to butterflies and native bees. A very tough ground cover. **CLIMATE:** Cool, temperate or sub-tropical. **SOIL:** In loam and sand, moist, well-drained or dry. Not clay.

Westringia fruticosa 'Smokie'

100-120cm
100-150cm

A small shrub with soft grey-green and white variegated foliage with small white flowers that are attractive to butterflies and native bees. Attractive as a specimen or flowering container plant; ideal for formal hedging and for mid-level screening. **CLIMATE:** Cool, temperate or sub-tropical. **SOIL:** In loam, clay and sand, moist, well-drained or dry.

Westringia 'Glabra Cadabra'

150-200cm
150-200cm

A small shrub with soft grey-green foliage and mauve flowers. Attractive as a specimen or flowering container plant; ideal for formal hedging and screening. **CLIMATE:** Cool, temperate or sub-tropical. **SOIL:** In loam, clay and sand, moist, well-drained or dry.

Westringia 'Jervis Gem'

100-120cm
100-150cm

A small shrub with soft grey-green foliage and mauve flowers. Attractive as a specimen or flowering container plant; ideal for formal hedging and screening. **CLIMATE:** Cool, temperate or sub-tropical. **SOIL:** In loam, clay and sand, moist, well-drained or dry.

309 *Westringia longifolia* 'Snow Flurry'

150-200cm
150-200cm

A small shrub with soft green foliage and white flowers. Attractive as a specimen or flowering container plant; ideal for formal hedging and screening. **CLIMATE:** Cool, temperate or sub-tropical. **SOIL:** In loam, clay and sand, moist, well-drained or dry.

Westringia 'Wynyabbie Gem'

150-200cm
150-200cm

A small shrub with soft grey-green foliage and mauve flowers. Attractive as a specimen or flowering container plant; ideal for formal hedging and screening. **CLIMATE:** Cool, temperate or sub-tropical. **SOIL:** In loam, clay and sand, moist, well-drained or dry.

310 *Xerochrysum* 'Cockatoo'

80-100cm
100-200cm

A small sub-shrub perennial with grey-green leaves and lemon-coloured everlasting flowers. Great general garden or pot plant and cut flower. **CLIMATE:** Temperate. **SOIL:** In loam and sand, moist, well-drained or dry. Not clay.

SpSA

311 *Xerochrysum* 'Dargan Hill Monarch'

80-100cm
100-200cm

A low-growing soft-wooded perennial with grey-green leaves and yellow everlasting flowers. Great general garden or pot plant and cut flower. **CLIMATE:** Temperate. **SOIL:** In loam and sand, moist, well-drained or dry. Not clay.

SpSA

Xerochrysum 'Diamond Head'

20-30cm
50cm

A low-growing soft-wooded perennial with small dark-green leaves and yellow everlasting flowers. Great rockery, border or pot plant. **CLIMATE:** Temperate. **SOIL:** In loam and sand, moist, well-drained or dry. Not clay.

SpSA

307 308

309 310

311

Xerochrysum 'Diane Everlasting'

A low-growing soft-wooded perennial with small dark-green leaves and yellow everlasting flowers that attract butterflies. Great rockery, border or pot plant. **CLIMATE:** Cool, temperate or sub-tropical. **SOIL:** In loam and sand, moist, well-drained or dry. Not clay.

Xerochrysum 'Sophie's Delight'

A low-growing soft-wooded perennial with small dark-green leaves and white everlasting flowers, with an orange centre, which attract butterflies. Great rockery, border or pot plant. **CLIMATE:** Cool, temperate or sub-tropical. **SOIL:** In loam and sand, moist, well-drained or dry. Not clay.

312 Xerochrysum 'Sundaze Bronze'

A low-growing soft-wooded perennial with small dark-green leaves and orange–red everlasting flowers that attract butterflies. Great rockery, border or pot plant. **CLIMATE:** Cool, temperate or sub-tropical. **SOIL:** In loam and sand, moist, well-drained or dry. Not clay.

313 Xerochrysum 'Sundaze Everlasting Gold'

A low-growing soft-wooded perennial with dark-green leaves and everlasting flowers that attract butterflies. Great rockery, border or pot plant. **CLIMATE:** Cool, temperate or sub-tropical. **SOIL:** In loam and sand, moist, well-drained or dry. Not clay.

314 Xerochrysum 'Sundaze Flame'

A low-growing soft-wooded perennial with dark-green leaves and everlasting flowers that attract butterflies. Great rockery, border or pot plant. **CLIMATE:** Cool, temperate or sub-tropical. **SOIL:** In loam and sand, moist, well-drained or dry. Not clay.

315 Xerochrysum 'Sundaze Gold'

A low-growing soft-wooded perennial with small dark-green leaves and everlasting flowers that attract butterflies. Great rockery, border or pot plant. **CLIMATE:** Cool, temperate or sub-tropical. **SOIL:** In loam and sand, moist, well-drained or dry. Not clay.

316 Xerochrysum 'Sundaze Lemon'

A low-growing soft-wooded perennial with small dark-green leaves and everlasting flowers that attract butterflies. Great rockery, border or pot plant. **CLIMATE:** Cool, temperate or sub-tropical. **SOIL:** In loam and sand, moist, well-drained or dry. Not clay.

317 Xerochrysum 'Sundaze White'

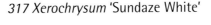

A low-growing soft-wooded perennial with small dark-green leaves and everlasting flowers that attract butterflies. Great rockery, border or pot plant. **CLIMATE:** Cool, temperate or sub-tropical. **SOIL:** In loam and sand, moist, well-drained or dry. Not clay.

Zieria 'Pink Crystals'

A dwarf compact shrub with small deep-green leaves and masses of starry flowers in spring. A good feature shrub or pot plant. **CLIMATE:** Temperate. **SOIL:** In loam and sand, moist, well-drained or dry. Not clay.

Native plant nurseries

AUSTRALIAN CAPITAL TERRITORY

Provincial Plants and Landscapes
Cnr Pialligo Ave and Fairbairn Ave
Pialligo 2609
Ph: 02 6262 6456
F: 02 6262 6006

NEW SOUTH WALES

Ausplants Nursery
51 Bunarba Rd
Gymea 2227
Ph: 02 9524 5532
Email: ausplants@myrealbox.com
Phone for an appointment before visiting.

Australian-natives.com.au
Contact: Mark Ferrington
Mob: 0438 284 448
Email: mark@australian-natives.com.au

Bilby Blooms
'Manna Springs'
Mollyan Rd
Binnaway 2395
Ph: 02 6844 1044
Email: bilby.blooms@tpg.com.au

Dealbata (cold climate) Australian Plant Nursery
Off Bloomfield St
Dalgety 2630
Ph: 02 6456 5043

Mole Station Native Nursery
Mole Station
Tenterfield 2372
Ph: 02 6737 5429
F: 02 6737 5443
Email: caldnsy@activ8.net.au
Visitors are requested to make an appointment.

Muru Mittigar Nursery
Old Castlereagh Rd
Cranebrook 2749
Ph: 02 4730 2774
(Louise de Lepervanche)
Email: nursery@murumittigar.com.au
Open Monday to Friday, 9 am–4 pm.

Newcastle Wildflower Nursery
260 Lake Rd
Glendale 2285
Ph: 02 4954 5584
Open 9 am–5 pm daily

Randwick City Council Community Nursery
Cnr Barker St and Day Ln
Kingsford 2032
Ph: 02 9399 0933
F: 02 9662 2658
Email: nursery@randwick.nsw.gov.au
Open weekdays, 9 am–3 pm.

Stocks Native Nursery
Lot 3 Symonds Rd
Harden 2587
Ph: 02 6386 2682
Plants for frost and dry weather, suited to Canberra, Wagga Wagga and Orange-type conditions.

Sustainable Natives
Indigenous and other native plants for the NSW Central Coast
Ph: 02 4372 2015
Email: snative@bigpond.com
Open by appointment.

The Sydney Rainforest
125 Dog Trap Rd
Ourimbah 2258
PO Box 259, Ourimbah 2258
Ph: 02 4362 2499
Retail nursery open Fridays

Sydney Wildflower Nursery North
327 Mona Vale Rd
Terry Hills 2084
Ph: 02 9450 1555
Open 7 days.

Sydney Wildflower Nursery South
9 Veno St
Heathcote 2233
Ph: 02 9548 2818
Open 7 days.

Wariapendi Nursery
Church Ave
Colo Vale 2575
Ph: 02 4889 4327

The Wildflower Place
453 The Entrance Rd
(cnr Puddleduck Ln)
Erina Heights 2260
Ph: 02 4365 5510
F: 02 4365 5514

Wirrimbirra Native Nursery
Hume Highway
Bargo 2574
Ph: 02 4684 1112
Located between Tahmoor and Bargo, eastern side of highway (3 km from freeway entry).

Wirreanda Nursery
Wirreanda Rd
Ingleside 2101
Ph: 02 9450 1400
Open 7 days.

Wombat Gully Native Nursery
1729 Coxs Creek Rd
Rylstone 2849
Ph: 02 6379 6202

NORTHERN TERRITORY

Inland Nursery
Alice Springs 0870
Specialist grower of native plants for dryland regions. Around seventy local species are grown and up to forty species of *Eremophila*.

QUEENSLAND

Fairhill Plants and Botanic Garden
Fairhill Rd
Yandina 4561
Ph: 07 5446 7088
Email: fairhill@bigpond.com
Open daily, 8.30 am–5 pm.

Gilston Nursery
Lot 6 Evanita Dr
Gilston 4211
Ph/F: 07 5533 2494
Open Tuesday to Saturday.

Kalangadoo Native Nursery
Eukey Rd
Stanthorpe 4380
Ph: 07 4683 7175

Nielsen's Native Nursery
49–51 Beenleigh–Redland Bay Rd
Loganholme 4129
Ph: 07 3806 1414
F: 07 3806 1706
Open 7 days.

Rainforest World
76 Bridges Rd
Morayfield 4506
Ph/F: 07 5498 5689
Open Monday to Saturday, 8.30 am–4.30 pm; Sunday, 8.30 am to noon.

Waratah Native Plant Nursery
PO Box 449
Kingaroy 4610
Ph: 07 4163 2268

Yuruga Nursery Pty Ltd
Peter and Ann Radke
Kennedy Hwy
Walkamin 4872
PO Box 220, Walkamin 4872
Ph: 07 4093 3826
F: 07 4093 3869
Email: nursery@yuruga.com.au
Open 6 days, closed Sundays.

SOUTH AUSTRALIA

Anne and Colin Dealtry
Lot 2 Trevilla Rd
One Tree Hill 5114
Ph: 08 8280 7079
Large range of tubestock plants. Display gardens. Phone to check if open.

Berri Native Plants
Sturt Hwy
Berri 5343
Ph: 08 8582 1599

Daisy Patch Nursery
Cnr George Tce and Richmond Tce
Coonalpyn 5265
Ph: 08 8571 1172
Mob: 0407 282 477
Phone for opening times.

Daryl Kinnane, Native Rainforest Flora
Summertown 5141
Ph: 08 8390 1155

Dealtry Native Plants
Lot 2, Trevilla Rd
One Tree Hill 5114
Ph: 08 8280 7079
Phone for opening times.

Malarus Native Nursery
Warrawong Sanctuary
Stock Rd
Mylor SA 5153

Mrs Uta Grehn, Mid North Native Plants
PO Box 767
Clare 5453
Ph/F: 08 8842 1874
Email: utegrehn@hotmail.com

Mount Barker Woodlots and Wildflower Nursery
2 Fletcher Rd
Mount Barker 5251
Ph: 08 8391 1971
Phone for opening times.

Natural State
Second Ave
Tailem Bend
(behind the football oval)
Ph/F: 08 8572 3049
Mob: 0439 727 057 (Matt Rose)
Open Thursdays and Fridays, 9 am–4.30 pm, or by appointment.

Nellie's Native Nursery
Randell St
Mannum 5238
Ph: 08 8569 1762

Nuthin' but Natives
Wholesale Native Nursery
Booleroo Centre 5482
Ph: 08 8667 2442
F: 08 8667 2489
Email: btwhellum@bigpond.com.au
Open to the public by appointment
only.

Poolman's Native Plant Nursery
Oliver's Rd
McLaren Vale 5171
Ph: 08 8323 8155

Provenance Indigenous Plants
27 Circuit Dr
Hendon 5014
Ph: 08 8345 0300
Open Sundays, 10 am–4 pm, or by
appointment.

Southern Native Plant Nursery
Chalk Hill Rd
McLaren Vale 5171
Ph: 08 8323 8259

State Flora Nurseries
Queen's Jubilee Drive
Belair National Park, Upper Sturt Rd
Belair 5052
Ph: 08 8278 7777
Open Monday to Friday, 9 am–5 pm;
weekends and public holidays,
10 am–5 pm

**Waikerie Native Wholesale
Nursery**
Ph: 08 8541 3163
Mob: 0401 948 737
Email: wnnm@bigpond.com
Retail enquiries by appointment.

TASMANIA

Habitat Plants
240 Jones Rd
Liffey 7302
Ph: 03 6397 3400
F: 03 6397 3074
Plants for revegetation, farm shelter
and wildlife corridors, public places
and home gardens. Contract growing
available.

Oldina Nursery
RSD 413A Smarts Rd
Oldina 7325
Ph: 03 6438 1266
Over 500 species are grown onsite,
including Tasmanian rainforest plants.

Plants of Tasmania Nursery
65 Hall St
Ridgeway 7054
Ph: 03 6239 1583
F: 03 6239 1106
Open 7 days, 9 am–5 pm (till 4 pm in
winter). Send four stamps to receive
a catalogue.

Pulchella Native Nursery
Tasman Hwy
Buckland 7190
Ph: 03 6257 5189

Redbreast Nurseries
1709 Channel Hwy
Margate 7054
Ph: 03 6267 2871
Native plant specialists for garden,
farm, forestry. Display garden and
farm.

VICTORIA

Australian Alpine Nursery
PO Box 143
Tawonga 3698
Mob: 0418 579 331
Email: jilldawson@alpineology.com.au
Mail order service (order online) or call
to make an appointment.

Barb Martin Bush Bank
Phillip Island Tourist Rd
Koala Conservation Centre
Cowes 3922
Email: bushbank@penguins.org.au
Ph: 0407 348 807
Open Wednesday, 9 am–noon, and
the first Saturday of each month,
10 am–1 pm.

Bushland Flora
110 Clegg Rd
Mount Evelyn 3796
Ph: 03 9736 4364
F: 03 9736 4716
Email: sales@bushlandflora.com.au
Australian native wholesale plant
nursery growing and supplying
general Australian plants and local
provenance indigenous plants for
revegetation.

Eucacia Native Nursery
56 Briagolong–Stockdale Rd
Briagolong 3860
Ph: 03 5145 5627
Mob: 0419 525 224
Email: plants@eucacia.com.au

**Granite Rock Australian Plant
Nursery**
Eleven Mile Rd
Sarsfield 3875
Ph: 03 5157 5633
F: 03 5156 8626
Open daily except Tuesday, 9 am–
4 pm.

**Greg's Indigenous Plants and
Landscape**
56 Derby Dr
Epping 3076
Ph: 03 9401 3696
Mob: 0414 318 470
Email: greg@gregsindigenous
landscapes.com.au

Indigenous Design
4 Webb St
Warrandyte 3113
Mob: 0419 178 219
Specialising in indigenous tubestock.

Kuranga Native Nursery
118 York Rd
Mount Evelyn 3796
Ph: 03 9760 8100
F: 03 9737 1968
Email: info@kuranga.com.au
Open 7 days. Delivery Australia-wide.
Free stocklist.

Lang's Native Plant Nursery
564 11th St
Mildura West 3500
Ph/F: 03 5023 2551
Email: langs@vic.ozland.net.au
Open Tuesday to Saturday, 9 am–
5 pm, Sunday, 1 pm–5 pm.

Mildura Native Nursery
Cureton Ave (near Apex Park)
Mildura 3502
Ph: 03 5021 4117
F: 03 5023 0607
Email: native@labyrinth.net.au
Open Monday to Friday, 8.30 am–
4.30 pm, Saturday and Sunday,
10 am–4 pm.

Neerim Native Flora
PO Box 95
Neerim South 3831
Ph: 03 5628 1419
Mob: 0419 100 805
Email: mikeh@sympac.com.au
Wholesale. Retail by appointment.

Pomonal Wildflower Nursery
Wildflower Dr
Pomonal 3381
Ph: 03 5356 6250

**St Kilda Indigenous Nursery
Cooperative**
C525 Williamstown Rd
Port Melbourne 3207
Ph/F: 03 9645 2477
Email: skinc@bigpond.com
Open Monday to Saturday,
10 am–4 pm.

Tambo Vale Nursery
Princes Hwy
Nicholson 3882
Ph: 03 5156 8310
Open 7 days.

Treeplanters Nursery
530 Springvale Rd
Springvale South 3172
Ph: 03 9546 9668

**Victorian Indigenous Nurseries
Co-operative**
Yarra Bend Rd
Fairfield 3078
Ph: 03 9482 1710
F: 03 9486 7155

WESTERN AUSTRALIA

Banksia Farm
Pearce Rd
Mt Barker 6324
Ph/F: 08 9851 1770
Email: banksia@comswest.net.au

Carramar Coastal Nursery
Mandurah Rd
Baldivis 6171
Ph: 08 9524 1227
Open 7 days.

**Eremophila Native Nursery
of WA**
20 Patricia Rd
Kalamunda 6076
Ph: 08 9293 2569
F: 08 6293 1665
Mob: 0429 325 693
Email: phil@eremophila.com.au or
ovnjames@iprimus.com.au

**Geographe Community Landcare
Nursery**
366 Queen Elizabeth Ave
PO Box 291
Busselton 6280
Mob: 0429 644 885
F: 08 9754 2049
Open Monday and Tuesday,
8 am–4 pm.
Nursery coordinator, Ann Bentley.

Jandakot Field Nursery
1071 Thomas Rd
Oakford 6121
Ph: 08 9439 2555
Open 7 days.

Lullfitz Nursery
Caporn St
Wanneroo 6005
Ph: 08 9405 1607
Open 7 days.

Tintuppa Nursery
PO Box 85
Balingup 6253
Ph/F: 08 9764 1066
Large range of Western Australian
species. Phone for an appointment.

Zanthorrhoea Nursery
155 Watsonia Rd
Maida Vale 6057
Ph: 08 9454 6260
Open 7 days.

Index

DEDICATION

To my mother Audrey, who has always been an inspiration and a support for my horticultural endeavours.

ACKNOWLEDGEMENTS

I would like to thank the following people for their assistance with this book.

Stuart Neal, Aziza Kuypers and Angela Handley at Allen & Unwin have done an amazing job in helping me bring the book to fruition.

The following people (roughly in order of the magnitude of their contribution) graciously either provided photos directly or allowed me to photograph their gardens for this book: Andrea Bishop, Sue Forrester and Bill Molyneux of Austraflora, Phil and Alexis Vaughan and family, Tom and Anne Raine, Jeff Cooke and Ryan Weber of RAMM Botanicals, Peter and Jennifer Ollerenshaw of Bywong Nursery, Yvette and Tony Gregorovich, Elspeth and Garry Jacobs, Todd Layt of Ozbreed, Bushland Flora, Richard Tomkin of Changers Green Nursery, Gordon Meiklejohn of Brimstone Waratahs, Graeme Downe, Plants Management Australia, Ed Bunker of Aussie Winners, Gordon Curtis, Sarah Walker, Graham Bowie, Alan and Carol Schwartz, Richard Anderson of Merricks Nursery, Peter and Margaret Olde, Brenda Ibels, and Jamie Durie.

I would also like to thank the following institutions for allowing me to photograph there: Australian National Botanic Gardens, Canberra; Kings Park and Botanic Garden, Perth, WA; Mount Annan Botanic Garden, Sydney, NSW; and Royal Botanic Gardens, Cranbourne, Victoria.

Lastly, and most importantly, I am indebted to Andrea Bishop for her amazing contribution to this book. She provided input on virtually every aspect of this book and it most definitely would not have happened without her.

This edition published in 2012
First published in 2010

Allen & Unwin
Sydney, Melbourne, Auckland, London

83 Alexander Street
Crows Nest NSW 2065
Australia
Phone: (61 2) 8425 0100
Fax: (61 2) 9906 2218
Email: info@allenandunwin.com
Web: www.allenandunwin.com

Cataloguing-in-Publication details are available from the National Library of Australia
www.librariesaustralia.nla.gov.au

ISBN 978 1 74331 023 6

Internal design by Liz Seymour
Illustrations by Lorenzo Lucia, Galaxy Studio
Printed in China at C&C Offset Printing Co. Ltd

10 9 8 7 6 5 4 3 2

PHOTO CREDITS

Aussie Winners: pp. 168, 190 (pic 93), 229 (pics 240–1, 243), 250 (pics 312–17)

Austraflora (Sue Forrester and Bill Molyneux): pp. 79, 170 (pics 1, 9), 173 (pic 11), 181 (pic 54), 183 (pics 56–7), 185 (pic 67), 186 (pics 71–4, 76), 189 (pics 79, 83–4), 193 (pics 102–3), 194 (pics 104, 111–12), 197 (pic 114), 198 (pic 129), 201 (pic 131), 201 (pics 136, 138), 202 (pics 143–5), 205 (pics 147, 149, 151), 213 (pics 182–3), 214 (pics 187–9), 217 (pics 195, 197–9), 218 (pics 204, 206, 208), 221 (pic 214), 222 (pics 215–16), 226 (pic 236), 230 (pics 249–50), 234 (pics 260–3, 266), 238 (pics 279–81), 241 (pics 284–6), 245 (pic 295), 246 (pic 301), 249 (pic 308)

Bushland Flora: pp. 193 (pic 95), 210 (pics 171–2), 218 (pic 204), 225 (pics 223, 229), 230 (pic 251), 246 (pic 305)

Bywong Nursery (Peter and Jennifer Ollerenshaw): pp. 193 (pics 97, 99–101), 201 (pic 133), 202 (pic 139), 204 (pics 150, 152), 206 (pics 155, 159–60, 162), 209 (pic 170), 213 (pic 181), 217 (pic 192), 217 (pic 196), 225 (pics 210–13), 222 (pics 217–22), 230 (pics 248, 252)

Changers Green Nursery (Richard Tomkin): pp. 201 (pics 132, 134), 202 (pic 142), 205 (pic 148), 206 (pics 157–8, 161), 209 (pics 164–5, 167), 210 (pic 175), 213 (pic 185)

Gordon Curtis: p. 91

Graeme Downe (*Telopea* 'Shady Lady Crimson'): pp. 6, 33, 126, 245 (pics 296, 298–9)

Jamie Durie Publishing: p. 41 (bottom right)

Gordon Meiklejohn: pp. 96, 127, 245 (pic 300)

Ozbreed: pp. 174 (pic 16), 178 (pics 39, 44, 45), 197 (pics 116–18), 198 (pics 121–4, 126), 225 (pics 224–8, 230), 226 (pics 231–3), 230 (pics 253–4), 233 (pics 255–6), 234 (pics 264–5), 241 (pics 287–8), 246 (pic 302)

Plants Management Australia Pty Ltd (*Acacia cognata* 'Fettucine' and 'Green Mist'): pp. 7, 99, 170 (pics 3–7), 173 (pic 12), 186 (pic 75), 198 (pic 125), 226 (pic 234), 242 (pic 290)

RAMM Botanicals: pp. 103 (top), 174 (pics 15, 17–26), 177 (pics 27–36), 178 (pics 37–8, 40–3, 46), 182 (pics 58–61), 185 (pics 62–6), 190 (pic 94), 193 (pic 96), 197 (pic 115), 198 (pic 128), 201 (pic 130), 218 (pics 200–1, 205), 226 (pics 235, 237), 229 (pics 242, 245), 230 (pic 246), 237 (pics 269–72), 238 (pics 274, 277–8, 282), 246 (pic 304), 249 (pic 306)

Sarah Walker: p. 80 (rainbow lorikeet)

PHOTO LOCATION CREDITS

Aumann's Nursery (Templestowe): pp. 32, 70–1 (top), 138 (bottom right)

Australian National Botanic Gardens, Canberra, ACT: pp. 19, 36 (top left), 55, 162–5

Graham Bowie: p. 46 (all)

Yvette and Tony Gregorovich: pp. 38–9, 138–9, 140–1

Brenda Ibels: pp. 40 (top right), 41 (bottom left), 48 (top right)

Elspeth and Garry Jacobs: pp. 130–3

Kings Park and Botanic Garden, Perth, WA: pp. 25, 28, 35, 37, 43, 45 (bottom and top right), 54 (bottom left and top right), 58, 61 (bottom and top right), 62 (bottom left), 66, 68, 87 (top left), 88–9, 150–3

Merricks Nursery: pp. 181 (pic 48), 182 (pic 55)

Mount Annan Botanic Garden, Sydney, NSW: pp. 10–11, 13, 48 (bottom right), 53, 56, 57 (top left and right), 69, 72 (top left), 77, 82 (middle and bottom), 158–61, 190 (pic 88), 242 (pic 292), 245 (pic 294), 246 (pic 303)

Peter and Margaret Olde: p. 213 (pic 181)

Peter Oyston: pp. 47, 48 (bottom left), 50 (top and middle), 57 (top left)

Tom and Anne Raine: pp. 20 (top), 36 (bottom left), 50 (bottom), 51, 52 (bottom), 57 (bottom), 65, 81 (middle), 108–9, 119 (top right and centre)

Royal Botanic Gardens, Cranbourne, Victoria: pp. 52 (top), 82 (top and second from top), 87 (top right and middle left), 119 (bottom left), 154–7

Alan and Carol Schwartz: pp. 14, 18 (top), 76

Phil Vaughan and family: pp. 26, 29–31, 101, 134–7